# GATHERING
# THE SOUL

For Steve -

Best Regards -

Connie

# GATHERING THE SOUL

Constance Simpson Myslik

To order additional copies of this book, contact:
Xlibris Corporation
1-888-7-XLIBRIS
www.Xlibris.com
Orders@Xlibris.com

# CONTENTS

SUPPLICATION ................................................. 11
INTRODUCTION ............................................. 13
PROLOGUE ...................................................... 19

I  At the Edge of the Underworld
Summer 1986
Connie ............................................................ 23
Mary Ellen ..................................................... 30
Fall 1986
Connie ............................................................ 36
Mary Ellen ..................................................... 46
Connie ............................................................ 51
Spring 1987
Mary Ellen ..................................................... 58

II  Spiraling Downward
Early Winter 1987
Connie ............................................................ 63
Mary Ellen ..................................................... 71

III  Divine Intervention
Late Winter 1988
Connie ............................................................ 75
Mary Ellen ..................................................... 82

IV  Descent Into Darkness
Spring 1988
Connie ............................................................ 85
Mary Ellen ..................................................... 91

V  Re-Membering
Summer 1988
Connie ............................................................ 94

Mary Ellen ...................................................................... 103
Connie .............................................................................. 106

### VI  Putrefaction
### Spring 1989

Ariel ................................................................................ 113
Connie .............................................................................. 120
Ariel ................................................................................ 123
Connie .............................................................................. 128

### VII  Help From Heaven
### Fall 1989

Ariel ................................................................................ 135
Connie .............................................................................. 141

### VIII  Reclamation
### Fall 1989

Ariel ................................................................................ 160
Connie .............................................................................. 164

### Winter 1990

Ariel ................................................................................ 169
Connie .............................................................................. 173

### IX  Expulsion
### Spring 1990

Ariel ................................................................................ 177
Connie .............................................................................. 188

### X  Healing Dreams
### Fall 1990

Ariel ................................................................................ 193

### Spring 1991

Connie .............................................................................. 200
Ariel ................................................................................ 205

### Fall 1991

Connie .............................................................................. 208

### XI  Choices
### Winter 1991

Ariel ................................................................................ 212

Connie ................................................................................ 217
                    Spring 1992
Ariel ................................................................................... 220

Connie ................................................................................ 223
                    Summer 1992
Ariel ................................................................................... 231
          XII  Seeds of Regeneration
                      Fall 1992
Connie ................................................................................ 235
                    Winter 1992
Ariel ................................................................................... 242

Connie ................................................................................ 248
            XIII  Going Home
                 Late Winter 1992
Ariel ................................................................................... 253
                    Spring 1993
Connie ................................................................................ 258

Ariel ................................................................................... 260
                    Summer 1993
Connie ................................................................................ 265
            XIV  Reunification
                   Winter 1993
Ariel ................................................................................... 270
                    Spring 1994
Connie ................................................................................ 277

Ariel ................................................................................... 282
                    Winter 1995
Connie ................................................................................ 284
                    Summer 1995
Connie ................................................................................ 286

*This book is dedicated to the women and men I have accompanied for a time on their journey home over the past twenty years, and to my many teachers, especially Betsy Halpern, Donald Kalsched, Nathan Schwartz-Salant, Barbara Brennan, Roseanne Farano, Jason Shulman, and Dani Antman. A very special thank you to Lynn Breedlove and Debby Taylor, clear channels who helped me enormously to connect to my guardian angels and mySelf.*

# SUPPLICATION

I honor the Great Mother
all pervasive space itself
the source of life.
Beyond death and birth,
masculine and feminine,
pain and pleasure,
dark and light.
To her, the essence of co-emergence
I offer this wedding song
of earth and sky, of body and mind,
of myth and self.
I offer it for the benefit of the earth.
May the ancient tale breathe new life into life.*

*by Laura Simms. From *THE LONG JOURNEY HOME*, edited
    by Christine Downing, Shambhala, Boston, 1994.

# INTRODUCTION

*Demeter, the Goddess of Grain, has a beautiful young daughter Persephone. Unbeknownst to Demeter, Zeus has promised Persephone to his brother Hades, Lord of the Underworld. One day when Persephone is playing in the fields with her girlfriends, she sees a beautiful, one hundred-petalled narcissus. She stops to pluck the flower, and as she does so the earth opens up beneath her. Hades, drawn in his chariot by eight black horses, drags her down into the underworld and rapes her. He keeps her captive, and ultimately she becomes Queen of the Underworld.*

*Meanwhile, Demeter is devastated and searches the world over for nine months in an attempt to find her daughter. She neither eats nor washes, disguising herself as a hag. In fact, she is deeply despondent. She will allow nothing to grow until Persephone is returned to her: fields lie fallow, plants die, the earth is barren. She is hired as a nurse-maid for a baby, Demophoon, and secretly tries to make him immortal; when interrupted by Demophoon's enraged mother, she reveals her God-dess nature and continues her search for Persephone. Hecate, the Crone, advises her. Zeus, alarmed at the desolation of the earth, tries to bargain with Demeter and ultimately sends Hermes down to the underworld to retrieve Persephone on the condition that Persephone has not eaten there. Persephone has eaten nothing for a long time but finally succumbs to the temptation of a pomegranate—symbol of fertility—and eats four seeds. Because she has done so, the Gods decree that she can return to her mother for only part of the year and must spend four months of every year with Hades in the underworld.*

*(This myth is variously seen as explaining the origin of the seasons and as the myth of initiation from which originated the Eleusinian mystery rites that were honored annually for many centuries. For the purposes of this book these other, important meanings have been set aside).*

Many years ago I went with a friend to a talk on spirituality. It included a group meditation in which we were each encouraged to allow a meaningful symbol to appear over our heads while we meditated, eyes closed. Much to my surprise I "saw" above my head a sheaf of golden barley, gathered and tied with a beautiful gold ribbon. The symbol meant little to me at the time, for I knew next to nothing about mythology. But later, when I began working with a Jungian analyst and told her my story, she suggested I read the myth of Demeter and Persephone. When I did so, I found that the image that had appeared in my meditation was the symbol of Demeter, Goddess of Grain. And I discovered that the myth is "my" myth, in that it contains many of the elements of my life history within it. Not only that, but as I worked with eating disordered women I came to understand that it is their myth as well. Not necessarily in all the particulars, but in the sense that it is a myth about mother-daughter separation, abduction into the underworld by the masculine principle that simultaneously seduces and abuses, loyalty to the aggressor, starvation and eventual surrender to hunger, bargaining with the Gods, and reuniting of separated aspects of the feminine.

Over the years I have learned that this myth is also about the different stages of womanhood: maiden, mother, crone. And I have seen that while in many ways as a psychotherapist I have been Demeter to my Persephone patients, many of whom had literally and others figuratively been raped and were held captive in the underworld when they began therapy, simultaneously, in my own personal process, I continued to gather up my own lost Persephone parts. The process of therapy can be seen as a consciously chosen descent back into the underworld to recover and integrate long neglected or stolen parts of the Self. My Jungian analyst was Wise Woman (Crone or Hecate) to me, and while assisting me to recover my lost Maiden also encouraged me to give up my overidentification with Demeter. While she was Hecate to me, and I was Demeter to many of my Persephone patients, at the same time each of us , as women, embodied consciously or unconsciously all three aspects of womanhood. I see more and more clearly that maiden/mother/crone overlap, interweave, and ultimately integrate in mostly mysterious ways. The first descent into the underworld, like that of Persephone, is often against our will, a literal or symbolic rape. Later, if we choose, we can descend into the underworld to be initiated time and again towards wholeness, neither negating nor overidentifying with any one aspect of being female. I see this in my own life, and in the lives of my patients and friends.

As I began writing this book, I was not thinking particularly about Demeter and Persephone. Then, when the myth rose to consciousness unbidden as the obvious guiding framework for the story I wanted to tell, I was humbled by the many versions and interpretations I encountered in the literature. Who am I, I asked myself, to suppose I understand or have the right to reimagine and use this well-known, ancient myth for my book? But I was reminded by a teacher friend that the reason myths have lived for so many centuries is precisely because they are open to individual interpretation; they are bigger than any of us and invite us to bring them to life in our own way. And so, because the myth holds great truth for me, and I believe for many women in our still-patriarchal society, I am using it to frame and enlarge the meaning of what I see as both a personal and transpersonal tale.

I chose to write this book as a story rather than as an academic book because I am hopeful that it will be read by "ordinary" people as well as therapists and healers, and also because I believe in the power of story to reach us in ways that go beyond cognitive understanding. I have therefore omitted analysis of the many dreams included as well as purely clinical commentary, and for this I hope my professional colleagues will forgive me.

*     *     *

It has been said that we draw those people into our lives who will give us an opportunity to learn. I am profoundly grateful to have been given the opportunity to learn and grow from my therapeutic relationship with a woman who called herself Mary Ellen— a name she hated and later changed to Ariel—beginning thirteen years ago. She came to me from a halfway house, newly sober and sorely troubled by her bulimia, because I was one of the few psychotherapists in the area who had chosen to work with eating disordered women. I had had a couple of years of experience in an agency, and before that, in a hospital internship, and I was reasonably knowledgeable, but also green. I had not worked with anyone as wounded as Mary Ellen for long enough to have experienced the full recovery process and what it was likely to mean for either her or me. Over the next nine years Mary Ellen challenged my knowledge, my skills, my patience, my beliefs, and my faith. From the hours, weeks, months working with Mary Ellen, my most difficult patient for several years, I learned how to work more effectively and more compassionately with eating disordered women, all of whom have been traumatized in some way. In the course of companioning her through her difficult and at many times uncertain recovery, I learned that it is possible, as a therapist, to serve as a bridge between terrible human suffering and spiritual recovery— recovery of the soul.

Mary Ellen/Ariel represents, in many ways, the archetype of a sexually abused, eating disordered female, abducted and held prisoner like Persephone in the dark underworld. Although this book is about her particular story, and her story is at one extreme end of the spectrum, it mirrors the experience of many women in our culture—their abuse, their pain, their collusion with the dark masculine, their shame and guilt, their self-destructiveness—and the potential for their healing. As such, it is both a personal and an archetypal story.

My work with Ariel coincided with, affected, and was affected by my own evolution as a therapist and a period of intense personal change. The urgency of my need to more deeply understand and help to heal the mind-body split so evident in all my patients, and critical in those like Ariel, led me into the realm of channeled guides and hands-on healing. Those initial experiences, in turn, led me to the Barbara Brennan School of Healing, to deeper personal healing, and to the work I now do, which is an integration of traditional Jungian-oriented psychotherapy and hands-on healing.

This book is a collaborative work. Although I take full responsibility for its final content, the chapters written from Ariel's point of view were reviewed by her, and her feedback on the honesty of the presentation was invaluable. Much of the material in those chapters was drawn from her journals, although I took the liberty of creating dialogue where none had been recorded. She also nudged me to write when there appeared to be no time to do so, and when I resisted because of the need to honor and complete the work of therapy with her first.

Why write Ariel's story rather than that of one of the many other women whose lives have touched mine so deeply? I cannot answer that fully. Perhaps in part because of the intensely archetypal nature of Ariel's experience; perhaps because reaching and helping others through this book has been seen by her as redemptive. I know that my desire to write about what I see as the emerging paradigm of partnership rather than heirarchy in therapeutic relationships, the parallel process that occurs so often in these relationships, and the spiritual basis for healing coincided with Ariel's desire to have her story told. It may also have been Ariel's way of ensuring continuation of our relationship after our formal therapeutic relationship ended. There may be other reasons I have not fathomed. What I do know is that this book is an expression of both Ariel's and my desire to offer our experience as therapist and patient into a wider arena, where it might contribute to an understanding of expanded reality, beyond our ordinary perceptions, and where those who seek to heal and be healed may be inspired to continue, no matter how difficult and painful the journey, on their souls' path to the light.

As I have often said to my patients: imagine that we are entering a long, darkened passageway, and you have been temporarily blinded. Hold my hand, and we will find the way with the candle I have been given. I know there is a light at the end of the tunnel. As we walk, who knows what monsters we will encounter in the darkness? But you will regain your sight, and as we emerge in the light, we both will have been transformed by the experience.

# PROLOGUE

The day Connie asked me how I would feel about her writing a book regarding my recovery process, my first reaction was disbelief. My second reaction was to ask myself, "am I that important to be written about in a book?" And then I realized what a great chance I had to make a difference in the world in a way I never had or thought I could. My immediate response to Connie's inquiry was a definite yes.

The realization that the book was being written made me contemplate deeply what going public would mean to me. We often joked about someday appearing on a talk show together promoting the book, but the importance of *Gathering the Soul* is much greater to me than my own story. Today I feel great joy to be given an opportunity to share my experience so professionals and people with difficulties and challenges like mine can see there is always hope. With good intentions, miracles do occur. I would like others to be inspired not to give up even when they feel hopeless and overwhelmed with low self-esteem, guilt, and shame.

The struggle was very difficult for me for a long time. When I look back today I see it was well worth my persistence to be free of the old baggage I carried inside myself for some forty years, but as I was going through the process I didn't always know that. I needed to feel the emotions of my childhood, kept tightly wrapped, that I couldn't acknowledge for so long. I had told myself it couldn't have been that bad and even if it was, it was all my fault. So I thought.

One by one, sometimes terror-stricken, sometimes intrepidly, I confronted my bogey men. They became smaller as I empowered myself to stand up to them. Moving through my fears, with Connie's expertise and understanding, I was able to see the reality of abuse that was harsh, but not as devastating as the effects of denying all that had occurred to me. My biggest boogey man had actually died some thirty years earlier, but I had kept him alive in myself all the time since then. With Connie's patience and my trust in her, and eventually trust in the healing process, I was able to let go. Wholeness came with coming to consciousness and letting go: of the painful memories, the false beliefs, and all the bad feelings I had about myself.

As I released the rage within, my trust in myself and others grew. Now I am able to interact with people without anticipation of being hurt and rejected. I am no longer afraid of pushing away those I care about.

In the past few years I have pursued and achieved a second career. Thanks to financial assistance from the State of Ohio Rehabilitation Services, intensive education in an Ohio medical massage school has allowed me the opportunity to become self-employed. I've settled in a small southwestern community and am building up clientele as a massage therapist. I am now able to give back to others, helping my clients to achieve physical as well as emotional health through bodywork and body awareness.

Connie, you have been my angel here on earth, giving me life anew.

To my pastor and his family, thank you for loving me and taking me in when I had nowhere to go.

To my dearest friend and sister, Denise, thank you for all your support, love, and most of all believing in me when I couldn't. I love you.

God has put so many people in my path who have given me emotional and/or financial support. There were those of you who gave me a shoulder to cry on as well as encouragement to continue. I couldn't have gotten to where I am today without all of you. Thank you from the bottom of my heart. All of you have taught me how to receive love.

Who would have believed that I could come to a point in my life of inspiring others? I have come to love myself, feeling confident I am on the right path. Today I am an assertive, self-sufficient and loving woman with a wonderfully full life. I pray that *Gathering the Soul* will inspire those reading it to tackle any bogey men lurking within themselves.

God Bless all of you.

Ariel

# CHAPTER I

## *At the Edge of the Underworld*

### Summer 1986

#### Connie

The ceiling fan whirred softly overhead, stirring the torpid July air just enough to make sitting at my office desk bearable. Usually I love my workspace, a very old building next to the 1753 farmhouse my husband and I live in, but we're in the middle of a New Jersey heat wave, and my clothes were clinging to me uncomfortably. Supposedly the building was once a slaves' quarters, but I feel none of the negativity I associate with slavery in it; instead, with its large stone fireplace at one end of the building, now a waiting room with a wood stove in it, and another wood stove in the office proper, and comfortable country furniture, it feels cozy and inviting, homey.

My next patient, who was new, was expected momentarily, and as I reviewed the brief notes I had made when I received the referral from a halfway house, I felt a twinge of anticipatory anxiety. Recovering alcoholic, recovering drug addict, bulimarexic, depressed, several suicide attempts. No wonder I was a little anxious: this sounded difficult. But not impossible. I am still filled with the enthusiasm and hopefulness (grandiosity?) that often come with relative inexperience as a psychotherapist. Although I've been working primarily with women with eating disorders—anorexia and bulimia—I know I still have a great deal to learn. I hope I can learn quickly enough to be helpful.

I heard the door to the waiting room open, and when I went in to greet my new patient, she had already settled on the couch with my fat and gentle orange cat, Fantastic. When Mary Ellen stood up I saw that she was very small and very thin, with the unhealthy pallor I had come to associate with bingeing and purging. Her dark hair was lank, and her tiny face had chipmunk-like swellings at the julienne. The smell of cigarette smoke reeked from her clothes, her breath, and the pores of her skin. Her expression was timid, defiant, and hopeful all at once, and as she followed me into the office and perched herself on the edge of the couch closest to my chair, I had the uneasy feeling that she was scrutinizing me at least as carefully as I was evaluating her. Her dark eyes had a devouring quality to them, they were vacuum cleaner eyes that looked as if they wanted to suck me in. I wondered, what then, would she spit me out as she did her food? I had seen that haunted, hungry look before, in the eyes of people who had been abused or abandoned early in life. What had happened to Mary Ellen?

I asked her to tell me a little bit about her family history, and she began talking readily, her normal tone of voice belying the abnormality of her experience. She told me she was in the process of getting a divorce from her husband of twenty-three years.

"I can't wait," she laughed.

"Oh?" I asked.

"Yeah, well, he thinks *I'M* sick, but he was almost as bad as my father. Never hit me, but he might just as well have. I have three kids, too, but they don't have much to do with me now. I tried to kill myself two years ago, and I guess they were pretty disgusted. They backed off. I used to be close to my daughter, but then I tried to kill myself again last year. I was taking Darvon, speed, Percodan—anything I could get my hands on."

Mary Ellen spoke rapidly, interrupting herself frequently to laugh, an ironic, dismissive laugh that I learned over time was one of the ways she masked her despair. As she continued talking she watched me carefully, scanning my face as if for approval, or to measure my reaction to some of the more shocking details. But except for an occasional sigh and the haunted look in her eyes, she might have been talking about the weather. I paid close attention to my own inner response, knowing that would be a more accurate way of sensing what was going on with her at a deeper level. I was aware of a knot in my stomach and emptiness in my belly, and under that, anger. No, not anger, rage. Deep, dark rage at what I was hearing and at something unknown that I felt in my gut.

It is fairly typical, I know, for patients to be "split off", or dissociated, from their feelings when they've been traumatized severely. They become numbed, no longer conscious of the emotions that would have been a normal response to their experience. They develop "dissociative disorders." But of course the memories are still there, somewhere, registered in the body, and they manifest in bodily symptoms and self-destructive behaviors. The key to healing is to help each patient reconnect with the traumatic experience and with the emotions that are so often buried along with the memories. If the patient experiences the therapist as providing a safe container and an understanding heart, over time healing occurs. Pain, shame, guilt, rage, and all their physical manifestations can be transformed; understanding and acceptance take their place. Slowly, the defenses developed for survival give way to an undefended Self. I truly believe this.

Although Mary Ellen apparently had a fairly good knowledge of some of her history, there were gaps in her memory, and the only real evidence that she had been traumatized by her experience was was her almost thirty years of addictive, self-destructive behavior. I can, for the moment, only guess at the extent and the kind of abuse she has suffered.

As with many of the women with whom I 've worked, Mary Ellen has made repeated attempts to fill her lifelong emptiness with various substances while simultaneously punishing herself for having any needs at all and trying to meet them.

"I used to drink seven or eight drinks a night, but I switched to mostly pills because Ceasar controlled my drinking," she told me, sounding almost proud. " Money, too, but that's another story. I started drinking on my first date with Ceasar, when I was sixteen. I always drank too much. My mother was a pill popper. Never any treatment. I guess she had a nervous breakdown when I was born. My Dad didn't drink much. My sister doesn't drink, but she's in Overeaters Anonymous. My brother Joe is a very angry man.

" My family doesn't deal with feelings, doesn't talk about anything difficult. I wanted to be close to my Dad, but he preferred my brother, and my mother preferred my sister. Dad was a corrections officer at the state penitentiary. He taught me how to cook, but he beat me a lot. Five minutes late from a date, he'd whip off his belt and beat me. My mother drives me crazy, whining and complaining all the time."

Two quick images flashed before me: my father's rifle kept in the closet by the front door and the fear I had of being even five minutes late for a date; my father standing behind me at the dining room table, belt in hand, commanding me to finish everything on my plate, or else.

"When my husband left two years ago, " Mary Ellen continued, "I was a mess. I took ninety-five Norpramine, and I was in and out of hospitals, I wanted to die. I couldn't seem to do it right though."

She laughed loudly, watching me. I smiled a little smile and shook my head, ruefully joining in the joke. I was good at laughing inappropriately, too. On the other hand, a sense of humor helped me get through a lot of tough situations, offered a sense of ironic detachment. I was glad Mary Ellen could laugh.

"That was a lot of Norpramine," I said. " It would have killed most people."

"Not me," she boasted. "I had a high tolerance. I was seventy pounds when I went to the eating disorders unit, though. I think I was always anorexic, a tiny baby, always skinny. I didn't grow at all between five and ten. I think I only ate to please my family. I purged by accident when I was about thirteen, and after that binged and purged on and off all my life. Always not eating or eating too much, nothing in between. I purged everything, got high on it. Felt clean, pure. Then I got into heavy laxatives and had rectal bleeding, hiatal hernia, malnutrition, anemia. Now I'm going to AA seven nights a week, and I'm living in a halfway house and trying to eat because people tell me to, but then I get on a roll and want ice cream, nothing but ice cream."

I wondered, why didn't she grow between five and ten? Failure to thrive syndrome? And what caused her to purge "by accident" when she was thirteen? And why the desperate need to feel clean and pure? These were all clues that would lead to the unraveling of a mystery, but they could not all be followed up on at once.

"What's so special about ice cream?" I asked, thinking sweet, soothing, like mother's milk. Did her mother literally withhold nourishment? Love? Both?

"I don't know—I started bingeing on it when I was a kid."

"What's your eating pattern like when you're not on an ice cream roll?" I asked, wondering how honest she would be able to be with me.

"No breakfast, just coffee in the morning," Mary Ellen replied promptly, proudly. "Not much lunch or dinner, except like last Sunday when I had six pancakes and syrup and ten slices of bacon for breakfast. I binge on candy and ice cream mostly. Sweets."

This is a fairly common pattern, skipping meals, denying hunger until it can't be denied, then bingeing on carbohydrates. I imagined her wolfing down food in a frenzied attempt to satisfy some primitive longing, fill some empty, cavernous space.

"What do you think of as your ideal weight?" I asked.

"One hundred and four," she said emphatically. "I'm five-four and I weigh about a hundred and ten now. I need to lose a few."

"Hm-m-m-m." I remained impassive, aware of the unrealistic, obsessive quality to her thinking. "When was the last time you had a period?"

"Oh, a few months ago. I've never been regular."

"What about coffee and coke?"

"No coke. I have about four cups of regular coffee and the same of decaf. I'm hooked on coffee and sweets."

Her voice was a strange blend of apology and defiance; her expression said "forgive me" and "I dare you to judge me or change me—I'll fight you every inch of the way."

"I guess that's better than alcohol and Percodan," I said.

We both laughed. Our time was almost up.

"I don't honestly know how much I can help you," I said seriously, feeling suddenly inadequate and overwhelmed by the gravity of her situation. After all, she's not an adolescent who is losing weight for the first time or even bingeing and purging for a year. This is a woman who has lived many years in a pattern of self-destructiveness; from what she has shared with me, it's all she's ever known. It looks like she developed a borderline personality disorder as a way of surviving—what?

Is it possible, even with the best of treatment, for her to recover? I have no idea. I paused, uncertain of how to proceed, then moved to what felt like solid ground: DO something.

"I'm going to ask you to do a couple of things," I told her. "I'm not sure how much you'll be able to do, but it will be a way for both of us to find out where you really are with food, what it means to you. First , buy a journal, any notebook that appeals to you. Write on the left hand side of the page each day what you eat, and any bingeing and purging that happens. On the right hand side, write what's going on with you. When are you hungry, when are you full, when do you crave sweets? What upsets you, when do you feel good about yourself? Any dreams you have—anything you want to write about. Especially your feelings."

"I've never done that," Mary Ellen said, looking frightened. "You can write as much or as little as you want to, and share only what you want me to know. It's primarily for you. Even if you only get a little down on paper, it will be helpful, a way of making yourself more conscious of what you're doing and feeling."

I stood up. "I think we should meet twice a week if at all possible. Can you do that?"

Mary Ellen appeared relieved, and as we worked out the details of appointments and fee—she could afford very little—I again felt her eyes on me, wide and devouring. It was decidedly uncomfortable. She seemed in no hurry to leave, so I moved to the door and reached for the handle, then turned and on impulse asked her if she'd told her whole story to anyone yet.

"No way," she responded, as if the question were preposterous. "I know they do that at AA, but I can't, at least not yet."

"If you can find the time and feel like doing it sometime over the next few weeks, I think it would be helpful to both of us if you were to write a brief autobiography. It may help to make your story more real."

Mary Ellen hesitated, then smiled shyly. "I'll try," she said.

I opened the door to the waiting room, and as I did so she leaped unexpectedly towards me, wrapped her arms around me, and clung to me like a small child. I hugged her briefly and stepped back, thankful my next patient had not yet arrived to see what had transpired. This is going to be, at the very least, intense.

# Mary Ellen

I've seen Connie five times now, and I've told her things I
never told anyone before. Like about my grandfather. She pays
attention, and she doesn't treat me like I'm crazy, but I felt so fat
and sloppy and sick to my stomach eating three meals a day, and
of course they were hardly meals, no fruit or vegetables like she
said I should eat, just milkshakes. I feel horrible, but not as horrible as I did before I purged. I couldn't help it, first I dreamed I
threw up and I thought I had, then I did. Only a few times, but I
had to. I felt like she was going to take away the things I wanted,
and I had to store up. I know I was substituting food, but I was so
scared, I knew I might drink or use drugs if anyone took away the
food. I know I binge when I'm horny, and I binged after a dream
about my brother and me having oral sex. In the dream he wanted
to have intercourse and I didn't want to, but I woke up feeling very
horny. I know the only time I feel connected, really connected to
anyone is having sex.

I told Connie how judged I felt at the halfway house and how
it reminds me of my home, always being judged and criticized.
And then my husband, the same thing. I know I get furious and
then snippy and sarcastic, and people back off in a hurry. Connie
said maybe it was easier to get angry than to feel the pain, and I
guess that's always been true. Once I started throwing up again I
lost my appetite, so I'm not eating much now. Connie talks about
eating three meals a day and taking multivitamins and cutting
back on the coffee and sugar as if I can do it, but it isn't that easy,
it's scary as hell. What the fuck does she know, she looks like she's
never had a worry in her life. I like her cat, Fantastic, and I try to
get there early so I can hold him for a few minutes. Connie's hair is
almost the same color as the cat's.

I just moved into an apartment with two women who are recovering alcoholics too, the halfway house set it up. One of them's
bulimic and the other is just plain nuts. I don't know if I can take
it, they treat me as if they think I'm crazy just like everyone always

has, but the bulimic one is stealing my food, so I stole some back, and the other one got in the middle, and she's weird as hell.

I tried to write my autobiography like Connie asked but it's too hard, so I'm just trying to tell her a little more each time, but of course it's not in order. She asked me about hospitalizations and I got them all mixed up because I was in and out so many times and took so many drugs and was drinking so much I can't remember. She's going to get the records from the rehab. But I told her about the state hospital, they committed me two years ago after I took all the pills and ended up on a respirator for a week and was sent to an eating disorders unit and slashed my wrists there. I guess I was really depressed, I hardly remember. But they diagnosed me as schizophrenic, I know that. When I told Connie that her expression didn't change, but she said she doesn't think I'm schizophrenic, and that's good news. I can always tell what people think by watching their expressions.

I'm supposed to go to to my sister's and then to visit my parents in New York State next weekend and I'm getting scared. I've always been the sick one in my family, and they treat me like shit, why should it be any different just because I'm sober? But maybe it will be, I guess I've always hoped it would be, just once they would be nice, but it's never happened yet. Connie asked me if I knew why they'd always treated me badly.

"It sounds like you were the scapegoat", she said. And she explained that in ancient tribes a goat was selected to be the scapegoat and the people hung medallions with their faults written on them on the goat, and then he was chased out to the desert, banished. That way, they could all feel good about themselves, and the scapegoat carried all the badness. That's exactly what it was like, all my life!

"I was only four pounds when I was born," I told her, "and I was a lot of trouble. I was so scrawny and sickly that everyone was afraid to pick me up, so I was carried around on a pillow. They nicknamed me "Bug" because I looked like a little bug on a rug. I'm told my mother had a nervous breakdown around then, but that's not real clear. I do know my father was away a lot and my mother wasn't well. Having a sickly baby was just more than she could handle. Apparently I wouldn't eat and didn't sleep much just cried a lot. The only way she could get me to sleep was to turn on the vacuum cleaner, so I slept with it under the crib. I still love the sound of motors running. I didn't want to eat much, and everyone was always trying to make me. Long periods of time at the table 'till all was eaten with lectures of take only what you'll eat so as not to waste it and how long and hard it was to get food then. Then I'd hear, that's not enough to keep a bird alive so got more put on my plate, then arguments of leave her alone and she needs to eat. I hated it."

Connie just sat and listened. She didn't say anything but I could tell it made her sad.

"I don't remember anyone ever laughing," I told her, "and I don't remember much about my brother until much later. I was always jealous of my sister Denise, so perfect all the time and everyone loving her. I remember once we were walking down the street and a woman stopped us and was ohhing and ahhing over Denise, what beautiful hair and pretty curls and how pretty she was. I was hiding behind my mother's skirt hanging onto her leg, I did that a lot. After being scolded and peeking out this woman said, is she yours too? My they don't look at all alike! Freudian slip, I think I felt like that a lot. I hated shopping, nothing ever fit and I looked awful in anything I tried on. I remember either hanging on my mother or hiding in the clothes on the racks, never taking my eyes off Mom. I wasn't so afraid of being lost but terrified of never being found. I still get that feeling of terror when I go shopping."

I watched Connie. She sat still, and she was paying attention. I liked that.

"I was very small when I started school, and I had to stay back because I had a nervous condition, that's what they told me, and everyone teased me and made fun of me. I was told later it was because my eyes blinked and I had developed nervous tics and the doctors said it was St. Vitus Dance. They said I should be under no pressure or harshly punished or it would worsen. I don't remember that, only always feeling hyper and afraid of being left."

"Were there any happy times?" Connie asked.

"Only with my friend Billy," I told her, because it was true. "He lived next door and he was my best friend. We climbed trees and played house and hide and seek. I liked running; I felt free. I was always out of the house playing or at neighbors and getting yelled at for never being home and stayed out of sight then didn't get yelled at or have to feel the tension of something going to happen. We were sent to the movies a lot on Saturday, to get us out of Mom's hair. All day matinees. In the summer we were sent to the community pool. Billy was my best friend ever, until we moved when I was in junior high school." I felt happy talking about Billy. But then I remembered what happened next, and I didn't know how much I wanted to tell Connie.

"What was it like after that?" she asked me. I took a big breath, remembering.

"My Dad left his job as corrections officer and became a sheriff. We got a nice new home, and we had a new image now to put forth: the wonderful family and good girls that do no wrong. I liked the feeling of importance and prestige—the sheriffs daughter—at least at first. Then it became a curse. My grandfather died right after we moved, and that was a big part of my life taken from me. The worst part was Gram just stopped living and was never the same again. I have a lot of good memories from my time with them, but I had lost both of them. I didn't feel like I fit in anywhere at school, not with the scholars and because of my father not with the black leather jacket kids. And there were no competitive sports for girls." I stopped for a minute, took another breath. "It was during the first summer in the new house that the involvement with my grandfather took place. He molested me. Thinking back the comments and gestures were made the summer before but the action took place that summer. Then when I was fourteen I was raped by a guy who was much older and had been kept back. I just remember being terrified of becoming pregnant and felt so dirty and couldn't get myself clean after washing for a long time. I told absolutely no one. My father would have killed me."

Time was running out, I saw Connie look at the clock over my shoulder, so I stopped, and I was glad I did because when I left I felt rung out. I'd said enough. She didn't press me for details, but she seems to care, who knows. She took some notes. I don't like that very much but I guess she has to.

I'm getting really scared about seeing my family, and I called Connie today and she finally called back and said it would be a good idea to find out ahead of time about AA meetings and go when I'm there, and also not to stay if it feels really hard. The problem with that is that Denise is driving and unless she wants to leave too, which she won't, I'm stuck.

I'm scared about something else too. Just when I'm beginning to get used to her, Connie's going on vacation for two weeks. How could she do that? I can see her supervisor, who's a psychiatrist, but who wants to? Anyway, it's a man. I'll never call him. Easy for her to say, but I won't. So what am I supposed to do? Ninety meetings in ninety days, I'm doing that, but I still don't feel like I belong anywhere. My new roommates listen to me sometimes but mostly keep their distance, even my sponsor acts like I'm too much trouble. Connie doesn't yet but she will. My sponsor says I'm wallowing in self-pity, what does she know. People at AA don't understand, don't want to. It always comes down to the same thing, I don't belong here, never did and never will. Where I belong I don't know, but it's not here on earth. I wrote a poem:

> I'm told my thinking is distorted.
> Sometimes distortion is better than truth
> It may have served a purpose to fool myself
> Not good you say
> Well let's hear the truth
> Abandoned by my mother, rejected by my father
> Used as a warm, pliable sex object by my grandfather
> A husband unavailable, just as needy as me
> Now my children have turned their back on me
> I keep chasing that golden ring of hope

That there's some connection on earth for me
Truth is coming forth no hope on earth for me
The only hope for me is eternity

People on earth are ugly, as good as they sometimes try to be
When you get through the layers of compassion and
        understanding
They're ripping the flesh with pity, surviving just like me

They have big words they use
Like resentment, understanding and love
But I don't think they really know what they mean
You can take your pity and shove it cause that's not what I
        need
Oh yes I think I understand
People although well meaning
Keep saying they're just not able
Truth: willingness just isn't there and they can't be my
        family

I can't let people close to me need to keep my guard up
So I know when the flesh is being ripped from me.
I can do it God, with your help
Truth is there's no "love" on earth for me

The pain's not easy, I won't pretend
I need to look up and feel you're there for me
Sometimes I wonder if that's reality
Truth is it doesn't matter
Each day gotten through is one day closer to you

Being on earth is hard, as you know
God, if you hear me, I want to be with you
I'll keep looking up, bearing the pain
So I can come home at last for eternity

# Fall 1986

## Connie

It 's always such a shock to come back from a vacation and spend an entire day sitting with patients, to reimmerse myself in their pain and struggles, to feel the weight of my responsibility to them. They are always angry at me for leaving them, whether they say it or not, and most of them act it out by "forgetting" appointments or canceling late or simply chattering on about superficial matters rather than sharing at a deeper level. It seems to take at least two weeks to return to a "normal" pattern, whatever that's been up until the break. So many of the women I work with have severe abandonment issues; with some all I have to do is look out the window for them to feel abandoned. I'm learning to be attuned to this, but it's hard; sometimes I don't even want to.

And after all the wonderful, strenuous hiking on vacation, it's really difficult to sit still for six or seven hours a day again. I want to get up and walk around to relieve the twitching in my leg muscles that builds over the hours, chase away the spiders that are crawling just under my skin. I'll start stretching and running again tomorrow, that always helps.

It's funny, *MY* therapist—Jane, an older female Jungian analyst I've been seeing for a few months—was on vacation for the entire month of August, and it felt fine to me. I thought of her occasionally, but not with any great longing or sense that I *HAD* to speak with her to get through any situation or day. Does that mean I haven't developed enough of a transference to her to have it matter yet, or is it that I've worked through my own abandonment issues? Or am I split off? She uses that term to describe me sometimes, the way I laugh things off, the way I defend my father. She said I have a manic defense, and when I talk about the things my father did she sees red—*EVERYONE* who knows anything about what my father did seems to hate him. Why can't I?

Mary Ellen is having a really rough time, and I don't think I can give her enough of what she needs, at least in the short run. She will probably have to be hospitalized so she can be in a safe enough environment to go through whatever she needs to go through without drinking, drugging, starving, bingeing and purging, or committing suicide. She's like a drowning person looking to me to save her, and I feel like I'm in over my head and inadequate to the rescue effort. I saw her the day I got back, and four times since then, and it's not enough. She had a very bad time of it while I was gone. The family visit went terribly, and apparently she just closed down, and she's been thinking almost constantly about suicide—" suicidal ideation" is the professional term—since she returned. It makes me anxious.

"If life is going to be this bad, I don't want any part of it," she told me. "I expected that sobriety would create a better life, happiness, all that good stuff, but all I feel is pain."

She looked pretty awful: disheveled, miserable, and jittery that session, and as we talked it was clear that her level of hopelessness and helplessness was indicative of a deepening depression.

"I was going to kill myself, but I couldn't think of a way that I was sure would work. I thought of driving real fast and crossing over the median and crashing into another car, I even had a dream about that, but I didn't really want to take anyone else with me. And if I'm going to do it, I don't want to do a half-assed job again, I want to be done with it."

I asked about her sobriety and her eating.

"No, I'm not drinking or drugging. I'm eating lousy, not much at all and then bingeing, but I haven't purged. My sponsor seems to be losing patience with me, tells me I'm still wallowing in self pity. I don't give a shit what she thinks."

She told me about her dream, and I wrote it down but didn't work with it. I kept thinking about all the cautionary words I've read about working with borderline dreams. Borderlines have so much chaos in the unconscious that exploring their often bizarre dream images can often exacerbate the tendency to fragment: read, fall apart. I would *LIKE* to work with her dreams, they're nightmarish but fascinating, but discretion is the better part of valor, so for now I won't.

But she was so anxious, I suggested we do a relaxation process, which she agreed to but had a lot of trouble with for the first ten minutes. Then she went into a deeply relaxed state and it was hard to get her out of it—when I counted to five and suggested she open her eyes whenever she was ready she sat there for a long time with her eyes closed. Finally I counted to five again and said when I snapped my fingers she would open her eyes and be fully present in the room, and that worked. But *I* had a couple of anxious moments when I thought she was out of touch with reality and might not come back. When she left she was much calmer, though, and was planning to go to a meeting at noon and another one at night.

The next day she called at 7 a.m., as I had requested, and told me she felt "bad" but professed to no suicidal plans.

"I'm trying to put it out of my mind," she said, sounding sincere. She was going to the beach with one of her new AA buddies and said she could talk openly to her. I asked her to give me her word that she would call me, her friend, or Dr. Z. if suicidal thoughts recurred, and she agreed. And I told her I would arrange to have her admitted to the hospital if she needed a place to be safe from her self-destructive impulses.

Meanwhile, I set up an extra appointment and told her we could use part of each appointment for progressive relaxation and begin to explore underlying issues, and she seemed to like that.

When we met next she still seemed very depressed but not as anxious. We did the relaxation process first and, again, it was hard for her to come out of it. But then she talked at length about her relationships with family members, and her sexuality, and her sense that she can't identify completely with being female, doesn't even want to.

"I always want more than people can give," she said, "and all my relationships, male and female, were always fucked up." She laughed. "I mean that literally. I've had sex with men and women, and sometimes I think maybe I'm bisexual, or maybe I'm just mixed up about what I am. Sometimes I think I'd be a lot more comfortable being a man. It sure is safer."

Identity confusion, I thought. Another classic sign of early wounding.

"I think all that will clear up in time," I said optimistically. "It's understandable that you would be confused, given that the bond with your mother was so tenuous and your father had so much power. How could you have wanted to grow up to be like your mother? It doesn't sound like she was much of a role model."

"I always blamed myself for my mother's sickness, but I hated her whining and always screaming, nothing I did was ever right. Then she'd complain to my father, and he'd beat us. There was never a time I didn't feel rejected and unloved. I can remember even as a little girl I would pray to God to take me. I don't know how I knew about God, but I did, and I always thought if I was just good enough he would take me away. But he didn't, so I must not have been good enough. That was always my goal, and it still is."

She suddenly began sobbing, and I lay my hand on hers. She took my hand and held it tightly as she cried.

"I've done so many terrible things," she blurted out between heaving sobs. " My son and daughter hate me and I don't blame them, but I miss them a lot. I'm so lonely without them. And my other son. . . . I haven't even told you about him. . . . he was born retarded and he's been in an institution since he was five. I. . . . I used to hit him, I couldn't help it, he. . . . he couldn't do anything right, and I would just get furious at him. The worst part is, he probably had. . . . fetal alcohol syndrome." She began rocking back and forth, tears running down her cheeks, nose running, and I reached for the Kleenex box and put it on her lap. She gripped my hand and, ignoring the Kleenex, wiped her eyes and nose on her sleeve.

"You've had so much pain in your life," I said gently. "No

wonder you wanted to escape, no wonder you drank and drugged and did all the other things you've done."

She looked up at me in anguish. "I feel so empty, and I don't know how . . . , it's like there's a big hole. When I was drinking and popping pills I didn't feel it so much, but now . . . I don't know what to do. I want someone to fill the empty space, but people have always let me down, so it's too scary, and then I pray to God to take me, but he doesn't. I don't know what to do," she wailed, " I just don't know what to do."

"One step at a time, one day at a time," I told her. "You're already beginning to heal from within. All this grief and guilt is coming to the surface to be healed; your tears help that process."

"I didn't have any sugar since Thursday," she said hopefully, looking at me as if for approval. "And I had a dream, that's what made me think about my younger son. I was trying to get him dressed, but his clothes were too big, and I was angry and frustrated. My daughter was angry with me for being angry. Then I had the same dream a second time." She started laughing hysterically. "Did you ever hear of having the same dream twice in one night? But the second time I wasn't angry, I was putting on his clothes easily and my daughter and I were laughing."

She laughed again, then abruptly switched back to tears.

"I don't want to get up in the morning, I just lie in bed and cry. It's getting harder and harder to get through each day, and I'm real edgy with people, I'm afraid they'll all push me away. Even you."

"I won't push you away," I reassured her. I could feel her desire to trust me, and her fear of doing so. "I want you to see Dr. Z. for an evaluation, though, just to help me know we're on track. Would you be all right with that?"

"Scares the shit out of me," she said. "What if he says I have to go to the hospital?"

"I'd like to be able to talk with him about you from time to time, and it would help if he knew you in person," I said, feeling the need for his backup. "If he makes a recommendation that you be hospitalized, we'll talk about it. He's not going to impose that on you."

"Will you go with me to see him?" she asked beseechingly.

I hesitated. It wasn't what I usually did, but in this case . . .

"All right," I said, "if he can see you at a time that fits with my schedule."

She left, promising to make an appointment with Dr. Z., but she hadn't done it by her next appointment.

"I was too busy," she said matter-of—factly. "I've been interviewing for jobs, and I might have one as a market research trainee."

She went on to describe the three jobs she'd applied for, sounding remarkably rational and moderately excited. I urged her to take her time and find something relatively stress-free, part time if possible, so that she would have the time and space to process whatever came up in therapy and to stay fully connected to AA. Her mood changed quickly, like a dark curtain coming down over her face.

"I'm gaining weight, I know it," she said disgustedly. "I hate the feeling of food in my mouth, I want to get rid of it, swallow it quickly or spit it out. I know I was bottle fed from the beginning and I had to be forced , that's probably why. I remember the feeling I had after my first purge, clean and pure, it felt so good. Once when I was a kid I ate twelve ears of corn at a picnic, everyone was impressed. I always liked family reunions, I got desserts and junk food if I ate enough of what they wanted me to. I want to weigh myself, can I?" She looked fearfully at the medical scale over in the corner .

"If you really want to," I said, pretty sure by the looks of her that her weight hadn't changed much, if at all. "Sometimes it's helpful to know, but not always. How do you think you'll feel if it's changed?" I knew, from my own years of daily, obsessive weighing what an impact two pounds up or down could have. If weight was up, it potentially led to severe restriction; if down, bingeing. Or sometimes the opposite. What a false but powerful God that hunk of metal was!

She laughed. "You know I'll like it if I've lost. And I'll hate myself if I've gained, and I already know I have."

"So you're looking for a reason to hate yourself?"

"Maybe," she said defiantly, getting up and sashaying to the scale. She had a decided wiggle. She took off her shoes, her watch, and her belt, stood on the scale, and held her breath while she fiddled with it until it balanced perfectly.

"Damn!" she exclaimed, jerking the marker to one side and stomping off the scale. "Shit! I knew it! I've gained two pounds, two whole fucking pounds, that's what trying to eat normal does for me!" She glared at me accusingly.

"Mary Ellen, most people who've been bulimic and stop purging gain water weight initially, I told you that before," I said patiently. "So it's probably water weight. And we talked about a range rather than one number as healthier and easier to maintain, and you're still on the low end of that range."

"Oh, fuck! What the hell do you know? If I eat three meals a day and don't throw up I'll turn into a blimp, that's what I know."

She stormed over to her chair and threw herself in it, then slumped down, looking thoroughly defeated. I waited. She was silent for a long time, almost as long as I could endure without saying something myself.

"I feel like a child," she finally said very quietly. "And I'm afraid of tomorrow. I feel like nothing's ever going to change, and I can't stand it this way. I don't want to eat any more, I just want to go to sleep and never wake up."

When she left a little while later I called Dr. Z. and set up an appointment for two days later . I knew I needed help, and I valued his judgment. Mary Ellen agreed, reluctantly, to see him, and so I met her there and sat with her while he did a psychiatric evaluation. Later he and I talked and agreed upon where she could go if her depression worsened and hospitalization was necessary. He confirmed my impressions and added some of his own, helping me to see even more clearly the extent of Mary Ellen's disturbance. I began thinking about in-patient treatment for her eating disorder even if potential suicide was not the issue.

At three a.m. the next morning my home phone rang, awakening me out of a deep sleep, and I heard Mary Ellen's voice, raspy and weak.

"I feel like I'm slipping away," she whispered. "I haven't taken anything, but I feel like I'm losing my grip on reality."

"Dr. Z. can get you admitted to the hospital right away," I said, suddenly wide awake.

"No. No, I don't want to go to the hospital," she said hoarsely. "I don't feel safe in hospitals. I feel safe with you. Can you see me tomorrow?"

I tried to mentally review my schedule for the next day, wondering how I would squeeze her in.

"Yes, of course," I said. "Can you come at eight in the morning?" I would have to skip my jog.

"I'll be there," she whispered.

I lay awake for a long time, afraid she was committing suicide, afraid she was going psychotic, afraid. . . . afraid of being responsible for what happened to her. I tossed and turned and questioned everything I'd done with her. Maybe she should be on medication . . . but no, she might stockpile medications, and anyway as a recovering alcoholic and drug addict it was unwise to open up the possibility other drug dependency. Maybe I shouldn't be working with her at all; it was probably too much for her to stay sober and relinquish her eating disorder at the same time. Maybe she just didn't have enough ego strength; she certainly no sense of a solid, integrated self. She was decompensating in front of my very eyes. I drifted off to a fitful sleep, planning to call the hospital I usually referred to for in-patient treatment of eating disorders. Maybe they would take her.

Mary Ellen arrived before eight and was sitting in my waiting room with Fantastic purring on her lap when I walked in. She looked tired, depressed, and unkempt. We talked about what had happened during the night, and she told me, slurring her words and speaking very slowly, that she had been turned down for all three jobs.

" I can't take any more rejection. And I threw up yesterday. Twice," she said despondently. "I'm cold." She reached for the plaid wool blanket that was folded over the back of the sofa and wrapped it around herself.

"Have you had anything to drink, or any drugs?"

"No," she said.

I wasn't sure I could believe her. The slurring . . .

"I want to throw things and cry," she almost whispered, "but I'm afraid if I do I won't be able to stop."

We talked about her anger, and her hopelessness, and how hard it was to face all the feelings she'd been able to escape from with her drinking and drugging in the past.

She was tortured over the pain she had caused others, especially her retarded son Johnny.

"I just feel horrible that I beat him," she said slowly, wiping her eyes with her sleeve. "After I was hit so much as a kid and it hurt so bad, how could I turn around and do that to my own kid?"

"Unfortunately, we often do to others what was done to us," I told her. "Parents who were abused as kids are much more likely to abuse their own. You never had a chance to deal with your feelings about being hit, nor were you taught how to parent more effectively and with better self discipline than your parents. It's very understandable."

"My chest hurts, and my stomach. It feels like a tangle of threads, all tied up in knots."

"We could do a relaxation process to help with that, " I offered.

Mary Ellen sighed. "All right," she said despairingly. "But why doesn't God just take me?"

I didn't even try to answer that one. Why some people who cherish life die and others who want to die live is a mystery I have never fathomed.

I led her through a progressive relaxation and then had her

imagine the tangle of threads in her chest and stomach being surrounded by a white light that gradually dissolved them, filling the space with light. It was a peaceful, natural process for me to lead and It took about twenty minutes. As usual I closed my eyes during the process to help myself focus, and I too went into a deeply relaxed state. When it was complete, I opened my eyes and saw that Mary Ellen was asleep. Her mouth was open and her head had fallen to one side. She looked like a forlorn, abandoned waif, a small orphan, pale and sickly amidst the folds of the blanket. No one was coming for half an hour, so I let her sleep.

# Mary Ellen

Feeling so many emotions and so erratic during the day laughing one minute, crying next, hostile in between. Feel like I'm going to go crazy. After talking with Angela guess they're just emotions of leaving Evergreen. Felt some better after crying. Just can't seem to cry enough without it shutting off. I think if I were able I could cry a river. Did a lot of calling about a place to live the last couple of weeks and was frustrated and petrified until went to New Jersey last week and found a place with a roommate also recovering. Hooray! I won't have to sleep in my car.

Feel the need to stay off to myself today so as not to strike out when my anger has nothing to do with them. Feel so bad after I do become hostile and hurt people. Felt good in assertiveness and talked about talking to son last nite. I have decided to go to his house for Thanksgiving.

Dealt with Grandfather violation in women's issues two days ago really let it out. Haven't cried like that for long time. Felt like shit but didn't try and make me feel better this time. Fell asleep in aftercare for short time. Felt absolutely exhausted and drained but afraid of sleep. That's happened a lot here. Felt so thirsty and bingy but knew why this time dealing with this issue I've denied feeling for so long. Kept thinking of a cold, tall bourbon and diet Pepsi but had grapefruit and apple juice instead. Know I'm going to be o.k.

When I think back on these weeks—almost seven—I can't believe all that's happened and the progress I've made. Lots of times I got very angry when in group and felt my views were negated and unimportant and left group a few times. Couldn't take it and wanted to lash out. Had a few real battles with staff especially with Gretchen who said one day when I was furious and ranting and raving that I should feel privileged to be here and want to participate. Became enraged I do feel privileged but feel she used one small example to make me feel guilty. Made angry smart comment and walked away. I notice I do that a lot. Went to

AA meeting that night and shared and went shopping, told myself I'm not going to feel guilty for buying something when I have no money as usual. I felt like I deserved something besides worry etc. Felt like I needed to defend my actions though so guess I did feel guilty. I've gone twelve days without bingeing or purging which is another miracle. Whether I can do that when I'm out of here is another story I'm really scared about that.

I wanted to stay longer and I was really pissed at them throwing me out and my lawyer for sitting on his haunches about alimony I have to kiss ass because everyone is doing me a favor and I'm to be grateful no matter what. But I got some insight when I talked to Angela about it's always felt that way like I get the crumbs and I'm supposed to be grateful. I will miss her and of course want to keep in contact but know as these things go it won't happen. I will see her in aftercare, I'll be able to get here every other week at least for a while.

I'm on Stelazine and Lithium, first they put me on the Stelazine because I was all over the place when I got here and wasn't making sense even to myself and I think they didn't even want me here once I got here even though they'd given me a scholarship. Then my moods went up and down so much they said they thought I might be manic-depressive, so they waited a few days and put me on Lithium and that's helped some. I'd be up one minute, like in Art Therapy which I never thought I'd like and did a lot and then I'd go to Community Group and feelings would come up and I'd feel so low I couldn't even talk, just curled up in a ball and wanted to disappear. Some nights I'd have horrible nightmares and have to sleep on the sofa in the group room. Then I'd have a good time going out for a walk with Patty and Kate my new friends and be high as a kite for a while. I'm still up and down a lot but it's not as extreme.

The hardest part after the first couple of weeks of feeling miserable all the time for one reason or another was trying to set up family sessions and getting rejected by both of my kids. Too busy, even when I gave them lots of different times they could come.

That hurt so much. Then tried to get Mom and Denise to come and Denise said she'd bring Mom, Dad was sick and couldn't come and I wasn't sure I was ready for him anyway, got in touch here with how afraid of him I've been all my life. I was so tense before Denise and Mom arrived I had to leave group, couldn't sit still. Felt irritable, bingy and purgy, and was so aware of how I've blocked all these awful feelings for so long, before if I felt irritable or tense I'd just take something and presto the feelings would disappear. Never mind the hangovers, they didn't matter.

Anyway, I was real edgy the day they came, what with weight going up and everyone encouraging me to keep eating normal and no outlet it got worse and worse until I could talk it out with someone, my roommate this time. The family session was very difficult. Had hard time knowing how to start but said what I needed to. Don't feel like there are things I should or wish I had said, told her about Grandpa and how I never felt safe or believed and always afraid of being punished for something. Felt content and relief it was all out. Feel sad and sorry for Mom that she'll never have this feeling of relief, Angela said she's a real stoic and has learned over a lifetime not to deal with feelings. Was and am very worried she'll become physically ill due to the emotional stress. Feel good about Denise's support and backing me up about G.F. Still feel that need for her to back me up. That night I was physically and emotionally drained and had a hard time even putting my thoughts together, so went to bed early and for a change slept for six hours straight without waking up.

One of the things I learned is that I carry a monster inside I call "Doom" that tells me how hopeless, helpless, stupid, and sickly I am. I worked hard in Psychodrama getting my monster out, really visualized it and for the first time said all the things it says out loud and not in bits and pieces to different people. I was terrified when thought the other participants were going to yell all those awful things back at me. It would be like my husband saying them to me affirming what my monster "Doom" already said to me. Instead most everyone joined me to yell at the monster it felt so good to yell at it but difficult at the same time. Started shaking and crying and have never sweated like I did then. Just poured off me. I felt a real closeness with the people in group and so happy they were there and felt support, genuine caring and support.

I'm not happy with my weight but at least I'm not bloated and feeling sick the way I was the first few days or maybe weeks. My stomach hurt and I had heartburn and indigestion almost all the time, felt like I was going to burst. Saw the doctor a couple of times and got stomach medicine but mostly they all said it would pass. I would fight the desire to purge for a long time and then finally give in just to relieve the horrible feeling. Time and again I would fight to keep my meals down, and it did get easier when finally the bloating started to go down. I hope I can eat and not purge when I leave here, that's one of the scariest things, what if I go back to bingeing and purging after all this.

Come to think of it the first two or three weeks are a blur looking back with only a few clear memories of things that happened. Mostly I was tired and probably off the wall a lot of the time. I'm so afraid of being that depressed again and being alone and feeling suicidal and having it just take over my thoughts and feelings. I will see Connie next week after I leave and I think that will be good but it's so hard to get close to people I either keep my distance lots of times with hostility or I open up completely, too much said and then I want them to be there for me forever and can't live without them. That makes it real hard to leave here. Angela said I have lots of boundary issues to work on over time, and of course issues with self-esteem and family that she said will take a while. Of course I want it to all happen now, I want to be o.k. now and I'm not and all this is damn fucking hard. But I've come a long way, and I have a new sponsor and a place to live and help promised from welfare and maybe even a part-time job as a receptionist starting in a couple of weeks so have a lot to be grateful for. And I am.

I'm still afraid I'll go back to the way I was. Sometimes my brain feels like a big cobweb, but it helps to talk and it helps to write things down. I'll bring my Progress Notes to Connie, and we'll see. As Gretchen said, if I give it my best shot and can't do it I can kill myself later if I want to, but not the other way around. That struck me as really funny and I laughed until my sides hurt.

## Connie

I saw Mary Ellen today for the first time in almost two months and was pleased and surprised to see how well she looks. We went over her notes and she shared a lot of what happened; also confessed that she had been bingeing and purging much more than she was able to acknowledge to me before her admission to Evergreen. She said she was given responsibility for her eating, which meant that she could binge and even purge if she wanted to, but there was always someone to talk to, and those patients who were committed to getting better did. She seemed proud of her accomplishments at Evergreen and only minimally depressed. Of course I had talked with Mary Ellen's Case Manager before her appointment, and I learned that originally when she was admitted, the staff questioned their judgment in taking her, as she alternated between being extremely suicidal and grandiose, was compartmentalizing and splitting extensively, and at times seemed out of touch with reality. The psychiatrist put her on Stelazine, and once that took hold she really worked hard and made an incredible amount of progress.

I asked her what her major concerns were now, and she was able to talk clearly and calmly about what she is facing as she tries to put her life together.

"I'm anxious a lot," she said, "and when I feel tense I struggle with whether to eat or not to eat. If I have a cigarette it helps for a while, and I remind myself that if I just stay on my food plan I can deal with whatever comes up, and if I binge and purge everything falls apart. I want to go to Friendly's and have a milkshake but I haven't done that yet."

I nodded, listening.

"I have so much to think about it feels overwhelming. My new roommate is nice, but I don't know how close to get to her. I'm waiting to hear about the receptionist job, and if I don't get it I'm up a creek. I'm trying not to think about my weight, but I feel fat. It was really sad to say goodbye to everyone at Evergreen, patients and staff, because I felt real safe there even though it was hard. The world seems like a scary place." She took a deep breath, seemed to think of something funny, and smiled. "Fantastic remembered me," she said happily. "I think, when I get a place of my own, I'm going to get an orange cat."

I smiled. Fantastic's unconditional loving acceptance was very therapeutic! When it was cold he often slept on the hood of whatever car in the driveway was warmest, and once he climbed in an open window and wasn't discovered until hours after a woman got home.

"I've been thinking about what I want to do when I grow up," Mary Ellen said, laughing at her joke. "I want to be in public relations. But I have to finish getting my degree first, so I'm going to apply to Carroll College, just take one or two courses a semester."

"That sounds exciting," I said, impressed that she could think about college on top of everything else she had to deal with.

"Could you make me a relaxation tape?" She asked tentatively.

I thought for a minute.

"Sure," I said. "I haven't done that before, but there's no reason why I can't. We can do a relaxation process next time and record it then. With music if you like."

"Yeah," she said, smiling.

We talked about managing her depression and working on developing better coping skills to deal with the challenges that would inevitably come up. We made arrangements to meet twice a week, and I stressed how important it was to continue going to AA meetings several times a week.

"My sponsor leads an OA meeting that's just for people recovering from anorexia and bulimia," Mary Ellen told me. "It's once a week, and I plan to go to that too."

"I think, at least for now, it would be wiser not to do any kind of regressive work," I told her. It was important to help her with containment until she was more stable.

"O.K., " she said agreeably. "What about my dreams, do you

want me to write them down? I've had some douzies."

"Yes," I suggested. "It would be good to write them down and bring them in, and maybe we'll work with some of them. Let's see how it goes."

She left, and came for her second session of the week three days later, still doing pretty well. She reported that she'd been eating three meals a day and had only binged and purged once, but that she had a lot of discomfort in her stomach and chest.

"I've committed to telling my story at an AA meeting Saturday," she said, laughing nervously, "and I'm really scared."

"What's the scariest thing about telling your story?" I asked.

"They'll think I'm a lump of shit, that I'm fat and stupid, and who cares about my story anyway, lots of people have worse."

"Hmm-mmm. I think it's time for you to have an affirmation to replace all those negative thoughts you have about yourself. Would you like that?"

"Depends," she said. "I'm not good at affirmations."

"O.K.," I said, thinking. I picked up my pen and wrote, then read aloud what I had written:

*My name is Mary Ellen. I am a beautiful, intelligent, shapely, and very important woman. I am capable and strong, and I am a survivor. I am learning how to live. Surviving is worthwhile.*

"That's great but it's not me," she said contemptuously.

"How about if you read it out loud every morning until we meet again, just try it on and see if you like it," I suggested. "If you find a lot of resistance coming up, let's talk about that part of yourself that won't let you believe good things about you."

"You mean "Doom"?" She asked.

"Who's Doom?"

Mary Ellen laughed. "He's my monster, and I learned at Evergreen how to shut him up."

"Great!" I said, glad she could work in the imaginal realm. "If you can replace his voice with affirmations you're going to feel a lot better about yourself."

"What about all those tangled threads that are back in my chest and stomach?" she said. "Can you help me with them?"

I looked at my watch. We only had twelve minutes.

"O.K.", I said, "Let's do a relaxation process."

Once again I led her through progressive muscle relaxation and then had her visualize the tangled threads melting, dissolving in white light.

"Now imagine the white light spreading out from your solar plexus," I said quietly. "and let it fill all your bones, all your muscles, your nerves, and your bloodstream. Let every cell in your body be filled with light, soothing white light that heals where healing is needed."

And once again, by the time we were finished, Mary Ellen had fallen asleep and I had to wake her before my next patient came. That night I had a dream:

*I am somewhere in a building with other people and small children. There's some activity and conversation I don't remember, and then I'm carrying a young child—maybe two or three years old—down a steep, open stairway like a ladder or a narrow fire escape. It's very steep, with platforms every ten or fifteen feet. The small child is clinging to my legs, and I hold on to her arm. I realize it's not a good way to carry her but for some reason it's the only way I can. The young child is terrified. I am not afraid, although I hold on to the railing with my left hand.*

I wondered when I awakened whether this dream was about me, and my inner child, or about Mary Ellen specifically, or was symbolic of my work in general, which seems to be working with the very young, wounded, and terrified parts of my patients. Maybe it's all of the above. And maybe there is resonance between parts of me and those parts of my patients that are in need of healing.

It has been a stressful fall, with many challenges in my practice. My group for eating disordered women has been difficult and volatile some of the time, and last week a lot of rage emerged, rage against men and the abuse most of my patients have suffered at their hands. I think I dealt with it well, but afterward felt very restless and somewhat disturbed and raided the kitchen cabinets— raisins, nuts, a bagel. I'd had dinner earlier and knew I wasn't hungry, but that didn't stop me. Am I , like my patients, sending my feelings underground? I've gained four pounds since the summer and I'm angry about that. Can't seem to stop overeating, especially Monday nights after group. Meanwhile giving wonderful advice to patients. I'm aware that I'm still SO NEEDY. I thought I was recovered, or transformed, but the truth is that despite so much growth and change I am still SO NEEDY. And probably a lot more angry than I'm in touch with. I identify more than I'd like to admit with the women in my group, and I feel as if I take on a lot of their feelings as well. I love my work and at the same time it is very demanding. My neck and shoulders are often quite tense by the end of the day, and by the end of the week I'm usually exhausted. I'm more and more aware of how difficult a patient population I've chosen to work with, and yet, and yet . . . I know this is right for me.

Maybe it has nothing to do with my work. My analysis with Jane is beginning to deepen; I'm becoming more honest about current relationship difficulties instead of glossing over everything in a desire to make everything o.k. when it isn't, as I did with my father, and I'm dreaming a lot. A couple of weeks ago I had a really strange dream:

*I'm in a house and have to have heart surgery. A man—my father?—someone I know—not my husband—is going to do the surgery. He is a doctor. Somehow the first part is that my heart is removed. I awaken and lie very still because I'm afraid I can't do anything with my heart out. The man is in another room with my heart and I wonder what he's found. My children know, but someone has taken the phones off the hook so I can't call my husband, and I wish he would come and be with me. The man is supposed to wait for an assistant, but he's decided to go ahead. I walk down the hall and look in the room and he has my heart on a piece of plastic on a bed and is examining it. He doesn't have sterile gloves on, and I tell him he should wear surgical gloves so he puts a baggie over one hand and I wonder how he can possibly perform the operation that way. Then a woman assistant comes— who? I know her too, and they get me ready for the operation. I am afraid and try to get to a working phone. I ask the nurse how it looks and she says there isn't atherosclerosis, it looks healthy, but she can see up around the left side of my neck and there are some swollen adenoids.*

I'm always amazed at how a dream which makes no sense initially actually has such depth of meaning when explored. Jane asks me for my associations, and before I know it the dream begins to be understandable symbolically. I've begun reading more Jung— I'd already read MEMORIES, DREAMS, REFLECTIONS, and now I've started June Singer's BOUNDARIES OF THE SOUL, which I love. Maybe I'll be an Jungian analyst when I grow up! The training program is six years long, though, which seems too long considering I'd have to commute to New York and even see patients in the clinic there. But Jung makes sense to me, more than anyone else I've read. His understanding of the human psyche, of culture, of spirituality in the broadest sense of the word, seems so TRUE to me. And I love working with dreams and the idea of the collective unconscious.

There is a less formal program for the study of depth psychology not too far from here that meets several times a year over long weekends; perhaps I could apply to it and then decide whether to commit to six years of study.

I just remembered a dream from last night, after going to bed consciously angry:

*I'm near a room and see there's a bear inside. He's big and brown and he's moving around, clumsily knocking things over. I'm watching from outside the room. There's a young child in the room—a boy— maybe two or so. I know the bear won't hurt him. But then there's a field, and a man and woman looking for their dog. I find the dog, a white scotch terrier, in the grass. He is dead; all that's left is his head and backbone. Then I realize the bear killed him, and if he did then the child in the room is not safe either. I awaken, afraid.*

Guess I'd better tell Jane this one.

# Spring 1987

## Mary Ellen

I've been doing a lot of thinking about what's going on with me. Trying to put pieces together. I think it's coming more together as far as the problem but no solution so far. I wish I could say the anger is gone. It's calmed down but just waiting to strike. I can rationalize in my head and know the anger is inappropriate and way out of proportion but damn the feelings don't stop and mushroom out of control.

I believe I have figured out, with the help of the dreams and situations happening today, the feelings under the anger. ABAN-DONMENT. Disapproval to me leads to abandonment. From birth nothing about me or what I did brought approval or acceptance. I was always feeling abandoned although didn't know it at the time.

Billy was the only stable part of my life, no matter what went on in my home. I know I could get up run outside and Billy was there till time to go to bed. I must have felt very abandoned and angry when he left me. I don't remember. When we moved and the molestation and rape took place I remember crying myself to sleep and fantasizing Billy would come back and we would marry. I was very angry with God cause he sure wasn't there for me or protected me. He had abandoned me too.

I know I'm rambling but this is all in my head and I need to get it out.

This anger has sure surfaced bigger than me like it's going to engulf me. I've held it in so long afraid of disapproval and more abandonment. But it's started and I CAN'T stop it.

My anger seems to be a defense mechanism I've developed so as not to feel abandonment, also so I can push people away from me before they push me away. So as not to feel abandoned.

I don't know if any of this is making sense. I HATE myself when I get angry and push the people I love away.

Connie asked me why I feel I can get angry with her. I've thought about this. I feel about her as a friend, confidante, a person I trust and when I begin to feel panicky that she will push me away I become very angry perhaps testing her and maybe self-fulfilling a prophecy that she will abandon me just like everyone else in my life but it doesn't stop there, then it boomerangs. I become angry with myself. Why shouldn't she abandon me? I'm such a schmuck and worthless that she couldn't really like me anyway.

Now what to do about all this. I know I can't turn it all around overnight although I'd like to but I need a starting point. I need to feel I'm doing something to stop the cycle and get rid of all this anger and right now don't feel that I am . Maybe there aren't any answers. Through all this I'm trying to say I hate and am sorry for my behavior with Connie. I know it's not her and want her to know that somehow. I hope she can help me stop it before I destroy anymore relationships and eventually myself. My bulimia is keeping the rage under control but I don't want to use the bulimia any longer. It doesn't feel good.

Meanwhile I did go 25 days without sugar and when I'm not in a rage I'm not bingeing and purging most of the time. It was hard to stop the sugar but it really does make me artificially high and then I come crashing down just like with alcohol and drugs. I did binge on fruit a couple of times and potato chips and pasta once each in the past couple of weeks. I feel fat in my stomach and hips and my boobs are getting big, which I hate, because men notice big boobs and I hate that kind of attention. I wish I were completely flat chested, which when I'm skinny enough I almost am.

My financial situation is terrible and depressing. Being poor never seems to end. After I got rear ended my car needed eight hundred dollars worth of repair, which took every nickel I had and borrowing from two friends who won't be my friends for long if I don't pay them back soon. The damned insurance company is dragging its feet and I'm sick of it, plus Ceasar's alimony checks are always late and since it took me three weeks to find the clerical job after I lost the receptionist job I'm really broke. Everything is such a struggle.

But I did go to visit my daughter Amanda in Delaware, and even though we didn't really talk about anything from the past it was so good to see her and to know we've taken the first steps to being close again. We WERE close, I know that's not my imagination, and even though she kept her distance and I know from everything I've talked about with Connie she's got a ton of stuff to unload sometime, it's a start. And I did write a letter to my Dad in the hospital telling him everything and forgiving him. That was real hard, and I just hope they read it to him because he's too sick to read it himself. I wonder if I'll ever see him again, I think he's dying but I can't handle being with them right now.

So some really good things have happened, it's just that the rest of it is still so fucking hard. A guy from AA, Gene, has given me a chance to work on some of my shit around men and sex. Connie says maybe he showed up to give me the opportunity to feel and talk about all the old stuff that comes up when I get close to a man. He's brought me flowers, and paid for dinners—mostly pizza but so what, and last Friday we went to Pennsylvania for a weekend, which I think now I wasn't ready for. We had sex and then I felt used and needed space the next day, then guilty because after all he was treating. But I get this feeling that I have to perform, that he expects something of me sexually. What man doesn't. Making love was hard, and oral sex made me feel as if I was "servicing" him and then I just wanted to get away, I went into a rage and it didn't make sense because he wasn't forcing me or anything, I just felt cheap and dirty and I hated it and him too. Then of course he got put off and we drove home hardly speaking to each other, and I don't understand why I feel this way. I suppose it has to do with my grandfather, and the rape. Connie asked me if my grandfather made me perform oral sex and I said no, not that I know of. I'm thinking that I never did like penises, they're ugly, wormy things when they're soft and worse when they're big and hard, like weapons. Yuck. I think I don't want a relationship, I'm not ready for it, and at the same time as I go through my therapy sessions I'm more and more aware that I'm not just ordinarily needy, I'm extraordinarily needy, and I reach out to people like Gene and then get so scared of my own needs and so afraid I'll be too dependent that I push them away before that happens. So, as Connie said, that's one reason I've always nourished myself in secret, inappropriately.

There have been times in the past few months when I've felt as if the child in me is going to take over, the frightened one, and I'm learning that there's an adult part of me that can take care of that child and needs to let the child know that. Once in a while that feels o.k. but mostly I don't want to have anything to do with her. But then there's that other part, the one that's so enraged it could kill, that really feels like a monster inside that if I let it out would destroy everything in sight. That's different from the scared little girl. I hate them both.

Last week I was so furious with Connie when she told me I could not keep calling her at home, I had to use my sponsor and AA for support in between sessions—as if they're always available— I stormed into her office and told her I wanted to break everything. She just calmly said I could feel the anger, I could stamp my feet and express it verbally any way I wanted to, but I could not destroy anything in her office. I don't know what she would have done if I had, but that would probably have been it. So I talked instead and calmed down eventually and as usual learned some things as I said above.

But when I think about it I still get angry, then it turns to rage and I feel like I could be violent. Then I get scared. But I don't know what the hell she's thinking, it's not like I call over a hangnail. And then I think, I do call her a lot, and I'm such a burden she probably wishes she'd never started with me, and then I think that if she rejected me now I probably would kill myself, I just couldn't do this alone. But I hate myself for being so needy, and such a pain in the ass. I'm back on the Stelazine, one a night,

Dr. Z's answer to these intolerable feelings that are supposed to be tolerable, as if he understands or cares. When I'm in a rage I feel so powerful it's scary. It does help to share at meetings and to hear that others had similar feelings like rage and grief even after one or two years in the program.

# CHAPTER II

## *Spiraling Downward*

### Early Winter 1987

#### Connie

Mary Ellen is sinking into despair again after maintaining a reasonable degree of equilibrium for weeks. As with so many of my patients, Thanksgiving and Christmas have triggered longings, old grief, and hopelessness. The holidays never seem to be the warm, joyful occasions they're "supposed" to be. The abandonment depression that is always hovering beneath the surface gets activated full force. Mary Ellen's job situation is not only tenuous but more pressured than she can probably handle, and her relationships with co-workers are testy at best. She's been visibly losing weight, and when I weighed her and discovered she was at the minimum recommended by Evergreen and her doctor here, I decided to confront her. When I asked her what was happening with food, she laughed at me.

"I can't eat, and when I do I purge," she said defiantly.

"This is the lowest weight that's acceptable if you're going to stay in therapy with me," I told her. "If you can't maintain your weight perhaps you need to be hospitalized. I know I'm not willing to work with you unless you're willing to maintain."

She looked at me in disbelief.

"I told you," she said, angrily this time, "I can't eat, and when

I do it goes right through me."

"Laxatives?"

"No."

I wasn't at all sure I believed her, but there was no way to know.

"I'm serious, Mary Ellen," I said quietly but firmly.

I watched her face and body shut down, and she sat unspeaking, withdrawn, through a long silence. I waited, knowing I had to take this stand now or her weight could spiral downward until there was no alternative but hospitalization. There had to be a commitment to maintain weight in order to do the work of therapy, not get caught in an endless, compulsive struggle over eating. There was what felt like an interminable silence, and finally she began speaking.

"There's lots of upheaval and uncertainty at work," she said. "And I'm really uncomfortable living with Therese, she's such a know it all. I have to go to court on the twenty-third, and if the insurance company comes through I'll find somewhere else to live, but I feel as if I don't know where I'm going, like I'm treading water."

She paused, and I was aware of how much more real she seemed than when she walked through the door.

"I'm just not sure I want to do this."

"What's the "this"?

"This. This life. Between the car wreck, and the medical bills, and the lowliness, especially not being with my kids, I just don't know if it's worth it. I feel alien, not human, like I can see people but I'm invisible to them. I don't know what they see, but they don't see me. Except that they're watching me, especially at work. They're training me on the computer but there's a lot of pressure to know it already and when I get nervous I make mistakes. I know they're talking about me, I just don't fit in."

I tried to see her through the eyes of an employer or a co-worker. Her long hair was straggly, her clothes were unattractive and fit badly, and her fingernails looked as if they hadn't been manicured for months. I could see why she wouldn't fit in in a corporate environment, but I didn't know what to offer that might be constructive and not heard as insulting. I said nothing.

" And I don't want to have anything to do with Christmas, it's such a joke," she said contemptuously.

I empathized with how painful the holidays must be for her: the sad memories, the unfulfilled expectations, the illusions that are encouraged by television and commercialism in general. I encouraged her to reach out through AA to find sober gatherings, to make plans and alternative plans for Christmas Eve, Christmas, and New Year's rather than risk isolation and further depression. By the time she left she'd agreed to maintain her weight and go to extra meetings beyond the three or four a week she'd been attending faithfully. As she walked out the door she handed me a piece of paper.

"Read this if you get a chance," she said dismissively.

It was a poem:

> In whom do we trust?
> I've trusted the best and eventually
> They bite the dust
> I trusted those close
> Those hurt the most
> Trust in the Lord, he'll always be there
> Although I know not where
> Down and out, no where to turn
> Need to trust or I'll just bust
>
> Life's got you down
> Nothing looks bright
> What little you had
> Has slipped away in the night
>
> Rise above you say, and go on
> The struggle gets harder with

Nothing left to give
The light goes through your fingers
Like a sieve

Each time I get close
To what I want the most it slips away once again out of
     sight.

As far as life is concerned I am such a mess
For right now I'm trying my best
Trying hard not to give up but without the light
Hard to see where I'm going
Too many dead ends it seems
Keep walking the blind path and hope
A door will open, giving rest at last

    I sat for a few minutes, feeling the weight of her depression. I felt such compassion for her, and I was also disconcertingly, increasingly, aware that she was looking to me to fulfill all her needs, and that no matter what I did I would be unable to do that. I experienced her need, her dependency, as a strong pull that she expressed in many ways: requests for extra sessions, periodic escalation of phone calls in between sessions, sitting very close to me in sessions, clinging hugs at the end of sessions, and often, too often for my comfort, those hollow, empty eyes turned toward me in unspoken supplication. I felt frustrated at my inability to give her enough to fill the gaping empty wound in her psyche, wondered how long I would have to provide the "holding environment" Winnicott talks about, wondered if I could be that "good enough" mother she never had. I had a strong sense that a lot of what I did, and did best, in my work was the kind of reparenting Steven Levenkron describes in his books about eating disorders. I believed that there was a level of dependency upon the therapist that was necessary for people like Mary Ellen to experience, and that when they'd had enough of that, like children, they would move into the next developmental stage. I trusted that, and my own experience of mothering was that. But oh! this was difficult work. I wasn't at all sure I had enough experience and expertise to help her.

The next session Mary Ellen was still despondent and, after telling me some of the details of the past few days, announced that she had saved fifty lithium tablets and had decided that if the insurance didn't come through she was going to kill herself.

"That sounds like a threat, or some kind of bargain," I said.

"I'm really pissed at God. If he wants me here, he'll provide for me, and if he doesn't at least do that then it's time for me to take things into my own hands."

"Oh," I said, feeling suddenly annoyed. "So you'll play God."

She stared at me, as if surprised by my words.

"The problem with the lithium is that it might not do the job," she went on thoughtfully, ignoring me. "But I have a better plan."

"What's that?"

"It's easy to get a gun. I wasn't going to tell you this but I will. I'm going to drive into your driveway on Christmas and park by the barn and shoot myself there."

I looked at her, aghast, and struggled to maintain my composure.

"I think that would be a very hostile act," I said coldly.

"The reason I'm telling you," she said, as if her words were reasonable, "is because I want to know if you'll come to my funeral."

"Your funeral?" I said, suddenly very angry and feeling very untherapeutic, a distant, inaccessible part of me aware that I was having a negative transferential reaction. "Are you kidding? You're going to drive into my driveway on Christmas morning and shoot yourself and you want to know if I'll come to your funeral? No, I won't come to your funeral, not only that but if you shoot yourself in my driveway I'll never speak to you again."

I heard the absurdity of my words but was not about to rephrase them. Mary Ellen just stared at me, stunned by my outburst.

"Look, Mary Ellen," I continued a little more calmly. "I hope you don't kill yourself, and I'm more than willing to get you admitted to the hospital for a few days if you need protection from yourself. But committing suicide, here? On Christmas Day? No. Perhaps next week we should talk about what that would mean to you, but right now we need to stop, our time is up."

I stood up and opened the door. She left without saying a word.

Well, now it's New Year's Eve, and she hasn't committed suicide and I don't think she will, at least right now, but she holds on to the idea of escape from life pretty strongly. Given what I know she's been through, and my sense that her abuse was much more extensive than what she remembers so far, it's certainly understandable. I've discussed in supervision my professional responsibility toward her, and if she actually takes lithium or in some other way attempts suicide and lets me know, I'll call the police and hope they get there in time. But if she continues to refuse hospitalization, there's not a lot I can do. I just wish she wouldn't keep calling me at night to discuss whether she will or she won't. So far I've talked her out of it, tried to instill hope.

New Year's Eve, the end of an intense year personally and professionally. The major work I've done in my analysis has revolved around my relationship with my husband and my father— in the latter case my internalized father, who's continued to affect every area of my life even though he died when I was eighteen. I've continued to defend him in a way that I see now is irrational in the face of his obvious cruelty to my mother and to us, and though it makes no sense logically, it's very difficult to change. But with Jane's help, at least I have come to understand that loving him and desperately craving his love was normal, particularly since I was only four and a half when my mother had him legally evicted for abusing her (and us). Though I don't remember it, I must have blamed myself, thought there was something wrong with me for him to have left. If only I'd been "better"—a good girl—he would have stayed. And of course the way he treated me all throughout my childhood only confirmed that I was not good enough to be loved by him. No wonder I spent so many years trying to earn the love of any man I loved, tried so hard to be "good" and therefore lovable! I know I was also terrified of my father's aggression, and with good reason, but I can't feel that, I only know I still go out of my way to avoid angry encounters, am afraid of aggression. And at some level I must have believed that some of the negative things he said about my mother were at least partially true.

So I decided, I wonder when, that my power lay in my capacity to understand, to make sense out of what was senseless. To know. A useful skill. The only problem is that in so doing I blocked out all the negativity I saw around me, allowed myself to register only the positive, saw life through rose colored glasses. And split off, big time. I was "good", but not whole. Twelve steppers call it Denial, and as they say, that ain't no river in Egypt.

My dreams have continued to lead the way; I'm astounded at the process that has unfolded through working with them: the remembering, the recording, the sharing with Jane, the active imagination with the dream symbols. The entire process, the Jungian approach, absolutely fascinates me, and I'm naturally bringing more and more of my learning into sessions with my patients, which enlivens and deepens the work.

One recent dream in particular stands out as a clear, true, and humorous statement about how I've tried to deal with potentially aggressive power, mine and others', and my growing awareness of how inadequate that is. It's my second lion dream, the first being my "opening" dream the week before I began working with Jane.

*I'm in a house of many rooms. There is a large male lion in one of the bedrooms, pacing back and forth, tail twitching. The room is smallish and has two bunk beds. I bring the lion a huge bowl of Purina Dog Chow. The lion is golden, the color of my golden retriever Yukon, with a large mane. He moves powerfully and gracefully, shoulder muscles rippling. I am standing outside the door, watching him, and there is someone standing on my right, I think a man. There are other people in the house. The man says the way to keep the lion in the room is to tie a pink ribbon to the door hinge (the door is open) and then we walk through the house, and as we pass each room he tells how to keep the lion in that particular room: for example, he suggests a small chair in one open doorway, a low gate in front of another, etc. I know they are all inappropriate, useless. I wake up.*

What is my vision for myself, as I begin a new year? To continue on my path as a healer, letting myself be led by whatever unseen force has led me thus far. To be open to new ideas, to keep my commitment to my higher self. To honor my body and care for it by eating and drinking only that which will sustain it as a healthy vessel. To exercise all of myself—mind, body, spirit—so as to be free to express the highest good. To seek fulfillment of those ideals which I honor in the wider world through community endeavors—church, peace and environmental organizations. To simplify my life so that there is time and space to attend to higher goals. To respect the earth. To depend on God alone.

# Mary Ellen

I feel like a robot. I feel like I'm in a dream. Other people seem real, the things around me seem real, but I don't feel real. I don't feel anything. Something's different since the hospital, I can't explain it. It's a chore to get through a day. No matter how hard I try, nothing works. It's hard to get out of bed, hard to get myself to work, hard to do the work once I get there. My boss told me I'm "not functioning on the job" and I know they're going to terminate me, why doesn't somebody terminate me and get it over with. I was taking Sinequan at Carter House and maybe it helped but I couldn't talk right, words wouldn't come to me, it was like everything was in slow motion. Connie said I was slurring my speech and my tongue felt strange, like it was too big for my mouth, so I saw Dr. Z. and he took me off it a couple of days ago. My mind seems to be clearer but I don't feel anything yet. I still think about suicide, ways to do it, and when I drive I think about crashing the car again but it's a thought, not like I want to do it or am about to right that minute.

I saw Connie today and I know she's trying to help but it's not getting better. I just don't care anymore, like nothing matters. I don't know if this is depression or acceptance. She seemed concerned and I'm supposed to see Dr. Z. tomorrow, so I'll go but don't expect any good to come of it. Connie thought I might have to be readmitted but I've only been out three weeks and it didn't help anyway so I'm not going back. I would cry if I could but I can't. I've been dreaming and writing them down and bringing them to Connie and now she'll work with them she never would before but she's changed her mind for some reason. Here's one from last night:

*I was in a hospital-type place but it wasn't Carter House. The nurses all knew me and liked me. I wasn't talking. All I kept saying is I'm not going to get better. They kept assuring me I would but I knew I wasn't. I kept saying but I can't cry. They would just smile at me. I was sitting on the floor in the room and there was a mattress beside me. All of a sudden they put a woman in there. According to them she was bad, a foreigner. I liked her and tried to protect her from them. Then it was time to go into a room for a lecture or something. I didn't want to go but went. I sat at the top of the stairs and all of a sudden started banging my head on the big column there screaming "See, I can't cry" repeatedly. This big woman came up the stairs toward me carrying a tray. As she was giving me a needle I woke up.*

I want my feelings to come back but I'm afraid of the sadness, the lowliness, the anger. I don't even care about how I look or whether I take a shower, it just doesn't matter. The nurses at Carter House had to remind me to wash, and I only remember taking one shower, maybe I took more, I don't really know. I know I was belligerent in the hospital towards the nurses and the doctors, I didn't want anyone telling me what to do, and I offended them. Tough shit. Connie came to see me twice in the ten days I was there, and even when she came I didn't want to get out of bed. I hate hospitals, I don't know why. Maybe it's because of when I ran across the street when I was ten and got hit by a car and broke my leg, and I was so scared because I hadn't stopped and looked and listened and my Dad was surely going to beat me. I had to stay home for a long time, couldn't go to school.

I'm trying to eat three meals a day and I'm not bingeing or purging for a change, at least not in three or four days. I don't care about food, it's an effort to eat but I'm doing it because I have to. I had a couple of other dreams, in fact I'm having lots of vivid dreams, like movies.

*I was in a bad place and I didn't like being there. I tried getting out and I took someone with me each time to get out. A machine with a big ball swung down and hit us, three times. They were men, and they all died. A person who really wanted to help me put me in a special car and I almost got away but the machine with the ball came and knocked me back again.*

I awoke from this one sure I'm going to die. I wasn't afraid, I was certain. I'm still not afraid, I feel protected from harm somehow even though I'm going to die. But I want my feelings back, I want to cry. And I don't even know why.

Connie asked me a lot of questions about the images in the dream, what the men looked like, and what did a big swinging ball mean to me, and stuff like that, and as we talked it seemed that the three men might be my father, my grandfather, and my husband, the men I thought would help me get out of the bad place I was in with myself ever since I was a child. And I thought maybe the person who put me in the special car was Connie helping me and putting me in the hospital, but this great big destructive force I have no control over gets me too. And I guess that's the way I think, kind of fatalistic, like there's no reason to hope I can escape death. Not that I want to.

Then there was another one that Connie helped me to understand was about three parts of me that do exist inside me, which made sense because a lot of the time I feel that way, that I'm a grownup sometimes and other times I'm younger, but not always the same age younger.

*I was playing three parts, all different ages and all me. The oldest had just gotten over being retarded, the other one, the middle one, said he had to go out on his own, and the little one said he wasn't going to go to school to learn how to be normal.*

I used to think I was retarded because I had such a hard time in school. Now I feel retarded at work, and people make comments that I don't like but it doesn't matter. Nothing matters. I had one other dream I wrote down that maybe was the worst because I can't stand rats and mice, they bite and carry germs and look at you with beady eyes. And you never know when they might attack.

*I was falling asleep, and then floating. I couldn't move or breathe, and I wasn't sure if it was real or a dream but I felt like I was smother-ing. I knew I had to get up. Walking was hard, and I ran into my bike that was in the hallway. I tried to call for Connie but I couldn't. I decided to call Laura and made my way slowly to the phone. I kept knocking things over. And then I saw a white mouse that looked as though it would attack. I tried to throw something at it but I fell. I woke myself up.*

We didn't have time to talk about this one much but Connie did say that white mice often show up in dreams and besides what I think of when I think of a white mouse, they have the same meaning for lots of people, I think she called it a universal mean-ing. So the mouse was an instinctual part of myself I'm afraid of, something inside me that might attack me. I suppose like my inner monster "Doom" in a way, only different. I do want to talk about my dreams I don't know why.

But I think I'll never be better, I'll always be depressed. I accept that. Is that depression, or serenity? Nothing's a big deal now, whatever takes place takes place. I'll do the best I can and if it's not o.k., that's o.k. I want to die. I'm ready. I've talked to God about it, and I know I was a good mother, I did my job. I just don't want to struggle and fight and lose anymore.

# CHAPTER III

## *Divine Intervention*

### Late Winter 1988

#### Connie

I'm not sure whether I made the biggest blunder of my professional career with Mary Ellen or, because I'd been called once too many times in the middle of the night, inadvertently did the most therapeutic thing possible. It may be a while before I know for sure.

Mary Ellen called me two weeks ago on a Friday night after I'd had a long, hard day and a long, hard week and said, once again, she wanted to kill herself, there was no hope. I talked with her for a little while, suggested she go back into the hospital for a few days if she felt she could not control the impulse to harm herself, etc., etc. And at a certain point I knew I'd reached my limit, the end of my patience with her ambivalence toward living.

"I can't take responsibility for whether you live or die," I said angrily. " Either you go back to Carter House and allow yourself to be taken care of until you get through this, or you attempt suicide and call me and I'll then call the police, or you just kill yourself, but I'm not going through this with you in the middle of the night any more. You decide if you want to live or die. It's up to you. Please don't call me in between sessions to discuss it again." And I said goodbye and hung up, furious and frustrated.

Of course I couldn't get back to sleep for a long time, but I'd actually been advised in my supervision group to take exactly this stand (only without the anger!) and hadn't been able to until now. I didn't know what she'd do, and I was afraid. Would she show up for her Monday appointment or be found dead somewhere? What a way to make a living.

She did show up the next Monday, looking extremely pale and tired but more together than she had in weeks. "I hated you Friday," she reported, for the first time in a long time maintaining eye contact instead of staring blankly at the rug.

I nodded. What I didn't say was I hated you too Friday.

"When you said you couldn't help me I called Dr. Z., and he yelled at me too. I didn't know what to do, there was no one, no one in the world to help me. I had the pills all lined up, the lithium and a lot of other things I'd saved, and I knew it was time to do it. And then I thought, I'll pray one more time, so I lay down on my belly and prayed to God, and then I fell asleep. I don't know if it was in a dream or I woke up, but all of a sudden I saw a bright white light, and I looked up and saw Jesus standing there surrounded by this white light with his arms held out toward me, looking at me with such love and compassion I've never seen before. And he said, "It's not time. I will cradle you in my arms, I am with you always." And I knew he was there for me, that he didn't want me to take my life, that he was guiding me in some way. And when I woke up I didn't want to kill myself anymore. And it doesn't matter any more if you're there for me, or Dr. Z., or anyone else on this planet, because Jesus IS there for me, and that's all that matters."

She paused, and I truly didn't know how to respond, so I just nodded. What did it mean? Was it "real"? Now what?

"Jesus Christ will always be with me," she repeated. "I can't count on anyone else."

Because of my training I felt an immediate need to understand her experience psychologically, but at the same time I sensed that she had truly had a numinous experience, one filled with divine presence.

"That's wonderful, Mary Ellen," I said, groping for words. "If you have truly connected with the light of Christ, anything is possible. Everything is possible."

"Do you believe in Christ?" she asked me.

"Yes, I do," I answered, a little uncomfortable with the question, and aware my answer was simplistic. I didn't discuss my religious beliefs with my patients.

Mary Ellen sighed, appeared relieved.

"I'm going to visit my sister for a few days," she said, reaching into a shopping bag at her side. "Will you keep these for me?"

She pulled out a large zip-lock baggie filled with pills of many shapes and colors and handed it to me. I took it, shaking my head in disbelief that she could have accumulated so much medication.

"It's my stash," she said, smiling faintly. "I won't need it any more."

"I'll turn it over to Dr. Z.," I said, thinking, he's not going to like this.

"O.K.," she said. "I'm still really pissed at him though."

I nodded. I was doing a lot of nodding this session.

We talked for a while longer, and when she left I was still in a state of shock. At the same time I had a strong feeling that this might be a crucial turning point.

When she returned from her sister's ten days later Mary Ellen seemed clearer in thought and memory, and she said she was beginning to think about looking for a new job.

"That was the deepest depression I've ever been in," she said thoughtfully. "I'm not sleeping much and I feel restless, but the depression is better, much better."

She said she'd had a good visit with her sister and wrote a lot while her sister was at work. She wanted to read to me, so I settled back in my chair to listen. She began tentatively, but her voice became stronger, more certain, as she continued.

"I've been thinking about pedestals, and how they hold things to be looked upon and admired. In my case they were always that, and the things on them also had qualities I wanted. When I was little I was sent to church so my parents would have a peaceful weekend without children. Like everything else, the messages I got there were confusing. I was taught about Jesus and all his wonders, that he'd protect me, love me no matter what kind of mistakes I made. So I put him on a pedestal, where he belonged, and wanted to be like him.

"With people, I could feel what was going on with them, and when they were angry, or hurting. If I used my brain I could do right, and please them, and they would love me. Or so I thought."

Mary Ellen looked up every few words, watching my face carefully. I tried to just listen, not respond actively to anything she said until she was done.

"I put my Dad on a pedestal to admire because everyone seemed to look up to him. He had such power. So I looked at the good qualities and disregarded the bad. He beat me, but he told me he beat me only out of love, told me I was bad. After a while I rejected him. I didn't want to believe I was that bad.

"And then horrible things happened to me, incest with my grandfather, and no support from my mother, and the rape that took away all my self esteem. I wondered where Jesus my protector was when all those things happened, and I couldn't figure it out. I was sure I was so bad that even he abandoned me. So of course I rejected him.

I stopped trying to be good, what was the use? To accept that I was bad was less painful, or so I thought. I lied, I stole, I enjoyed taking advantage of people. I found alcohol and drugs and found they gave me self-worth, they said I was o.k. The pain went away, and there was no fear of retaliation.

"Somehow, in all this haze I got pregnant and became a wife, only to discover I'd married another father. He abused me emotionally, always out of care and love, just like my father. I was convinced I was getting all I was worth, and to kill the pain I used more and more alcohol and drugs. I tried to be the best mother to the children I could be, to protect them and love them the only way I knew how. We were close and that felt good, but when Johnny was born and turned out retarded Ceasar hated me with a vengeance and things got worse and worse. After a while alcohol and drugs no longer killed the pain and I felt Wayne and Angela to be slowly leaving me. They tried to be kind and said they loved me, but they had lives of their own. When they were both gone I felt so abandoned, all alone. I was a mess, and when my "friends" no longer helped—not the alcohol, not the drugs, not the bulimia—it seemed the only way out was to reject life. I didn't know it then, but my higher power said no. I was running scared, felt all alone, and somehow even with all the times I tried to kill myself He finally got me into the program so I could slow down long enough to listen to Him.

"I struggled to find a higher power, I tried to use the program as I was told, but there was a huge problem. I kept putting people on pedestals, only to find human frailties, and rejection of me. I groped, I hung on to people, and I scared them with my expectations. And then . . . "

Mary Ellen paused, a catch in her voice. She took a deep breath and continued, a tear sliding down her right cheek.

"And then the person I had on my highest pedestal said 'I can't help you, don't you see'. In all my confusion I said 'if you can't who can? I know my higher power sent me to you."

I felt such an ache in my chest, and tears filled my eyes. I struggled to hold them back. Mary Ellen noticed, continued reading.

"Consumed with rejection and pain, filled with anger and hurt, I decided to use my plan. Face to face with death I felt much confusion. I was not afraid of death but a small part of me believed my higher power, that life might get better. I decided to pray. I prayed for death to take away the pain, but I was afraid to kill myself because it felt like Satan's work. And then Jesus came to me, just stood there, loving me, and I've never felt such joy."

"I know now that I want Jesus' love, and to know the wonders of life. It took so much pain for me to get close to him, to truly feel his presence. And now I know he's carrying me, and I find comfort in knowing that he's there. My pain isn't gone, but I know that I still need it to remain close to him.

"And the other thing I know . . . " she paused again, looked up at me, and laughed uneasily. "This is hard. . . . The other thing I know is that I mistook Connie for my savior, and that got us in a lot of trouble. She listened so intently, and helped me express myself, she opened the lines of communication so I could look at the feelings within. She listened to my secrets with care in her eyes. She made me feel she could see some goodness in all the darkness buried in me even though I felt so bad about myself. She brought out my sense of humor, encouraged me to write. Imagine the pressure she was under, me thinking she was my savior! I expected her to be able to save my soul. When she said she couldn't help me, I was at the bottom and had no strength left to hold on. I was forced to let go, but I didn't have very far to fall because Jesus wrapped me in a blanket of love and held me."

"I believe in angels on earth, and Connie is one that God has put on my path." She looked up and smiled at me.

" Of course with human frailties," she laughed.

"There's so much work ahead to find a oneness of my body to match the peace that is within. Hopefully to find God's unity. I hope that my angel will stay by me, guiding me with therapy. Our relationship can take on new meaning with both of us remembering our human frailties. Now that I'm getting to know my savior I think we can work better together. Thank you, my angel, for staying by me."

I reached for the Kleenex box and took one, then two, and handed the box to Mary Ellen. We both wiped our eyes, blew our noses, and then began laughing. I reached out my arms to her and we hugged. There were no words needed. I had no words.

That night I had a dream:

*I am standing on a dock, like the one in Sutton Manor where I lived as an adolescent. Mary Ellen is in the water, under the surface where no one can see her, drowning. Several people rescue her; I am part of the rescue effort. Then I am sitting in a chair holding her on my lap. She is cold and pale, and she has her head on my shoulder and I have my arms around her, comforting her. I think to myself that she is awfully big to be on my lap, but that's what's needed.*

## Mary Ellen

I've been writing a lot, and crying a lot—good tears—and sometimes feeling such joy I can't believe it's me feeling it. I've written letters to my kids, and I'm turning some of my journal writing into poetry, and I've been going to church and maybe will be baptized in the fall. They do it in the water, I think in a swimming pool! Maybe I'll change my name for the baptism, I always hated Mary Ellen, I can still hear my mother yelling "Mary Ellen, don't do this" or "Mary Ellen, do that" . My name was always said with such spite, such disapproval, never with love. I hated it. I don't know what a better name would be, but if I am going to be new in Christ by being baptized, I need a new name.

But something else about the name Mary Ellen bothers me. Lately I've been waking up in the night, as if I've been dreaming but I'm awake when it happens, and I hear a voice—my grandfather's voice—saying my name, and it gives me the shivers. It's this soft, soothing voice, but it scares me, and I don't know why. Connie says she wonders if there was more than the one incest experience I remember with my grandfather, and I have this awful feeling there was, but it's just a feeling, a sick feeling in the pit of my stomach, and it makes me want to throw up. Like I know something awful that I can't remember.

I told Connie that I do remember not wanting breasts or a round bottom because I vaguely remember my grandfather watching me and being very uncomfortable with that. But the only thing I remember is the one time, when I was in bed between my grandparents. I cried so hard when I told Connie about it, and I feel so ashamed when I think about it, because I remember him touching me, and it felt good, and at the same time I was afraid and I knew he shouldn't be doing it. Connie asked me what I was doing in bed with my grandparents when I was twelve, and I don't know, I don't remember, all I remember is that my grandmother was asleep and my grandfather was touching me on my belly and then my breasts and between my legs, and I could feel it but it was like I was frozen there too, I wanted to get up and run but I couldn't. Why didn't I?

Connie said there's an incest group I can join but I don't want to. I'm aware that I want my body to be clean, and it doesn't feel clean, no matter how many times I wash. I'm ashamed when sexual feelings come up, I can't feel aroused without feeling shame and terror. It didn't used to be like that, when I was drunk, which is probably the only time I had sex come to think of it, I could do anything and not feel ashamed. At least till later. But now I feel ashamed every time I think of sex. Is it because of that one time with my grandfather, and the rape? It feels like there's more, but I don't know what it is. It feels like there's something stored in my body, I feel pain and discomfort especially in my abdomen It's more than bloat from food or water weight.

I keep praying that Jesus will heal the damage I've done. I'm eating better, and I've gained a couple of pounds and I'm trying not to let that bother me. I talked to Connie about having some body work done, and she thought it would be a good idea but need to work with someone who knows about incest and how to deal with what might come up. She's going to talk to people she knows and recommend someone.

I went to see Dr. Moore for a check up because my chest felt funny, a strange kind of discomfort that felt normal and yet abnormal for me. He said my pulse rate is down twenty points, and my blood pressure is normal, and even the electrocardiogram was normal. He gave me a clean bill of health! And said I look very well. I do feel different, and I can't explain it, just that something is changing in my body, and lots of the time I feel calmer than I ever have in my life. It's very strange.

I had a terrible dream that made me think more about hospitals and why I can't stand them, why I don't want to be touched, why I go into a weird rage when I'm in the hospital no matter what's happening. In real life I had my tonsils out when I was four and then of course hit by the car when I was ten, otherwise I wasn't in the hospital until my kids were born.

*I was a very little girl, maybe four or six years old. There was a man who kept coming at me. His face was close to me; his face kept getting bigger. I kept screaming don't touch me, don't hurt me. Then there was a very large schoolboys passing close by. Then I woke up, terrified and thought, did something happen at that time? I tried to push the thought away.*

# CHAPTER IV

## *Descent Into Darkness*

### Spring 1988

#### Connie

I heard Mary Ellen come into my waiting room and wondered if her recent conversion experience was going to last or if, once again, she would sink into deep despair any day now. The past few months have been so difficult for her and with her. Despite the deepening of our relationship, I often feel inadequate to deal with the deep wounds she has suffered. I don't know if I have enough of what it will take to companion her through her process of healing—enough understanding, enough patience, enough skill, enough faith in the therapeutic process. If she continues to feel she has made a spiritual connection to something beyond me—in her case, Jesus—her recovery might proceed in a very different way. We might be able to venture into and work through painful memories she couldn't approach before without the danger of fragmentation and possible psychosis. She has told me that she feels "held" by God now, safe no matter what happens, and this can only strengthen the container within which a deep process—in Jungian terms an alchemical process—is taking place. As her therapist, I know one of my major functions is to provide a safe container, a sacred space in my office and in our relationship. But now the transpersonal, the transcendent, has entered this space in her consciousness, and our relationship is already being transformed by it. I am so grateful.

And I'm also grateful for the excellent supervision I'm getting both here and in New York, and the Institute for the Study of Depth Psychology for its Jungian program. It's helped me so much with patients like Mary Ellen! I've been able to interpret to her that because she had both an intrusive and an abandoning mother, whenever she experiences intense contact she becomes terrified of engulfment and also of loss. Closeness produces panic, and love becomes insatiable hunger because the terror is that the object world will vanish, absolutely vanish. And there is constant testing going on to see if I, as her therapist, will survive her aggression and her need. Her mother either retaliated with aggression or ignored her needs. There is such extreme terror, the terror of annihilation, under all of the acting out. I need to hold on to a deep understanding of all of this to work with Mary Ellen, and I need to help her to understand her abandonment depression as fully as possible so it doesn't, like quicksand, pull her under. I'm learning, and everything I'm learning with Mary Ellen is helping me with my other patients.

It's an enormous relief for me to come down off the pedestal I've been on for so long. I knew I was being seen as all good and all powerful, a necessary idealization for her in the beginning stages of therapy. But sooner or later I was bound to fail her, and I did. I also know that the crisis that developed out of her disillusionment with me as savior could have resulted in her death; instead, it offered new life.

"Please, God, let it be real," I prayed silently as I went to open the door. "I need all the help I can get."

Mary Ellen practically leaped out of her chair, startling Fantastic onto the floor. A wide grin enlivened her face; her eyes sparkled with joy. She looked younger, healthier, than I'd ever seen her.

"I've been crying a lot," she said, laughing.

I looked at her, puzzled at the inconsistency, but I couldn't help smiling. What a refreshing change! She flopped onto the couch as I settled myself in my chair.

"They're good tears, tears of joy," she said. "I feel like a new person, like I've really been reborn."

"You do look different," I told her truthfully. Except when she was in the midst of emotional process, which she seemed to recover from quickly each time, she had been remarkably cheerful the past few sessions.

"I have a clean bill of health from my doctor. First time in my life," she said happily.

"I know Jesus is with me. I KNOW it. He's trying to heal the damage I've done. I have to help, though."

Suddenly her smile faded; she looked drained, exhausted, and her eyes filled with tears.

"I want my body to be clean," she said. "You tell me what happened to me wasn't my fault, but I'm so ashamed, it still feels like my fault."

"Do you want to talk about the shame?" I asked gently.

There was a long, full silence.

"This is so hard," she said, looking away. "I know I couldn't have stopped my grandfather, at least you tell me that . . . though when I think of a twelve year old I think why not, why didn't I just get out of that bed? I was old enough to do that. I know my grandmother might have woven up and known what was going on, but why didn't I want her to?"

Mary Ellen stared at a spot on the braid rug for a long time.

"But it's worse than that." She glanced up at me, then at her hands, which were clasped tightly on her lap. "I don't think there was only one time. I think it might have happened a lot more."

She looked up at me again, and I nodded assent. I had felt this to be true for a long time, based on the severity of her symptoms.

"And sometimes, sometimes . . . what he did felt good. I can't believe I can say this, but it's true. Even though I was terrified of him, and I hate him for what he did, if it felt good, even for a minute, I feel so guilty and ashamed I can't stand it."

"The fear and the pain and the pleasure got all mixed up, didn't they," I said. "That's what's so horribly damaging about incest—love and abuse seem to mean the same thing. You were looking for love and you got abuse instead. That wasn't your fault, not for a minute! He had all the power."

I heard the anger in my voice, felt it course through my body. How often I, as therapist, was required to give voice to my patients' split-off anger, modeling what they had never had permission to express! And how much easier it was getting for me to do this as I got more in touch with my personal rage at abuse in all forms and the devastation, the soul theft, it created!

Mary Ellen began to rock back and forth, tears coursing down her face. She wiped her eyes and nose with her sleeve; I handed her a Kleenex box and said softly, "You were a child. What could you possibly have done differently?"

"I don't know, I don't know," she wailed, ignoring the Kleenex, wiping her face on her other sleeve. "It MUST have been my fault."

Suddenly she stopped rocking and stared at me with hollow eyes. She whispered, "I don't want to remember any more, but I know I have to."

"What are you remembering now?" I asked.

"I don't know, I don't know!" she wailed.

I waited silently, feeling a knot in the pit of my stomach, not sure if it was my anxiety at what was beginning to unfold, or her anguish.

"I was home after school," she began in a soft, hesitant voice, holding her hands tightly together on her lap. "I heard him downstairs, walking around . . . and I hid in my room. I must have been twelve. No one else was home. I heard his boots on the stairs, he always wore these big, heavy black boots. I was SO SCARED! I heard his footsteps and I hid behind my bed. I knew he was coming for me. He came in the room and found me, he always found me, and pulled me to a chair. He sat down and held me on his lap and . . . and . . . put his finger in my rectum. I started to scream and he put his hand over my mouth. I couldn't breathe, I couldn't get away, it hurt, it hurt, it hurt!"

Mary Ellen was sobbing hysterically now, rocking back and forth, tears flowing down her face. My stomach was tied in knots. I reached out to her, laid my hand on her arm to comfort her.

"Oh, God, why did he do that to me? He took away my body, he . . . " suddenly Mary Ellen's voice changed, became childlike with a sing-song cadence. Her face, too, altered somehow, and her eyes glazed over. I had the eerie sense that she had left, that her consciousness was elsewhere, and when she spoke I realized it was true. She had spontaneously regressed to become the child she once was.

"Don't pee in me, Grandpa, please don't pee in me," Mary Ellen pleaded as she curled up in the big chair, staring ahead with unseeing eyes. "It hurts when you do that," she whimpered, "please don't do that."

I made an attempt to reach her.

"Mary Ellen, what's happening? Try to tell me."

But she was clearly in her own world, and even if she heard me, could not respond. I watched, and waited. She began to writhe in the chair, screaming once as if in excruciating pain and then, frantically to pull at her mouth, twisting her head violently from side to side. Her eyes were wide with terror, and as I watched I felt anxious and frightened, not knowing where this was leading.

"Mary Ellen, Mary Ellen," I called to her uselessly, "try and tell me what's happening." But she appeared to be totally unaware that I was there, and then she began to cough and choke and clutch at her throat, and I became truly alarmed.

"Come back, Mary Ellen, come back," I repeated insistently. "You're forty-one years old, you're in my office, you just remembered something, and it's over now. Open your eyes and be here, NOW!" While I spoke to her I anxiously tried to remember my CPR skills, which I hadn't had to use since I took the course years ago. I would do mouth-to-mouth resuscitation if I had to. Her face had a bluish tinge; she was either holding her breath or couldn't breathe.

"BREATHE, Mary Ellen," I commanded her. This was getting really scary.

But whatever was happening ended spontaneously and abruptly; suddenly her entire body went limp. I spoke to her, but there was no response, only the sound of her rasping breath. At least she was breathing, thank God, I thought. She lay there for a few minutes, then began crying softly. I felt her sad desperation.

"God, please take me away," she cried in that same singsong child's voice. "Grandpa took away my body, it's not mine anymore, not mine to keep or give away. God, why don't you take me? I've been asking you for so long. I don't want to be here, don't you understand?"

She began retching, and I reached for my wastebasket, but she didn't vomit, just heaved and heaved, her face ashen and drawn. Finally, still apparently oblivious to her surroundings, she curled up in a fetal position and was silent. I covered her carefully with a blanket and kept watch while she slept.

## Mary Ellen

The pain was awful when I left Connie's office. My vagina and abdomen hurt so bad I didn't think I could stand up. And I was cold, and sick, so sick. I kept wanting to throw up, even though I didn't want to do that anymore. I was so nauseous, I don't know if it was from remembering what happened and feeling it again in my body or from knowing for the first time that he had intercourse with me.

When I was in the chair, reliving it, it was as if I was watching from someplace outside my body. I saw Connie, but I couldn't talk to her. But I remember it all, I'll never forget it again. I want to kill him; if he weren't already dead I would I think. But I'm scared, too, scared of my anger. If I feel that angry I'll be punished, I know I will.

I called Connie that night because I couldn't stop crying. I know I still call her too much, but I couldn't help it this time, there was no one else who would understand. No one. It was the twelve-year old in me that couldn't stop, and I was so angry at her for not stopping, I wanted to kill her too. I just didn't want to deal with her. And I wanted to throw up in the worst way. I felt so turbulent, out of control for the first time since Christ came to me. Worrying about the twelve-year old takes me from the Lord. I told Connie that, and she said maybe the reason I'm able to remember what happened to me at twelve now is because I feel connected to God in a way I never did before. I know she's right, but I still don't want to deal with that twelve-year old. I told her how sick and dirty I felt, and she suggested a ritual of some sort—a bath or a douche—to cleanse myself of his energy. But I haven't done it yet. It felt like I had to do something else first.

When I went for my next appointment I told Connie about my anger, and how afraid it makes me. She asked me if I had any idea what I would say to my grandfather if he were in the room. At first the idea of him in the room terrified me, but she put a big pillow on a chair and said I could say anything I wanted to him, that I wasn't a child anymore and he had no power over me. She just sat there looking calm and I wanted to scream, "That's what you think!" but I didn't. I stood in front of the chair and stared at the pillow and, sort of like the last time, I went into a kind of altered state of consciousness (that's what she called it later). I could feel my anger (rage) coming up, and at the same time I felt very, very powerful. Words just started coming out of my mouth. This is what I said:

**"Old man, look at me. LOOK AT ME! Look what you've done! You plucked this unripened fruit from the vine! I cry tears of dried blood for the agony you inflicted on me! You are a cruel beast, a horrible excuse for a human being. How could you do what you did to me? I was a child, and I thought you loved me. You knew nothing about love, NOTHING! You took away my childhood, you took away my virginity, you used and abused me! You had no right to do that!**

**Old man, I take this red hot poker and I cut off your hand. I put your dirty filthy hand up your rectum and sew it up tight. I take this red hot poker and CUT OFF YOUR FUCKING COCK! I put your dirty filthy penis in your mouth and sew it up tight! I want you to suffer the way you made me suffer! Maybe God will forgive you someday, but I hate you, hate you, HATE YOU!"**

I was shaking from head to toe before I finished, and sweating, sweating. It took a while to settle down again, and then I was so tired, bone weary, but I felt different, stronger somehow. I called my sister later and told her what had happened and she said "he's got his hand up his ass and he can't even whistle Dixie." We both started laughing and laughed until we cried.

Then I had a dream, that I had "faulty steering" in my head. It seemed funny, I don't know why, and I woke up laughing. It seems like I'm either laughing or crying all the time. I went back to sleep, and I felt, rather than heard, the words "You need to be patient, you kept making detours with wide turns and it took a long, long time to get here." Then I heard clearly, "Time is the Lord's, not yours." So strange, the voice was so clear. I had been trying not to be angry at God, but this is so hard, I guess I am.

I thought that session would be the end of it, but it wasn't. Will it ever end? After a couple of days I started feeling the turmoil again, and I felt nauseous and kept having the dry heaves. I tried to call Connie and she was away. That still pisses me off, excuse me, makes me angry. How come she gets to go away and I don't have the money to buy a fucking hamburger at Friendly's? I'm trying to cut down on the swearing, that's another thing I pray about a lot, but it's hard. I guess I can't do any of this without His help.

Then I got scared so I went to my minister at church, he was the only one I could think of with Connie away. I sure wasn't going to call Dr. Z. I guess I went into a trance again with him and relived more of the stuff with my grandfather. Now that the memories have started coming back I can't seem to stop them. I saw Jesus with open arms looking at me when I prayed in the minister's office, and when that happens I know I'm safe. But a lot of the time I don't feel safe. I don't know how to live, I feel like an alien so much of the time. When I tell Connie I'm an alien she just smiles, but it's really the way I feel, like I'm from someplace else and I don't belong here.

I keep hearing my grandfather's voice, soft and soothing, and it gives me the creeps. He would always start with that voice. I remember that from the age of twelve on I thought I couldn't be a woman, like he had taken everything away and left nothing but a shell. I don't know how I knew that, but I did. I've felt that way for so long, I don't know if I can ever feel different. If I just keep praying, He'll get me through this.

# CHAPTER V

## *Re-Membering*

## Summer 1988

### Connie

I continue to be awed at the process that's unfolding with Mary Ellen. Powerful dreams, spontaneous regressions in session, painful memories all pouring forth along with incredible grief, rage,—and healing. I feel as if I am a witness more than anything else, as if her process has developed a momentum that has little to do with me, other than that I continue to be as fully present as I can. This is a depth of therapeutic encounter I have not experienced before, and although I've read a great deal, I know my ability to stand back and be objective, to see clearly and fully the road map for what is happening and accurately assess where we are on this journey, is lagging far behind what's actually occurring. Along with everything else, the transference is intense, and were it not for good supervision I doubt if I could handle it.

I had suggested a while ago that Mary Ellen write and draw as a way of expressing herself in the moment when she is home alone, and she's been writing a great deal—dreams, journal entries, and poetry. Several weeks ago she brought in a spontaneous drawing of herself, and we spent most of the session talking about it.

"The small yellow circle on the little antennae is a stunted halo," Mary Ellen told me, "and the horns instead of ears are the devil in me. "There's love in those yellow eyes, and they were always opened to a lot. They saw everything. I could see but no one could see what I was saying . . . the nose is angry, see the flared nostrils?"

I nodded. To me the eyes were desolate, hollow.

"There's fire coming out of her mouth because there were lots of people she wanted to burn. She's holding her heart because it's been ripped from her and it's bleeding. The black heart is where her real heart is supposed to be."

She stared at her drawing quietly for a moment. I held one corner of the paper, and we looked at it together. There was a strange, E.T. quality to her self-portrait.

"The body is stunted and deformed, she doesn't want her body because that's all people see. She wants people to see the real her."

I sat quietly, feeling the emotion that was building in Mary Ellen as she stared at the drawing.

Suddenly Ariel let go of her drawing and began sobbing, her head buried in her hands.

"She's that wounded inner child you talk about, she's part of me I can't stand. She won't let me hate, she says I'm not supposed to hate. I HATE her. . . . I want her to leave me alone. . . . I want to hurt them so they know how I feel, they never told me why, they just hit me. I want it back, I want my body, I'm not bad, people just think I am, I'm not bad, I'm not, I'm not, I'm not," she cried, stamping her foot at the end.

I said nothing, just waited until she calmed down somewhat.

"What you drew seems very real to me," I told her, "very honest. It takes a lot of courage to share what's on the inside even when you don't like it."

She looked up at me and stopped crying. We sat in silence for a little while.

"You know," she said, "I hate my breasts and I hate my stomach. The reason I wear tight clothes is not to look sexy but they keep me flat and there's no jiggling to make me aware of my breasts. So I'm more comfortable. When a man touches my stomach it feels so good and soothing and relaxing but then horrible things happen and it hurts and especially if he smiles while touching my stomach I get enraged."

She paused.

"Why does everybody want me to wear a bra? I feel total disgust inside when it's mentioned. When I look at other women, in particular, I'm struck by their breasts and crotch. I watch to see if they jiggle and if they're wearing a bra. Then I look at them wondering if they feel like me. I look at their crotch and envision them with the same body parts I have, vagina, anus, and so on and they have the same body function I do. Most of the time I feel I'm the only one with these disgusting things. By doing this I reassure myself I'm not disgusting, I'm really o.k. But I don't feel o.k."

She looked up at me and laughed self-consciously. I smiled, feeling self-conscious about my own body and her observance of it and aware, at the same time, that she was groping for some kind of positive identification with being female.

The next session she talked about how much she basically dislikes and mistrusts people.

"I always thought I loved people," she told me, as if puzzled. "But I don't. I really don't. There are a lot of mean people, and I'm discovering there aren't a lot of humans I can trust."

She told me about an incident at work in which she felt maligned and betrayed, and we talked about the formation of basic trust and mistrust in infancy, and then she haltingly relayed a dream:

*I was upset, and you said I could come and stay with you in your house. I was in your office, crying, and you kissed the back of my neck. You were sitting on the floor getting dressed. I asked you what is NASA? and you said it was a seminar, too bad you can't attend. I was furious and went out. There were children there, and then adults. I wasn't part of it. The woman I was going with said it's rather warm out there. You kept putting clothes on—a raincoat, galoshes, an umbrella, just doing what you wanted.*

I asked Mary Ellen for her associations, and she said NASA represented the moon, peacefulness, and the beauty of space. She said she never got straight answers at home, and in our last phone conversation she had felt misunderstood and unable to communicate. Plus, she felt left out of my normal life.

"You don't always give straight answers," she said accusingly.

I took that in and mentally tried to find the grain of truth in her words. We discussed the conversation in which she had felt that way. I acknowledged I'd felt impatient and had not wanted to have a long phone conversation with her.

"What about me kissing the back of your neck, and having you stay in my house?" I asked, noticing she had not offered any associations to that part of the dream.

"Well," she said, looking embarrassed, " kissing the back of my neck felt loving, but also sexual, so I was uncomfortable. And sometimes . . . sometimes I imagine what it would be like to live in your house, and that feels good, safe."

I nodded.

"Sometimes I think I know you, but other times I feel like I don't see the real you," she said. "But last week when I got here early and you were going jogging, I did. It makes me wonder what you really think."

"And where do you go with that?" I asked, aware that her disillusionment with me as idealized object was continuing.

"Well, most of the time I think you really care about me. But then I think, you only see me twice a week, and you have a life I don't know anything about, and I think I'm just a patient and you don't even think about me except when I'm here. And maybe you think bad things about me if you think about me at all, and . . . "

She stopped, shrugged her shoulders, and smiled faintly. I wondered how to respond.

"It seems like this is the same issue of trust you've been talking about," I said. "Can you trust I am who I seem to be? Can you trust that I won't abandon you? You seem to be struggling with those lifelong issues . . . " I paused, reflected. "First, I really do

care about you, I care about you a lot. And of course I think about
you in between sessions. The other piece is harder, because, yes, I
have a life you don't know anything about, and it's important that
I bring as little of my ordinary life as possible into our sessions. I
need to maintain healthy boundaries, mostly for the sake of the
therapeutic relationship, but also for myself. It's one of the odd
realities of psychotherapy: I get to know you really well, and you
get to know only what I want you to know. It's really lopsided in
that way."

As I was saying this I realized that even though I was trying to
be honest, my words weren't entirely true. Mary Ellen and other
people I worked with knew a great deal about me, no matter how
hard I tried to keep my professional and private lives separate.
Mary Ellen's antennae were fine tuned; she was always scanning
my face, my body language, my voice for clues. Actually it was
sometimes quite unnerving how much people picked up. Especially people like Mary Ellen.

Mary Ellen seemed satisfied with my answer.

"I had another dream," she said. I nodded encouragement.

*I don't know where I was, but you and I were there. I had three
huge cysts on my stomach. I popped the top one and all kinds of disgusting stuff spurted out. You said leave them be, they'll come by themselves;
I said no, I have to pop them. I ran away from you. In the dream I was
furious with you; I had to squeeze them.*

I knew that cysts popping were one of the classic signs of regression. And I felt her impatience with her process, her desire to
rush it.

"What do you associate to cysts?" I asked her.

"Well, pockets of infection that have to be opened to heal,"
she said. "I think the first one is all the stuff about my grandfather.
I don't know about the others. I keep remembering more and more
from my early childhood, it's like the memories just come any old
time. I remembered yesterday that my brother and sister put me

in a wagon and walked up and down the street trying to sell me when I was about five. No one would buy me, so they tried to give me away. The mailman said, 'you seem like a nice little girl, but you won't fit in my bag, otherwise I'd take you.' I felt so bad because he wanted me but he couldn't take me. I remember telling Santa Claus to bring Daddy home, if Daddy came home Mommy would be all better. But he didn't bring Daddy home and I remember I said I was going to tell everyone there was no Santa Claus. Dumb stuff like that I'm remembering."

Each week she's remembered more, filling in pieces of the puzzle. Her eating pattern seems to be very much related to this process and ranges from eating huge meals at which she feels she can't get enough for days at a time, to skipping breakfast and waiting until she's starving and then munching on cookies and ice cream, to eating fairly normally for several days at a time. She says she's not purging, and I think she's telling the truth; in any case, she's maintaining her weight. Slowly, slowly her eating disorder is losing its grip. But she continues to be very self-conscious about her body, and when people tell her she looks good, much better than she did (which is true), she interprets it as "I'm getting fat and they notice." This is so typical of anorexics; any comment about appearance is interpreted negatively. In fact Mary Ellen *DOES* look different, more fit. The slight forward slump to her shoulders that was probably an attempt to hide and protect her femininity is gone, resulting in a visible expansion of her chest and better posture overall.

Most recently Mary Ellen brought in a dream in which it was clear, listening to it and to her associations, that her infantile longing to bond with me as "mother" and her fear that touch from the "mothering one" will lead to abuse was ready for conscious attention. She was clearly embarrassed as she read me this dream, and said it was so hard to tell me she almost decided not to.

*We were talking in a park. You were putting your fingers through my hair. I said don't do that, I don't like people touching my hair. You said all right, and stopped. We talked some more. You said there must be something from your past we need to look at. I knew we'd already looked at all this other stuff. I said we've looked at enough, I don't want to look at any more. You talked calmly, the way you do, and said to me, can I comb your hair, and I said yes, so you combed my hair, but then I said no, and you said very softly, I think there's something we need to look at and you persuaded me to take off my clothes. You patted me on the stomach, and I got all funny, and you touched my back, and I said don't do that, and I ran away, and I said to myself I have to call Grandma, and I ran to a phone and some of the buttons were on one side and some on the other, and I dialed 9054. I knew it wasn't Grandma's number, it was our number, and I couldn't get Grandma. I ran and ran and all of a sudden I was in their house, and my brother was there, and he went up some stairs to the attic, and came down and said Grandma has two huge holes in her head, you can't talk to her. Then I woke up. I knew she was dead.*

"I felt terrible when I woke up. I kept thinking there's something else in my past I have to look at but I don't know what it is and I don't want to know."

Mary Ellen looked at the floor.

"I feel really ashamed of the dream."

Along with a "heating up" of the transference, the conflict between her urgency to know and her resistance to knowing was evident in these dreams,

"Can you talk about it?" I asked, sensing how sensitive an area this was for her.

"I don't usually have sexual feelings for you," she said, avoiding eye contact. "But . . . but sometimes I wish you would hold me, it's such a longing. And then I get scared, because anything with my mother or father that felt good ended in pain. And I know you're my therapist, not my mother, so I shouldn't want you to hold me, but I do."

"That's a very natural longing, to be held," I said. "And it doesn't look like you ever had that longing satisfied except when there was sex involved."

She nodded assent.

"I never felt so close to anyone," Mary Ellen said, looking at me imploringly. "It's so scary. I don't know what will happen. I'm afraid to tell you how I feel, because you might send me away."

"Send you away?" I echoed.

"Yes, you'll be disgusted by the way I feel."

"In babies," I explained, "sexual feelings are not separate from feelings of love and desire for love, they're experienced by the baby as the same. There's a desire to merge with the mother, and in fact it's as if from the baby's perspective there is no differentiation, no difference, between self and other. You didn't experience enough of that merger with your mother to be satisfied. So now, because you feel safe with me, and close, all those unfulfilled longings are coming up in you, and they feel sexual. I would say they're not sexual in the adult sense of the word; it's a very young, infantile sexuality. And I'm not disgusted or repelled by it; I think it's a phase of development you're going through, and those feelings will change into something else as time goes on."

Mary Ellen was listening, holding her breath and watching me carefully. When I paused, she let out a huge sigh. Fortunately, I felt I understood her longing at a deep level and was not disturbed by it; nor did I have any confusion about my own sexual identity. Her feelings and words triggered no complex in me. She seemed reassured , but I noticed she didn't ask for her usual hug at the end of the session.

For some reason I thought of Mary Ellen today when one of my other patients, a young woman named Heather who I've been seeing for a year or so, brought in a tape of a session she'd had with a psychic in California . She asked me to listen to it with her, so that's how we spent our session. I was absolutely amazed at what the psychic "channeled" about Heather's life without, apparently, being told anything in advance. The thing that's so uncanny is that she not only confirmed a lot of history—factual and emotional—that Heather and I have slowly uncovered in our work together, she added pieces of information that fit perfectly with and expanded my understanding of Heather's early life, particularly the sense that she had experienced a traumatic separation in the first three or four years of life. According to this psychic, (who worked by phone!) Heather's beloved nanny left suddenly when she was three, and Heather's chronic separation anxiety stems from this experience. There was a lot more, too, that could not have been known by ordinary means. I've never talked with a psychic; my skepticism has always been too great. But I was very impressed. There are so many unanswered questions about my own childhood, maybe I'll work up enough courage to call her.

## Mary Ellen

I feel as though a Pandora's box has been opened bigger than ever imagined, entangled and confusing. With nowhere to go for answers to help put everything in order. I want to put it all back in the box, close it, and burn it. But it's too late for that. I find I'm telling myself, you lived through this alone and survived, God's will. Now aware of the Lord and joined with him you can go through this, the answers you need will be provided. Through Connie. The Holy Spirit will see this provided so you can get order and put it where it belongs. This will be provided even if Connie isn't available and you will get through it. God, please keep reassuring me that you are my Father and that you love me no matter what.

When I asked my sister how Mom was around my grandfather she replied "I remember being afraid of him, not liking him and not being in a room alone with him. I always wondered if he had done something to her." She does not remember how it was when Dad came home from the war after I was born. Just anger. I told her I don't always think Dad is my Dad, and she said she didn't know. There are too many secrets in our family, things not to be talked about.

Why was I born into this world, that family? I used to try to fool God by pretending I loved him, while I really hated him. Now I can tell him I hate him, and he understands. He can forgive even my hating him. All my life I've felt abandoned by him. Why? There must be a reason. But he must love me for it to be all right for me to hate him. And that helps me to really love him. I don't think I'm making any sense, but I am.

I'm pretty sure this life is temporary, that there's a reality else-where. I don't know where it is, but I feel it so strongly. I remember as far back as ten years old I wanted to die and be with God, wherever that is. I still want that, but I'm beginning to think I'm here for a reason, that he'll take me when he's ready, not before.

I've always been so terrified of humans, not just scared, *TERRI-*

*FIED,* of something I've had no words for. I'm finally beginning to understand why. I've had some horrible memories that I still don't believe can be true. A couple of weeks ago I started having pains in my arms and legs, and my hands kept curling into fists and cramping. The pain was excruciating, and I couldn't sleep, and I had an awful pain in my vagina. None of it made any sense, but it got worse and worse. And all the time I wanted Connie to hold me and stroke my hair, I couldn't think of anything else, just longed for her to hold me and at the same time I was so afraid, terrified of her even touching me, and the pain in my arms and legs and vagina got worse and worse until finally I called her, and all I could say over and over again is "I can't be with people and I'm afraid to be alone." When I went to her office I went into another regression, I was lying on a pillow all alone, on my back. I felt really little. My arms were up, I wanted to be picked up, but I was terrified of being hurt. I kept saying Mommy doesn't want to pick me up, she doesn't come, she doesn't come. And then she grabbed me by the arms and held me real tight, she squeezed me. She didn't keep me, though, she gave me to somebody else. Everybody was mad at me, everybody was mad at me. I wanted to be put back on the pillow, I wanted to be safe. And I knew I was connected to God, and I wanted to leave and go to him. And then there was a big man there, and he talked to me so soothingly, and he rubbed my stomach. I felt good and relaxed. Then he did something to my vagina, and I could feel myself go tense. He stopped, and I cried, it hurt. And then my mother picked me up by the arms again, and that hurt. She put me back on the pillow and I felt better, I sucked my thumb. And then when I came out of it I cried and cried, I couldn't stop crying, and finally I asked Connie if she would hold me, and she took me on her lap and I put my head on her shoulder and cried and cried some more, and she just held me until I stopped, and stroked my hair and I felt like such a baby but it felt so good, so safe and comforting. And then she talked about my abandonment depression and terror and longing and somehow by the time I left I felt different, so exhausted but different.

I still can't believe my grandfather abused me when I was a baby, but maybe he did. I learned that after I was born my mother had pneumonia and we stayed with my grandparents for a while. Did it happen then? How could my mother have let it?

The strangest thing has happened though. I was in the shower last week and I suddenly said out loud "I think I want to be female." This was at the end of a day when I was up and down and all over the place—from calm to rage to tears to joy several times for no reason I knew. When I told Connie she asked me what it would mean to be fully female and I said it would mean more freedom to be strong and independent and fragile at the same time. To be strong means I'm going to be o.k. and I can make decisions without compulsion. It also means I can make mistakes and it won't be the end of the world. It's the first time in my life I've ever really wanted to be female.

The other thing I've been thinking about is what my new name is going to be, and I'm thinking of something really beautiful like Ariel. It kind of comes from Mary Ellen, but it sounds completely different. And I want Constance to be my middle name. I wonder if Connie will like that or be mad if I choose her name for my middle name. I don't have to decide right now, just sometime before my baptism in the fall. I can't wait. The other thing is I have a chance to get a kitten, and if my landlady doesn't object too much I think I'm going to. It's orange like Fantastic, and I already have a name for it. Pumpkin.

I drew two pictures, one of my grandfather and one of me in the crib. I hate both of them.

## Connie

I'm learning so much in the depth psychology program at Wainwright House. It has both a strong intellectual component and a lot of opportunity for personal process; my dream life is always stimulated in surprising ways. Here are two that are so different it's hard to believe I had them in the same long weekend:

*I am with my children outdoors. It is summer. I cross a small, low bridge with a low wall. There is a grassy embankment on the right, and as I glance down I see a long-haired black, white, and brown guinea pig, small, scurrying out of a hole and across the grass. I recognize it as the guinea pig that escaped and disappeared in our back yard when the children were younger and we had pet guinea pigs. I am so surprised and pleased that he has survived. I notice he has many scars; wounds that have been sewn up. Then I see a larger white guinea pig nearby—it is Papa Dink! The father of all the guinea pigs we had. I scoop them both up and carry them to my children to show them, excited and happy.*

*I'm in ocean water, deep. There is a bulwark in front of me. I'm with someone, and we're each carrying a baby. We're trying to swim somewhere, but the tide is pulling us farther and farther out. There are huge boats nearby; we're in the boat channel. It's hard to swim carrying the baby. Then I realize all of a sudden I've forgotten the baby. It's under water. I hold it up, and it's become a limp balloon; there's nothing left but the skin.*

Hmmm. The first one seems to be about recovery of some lost, lively instinctual part of myself; the second, if I had to guess, is connected to my marriage and the path of individuation I'm on. Which is it going to be, swimming against the tide or saving the baby? Is it possible to do both? I'm looking forward to sharing both of these with Jane.

One of the best lectures this past weekend was by El Mattern, a wonderful Jungian who lived in Zurich for many years but is now in Maine. She talked about the stages of regression in a way that really helped my understanding of the process that's been unfolding with Mary Ellen and other patients I'm working with. First there is resistance, in which the patient may get sleepy, eat compulsively, or otherwise act out as a way of avoiding regression. The patient is likely to be afraid of destroying the therapist, ashamed of her own needs, and afraid of dependency. She is also likely to be afraid of her own madness, though this may not be conscious, and the therapist may unconsciously collude with her resistance out of fear of her OWN unrecognized mad self.

Three things usually appear in dreams at the beginning of regression: symbols of the Self; a positive attitude towards a child; and images of a dream child or a dream mother showing positive trust toward the therapist.

The actual beginning of the regression may be signaled by dreams of fainting, falling, being a child, watching a mother figure hold an infant, or the dreamer melding into ocean or space. Glass may break or ice melt. The middle stage is marked by bottomless grief and sadness, and the patient discovers the trauma that had to be cut off. There are dreams of helplessness, cysts breaking, violent urinating, shitting, menstrual bleeding, being in a dungeon crying, etc. Sometimes a door opens and a small child is found; sometimes there is a tidal wave.

And then, towards the end, images from the positive pole of the mother archetype are constellated: food, shelter, warmth is given or stolen, a drowned child might be found alive or the dreamer might be caring for animals. Sometimes the therapist is comforted by the patient in a dream, or the patient may discover a secret room that turns out to be the patient's own room.

It is all quite amazing, and it really helps to put what I am so close to and part of in this context. I'm not capable of being totally objective with my patients. Is there even such a thing as total objectivity? I doubt it. When I think back on all that has happened with Mary Ellen over the past few months, I see much more clearly that the whole process has been a regression, not just the individual sessions in which spontaneous regressions have occurred.

As usual, life is extremely full, and as usual, I am probably packing more into each day than allows enough time for rest and reflection. I can't believe I orchestrated my daughter's wedding for two hundred people while working full time until the last two days! I guess doing it all, and doing it as well as possible, is a lifelong pattern. Over responsible? Who, me? Seriously, I'm more and more aware of how I mothered my own mother, became an over responsible child quite early. Even though she loved us, in the end she was inadequate, thoroughly defeated. When she finally gave us up to my father, I think she had been overwhelmed for years. Who wouldn't be, with four small children and an estranged husband who was determined to prove she was an adulteress and unfit to be a mother in order to get his way? Jane says it's a horror story, and I guess it is. Maybe the worst part for me was being totally cut off from her for so long; when I told Jane I didn't see her for twenty years she was speechless. Do I mother my patients because I wasn't mothered enough myself? Do I help them deal with their abandonment issues because I understand them deeply, or because I need to deal with my own? Who is the healer and who the healee?

I've been reading about quantum mechanics. The most recent issue of Psychological Perspectives has a fascinating article that explores in depth the acausal connections that exist in the world, the synchronicities Jung talks about. There is a strong link between Quantum Theory and Jungian Psychology that makes absolute sense to me. I would like to know more about this.

Also, I finally called Lynn Breedlove, the psychic my patient Heather told me about, and had a phone session with her. Without any information from me, she talked extensively about my children, my husband, my parents, and me. It was an incredible experience, and I was—impressed is too weak a word—deeply affected by what she had to say. It helped me to understand what each of us brought into this world. She talked about "cycles of time", meaning other lifetimes, and for the first time I saw my life from a perspective that goes way beyond what I have understood to be my personal reality based on a combination of the traits I was born with and my early environment.

Just a few of the things she told me:

My ability to "see behind people's doors" started early. This is what was "channeled" about my father after Lynn said yes, I was terrified of him, and yes, he was extremely controlling of everything down to the minutest detail out of his terror of life, but that I had built up enough strength so that I could be with him without being destroyed by him by the time I was ten and we had to go live with him. And that I was a gift to him because I understood who he was behind how he acted, and I was the only one who did in his last years. I cried when I heard the guides' words.

*You knew him. You understood him. You are a child to him many times before in previous passages. You have been mother to him also. You have understood his sorrow and his pain and the anguish which he undergoes in his bones. You have felt with him the terror that dwells within him and the fear that he will not remember his source. You are a guide to him and counsel. You are also sister and child. You have traveled with him many times before. You do not honor within yourself the knowing that goes there, the wisdom that lives deep inside of you. You came from the earliest time into this existence wishing to counsel those who are in pain. Your mother and father do many battles with one another and stab in the heart one another. In previous times there is killing of each other and this continues to play forth in this period, this frame of time called now. They are to each other enemies and brought forth in this time the greatest battle of all, the loss of child one to another, and the hated words spoken with great vileness. He is wishing to kill your mother, and she is hiding. She owes a great debt to him also. This is the cycle between them, to take each other's life, and in this frame of time the taking of each other's children. They are bonded together in the earliest time and said make peace in this time and they play out their agony again and again until there is resolution. They are*

*bonded together for many cycles of time and you have seen them sepa-*
*rately and together. You have been on both sides of the battle in previous*
*time, first on what was called your mother when she was in the form*
*not of woman but of man. You walked beside her and counseled her*
*and you held her head on your lap as she was slain. You also walked*
*with one called father, walked beside him and also saw him strike the*
*blow and receive the blow from this one. They have gone this route*
*many times before. You have held the head of each as they bled and lay*
*weeping on your lap. You have watched them pass from the realm and*
*have come to understand that the enemy is not the enemy but one to be*
*seen clearly from both sides. You changed camps in the middle at this*
*time so that you too could pass and understand that loyalty is given*
*easily and changed easily and it is not the issue . It is the wisdom and*
*ability to see the truth in the moment that allows the truth to be born*
*and brought to the light. It is your ability to change loyalties which will*
*save you and your ability to see things from many sides. You must forgive*
*yourself a child's need to make loyal which party she is with, for you*
*have been unforgiving of yourself in this time and in previous times*
*also. You are like a child raped.*

In my therapy group, with Jane, people question my "nice-
ness" and say they would feel more comfortable if they could see
more of my dark side. Lynn said my experience is that I have wit-
nessed people's dark sides so much both in this lifetime and in
past lifetimes that I'm acutely aware of where acting out the dark
side leads, and my job in this lifetime is to help people integrate
their dark sides. This makes sense, although I'm also aware there is
darkness in me that is coming to the surface to be healed and
integrated.

I asked about whether applying to the Jung Institute would
be the wisest next step for me, or whether there is something else,
because I keep feeling there is something else but I don't know
what it is. I would like to find a way to work more with what is
stored in the body, as I think that, particularly with eating disordered patients, there is a mind/body split that needs healing. The

body is seen as Enemy Number One; control by the mind is the only thing that matters. Lynn said it looks like there is a special field calling to me and the process will be as important as what I am actually taught. We talked about many possibilities, all of them involving mind-body integration, and she reassured me that I would be led. Then the "guides" spoke through her:

*You will be drawn in the time ahead into the arena which will guide you. This is not the time to make the decision and that is why the answers aren't clear or laid out in black and white. You will find in the time ahead a clearer direction and what you must do and where you will go. There will be people who will come into your company and direct you. Your fascination with what goes in the body is of utmost importance and your understanding of what comes in the mind and what develops in the personality is already laid out clearly. You must trust yourself f more fully in the time ahead and understand that the work that you do is profound and healing to many. When you have understood this and accepted this clearly and laid aside the concept that it could be better or different you will have seen many things and will have understood the profound awe of the work that you do. Lay your hands on people and you will have an experience and an understanding of what comes through them. Train your hands to touch and receive the message that the flesh holds. Those who hold still their bodies and refuse the intake of nutrients are most sick from the earliest time and deny the mother and the connection to the mother and become bonded to the father and identify with him and then become confused about the intake of food. The mother turns away and the liquid kiss becomes cold and ungiving and the child turns her eyes to another form and though there is no nipple there bonds and cleaves to this one, cleaves to the hairy chest and becomes confused and bewildered about nourishment. You will find a greater understanding of this in the time ahead and you will see it more clearly. You are capable of rebonding the mother and the daughter one to the other, not in this flesh but the child to a more divine mother who is able to nourish and feed the child and she does not starve herself in anticipation of an early death. The mother is the key in this and her withdrawal from the child is of utmost importance. The jealousy that comes at the earliest period has great importance. We would offer you this at this time , that the mother who says I am no longer a child, I am no longer a girl, I do not wish to nourish this one or give her the liquid nourishment , this mother then says to the child you are not wanted here and the child cleaves to the other form that cannot give her milk. Look into the earliest time and you will see that the child is brought forth from the mother and the mother's girlhood dies and the blossom of youth goes from her cheek and she says I am no longer treasured and adorable and it is this one that has taken my childhood from me, and the mother then turns the kiss away from the child and the child is bewildered. You will understand these things even more fully in the time ahead and hold them dear to your heart. This particular aspect of human behavior will teach others in greater realms and greater understanding. What is called now bulimia and anorexia is the groundwork for something coming in the time ahead more fully understood and more fully seen. It is the beauty of the mother, the flower gone from her cheek, that starts this cycle, and her anguish and pain and refusal to nourish the daughter.*

I was and continue to be incredibly moved by these words. I *FEEL* their truth, and at the same time have many questions, not the least of which is how could I, as a traditional psychotherapist, "lay my hands on" people, even if I understood what that would mean? What this means in terms of the path I am on I do not know; I do have a much stronger sense that I am, indeed, being guided by some unseen force, and that if I can trust, the particular form of training that is best will become clearer in time. I've always thought people who talked to psychics and listened to "guides" were a little weird, but this feels like a profound level of truth.

# CHAPTER VI

## *Putrefaction*

## Spring 1989

### Ariel

So much has happened in the past few months. Some of it has felt real good and other parts awful, like the way my body's been the past few weeks. It feels horrible, strange aches and pains like I've never had before. But thinking back I know I've done a lot of work on my wounded inner child, and forgiving my parents, and what Connie calls "working through" all the mixed up feelings about my grandfather and what he did to me. But I still get angry, so angry people back off and I lose jobs and relationships. Connie hasn't abandoned me yet, but I get so enraged with her sometimes I don't know why she doesn't just tell me never to come back. I keep expecting it. If she tells me not to call between sessions—which I don't do as much—or brings up money, which I never have enough of to pay her regularly, I get so furious I want to never see her again, and then I get depressed and suicidal and then I realize she's still there when I go for my next appointment and I begin to get over it—until the next time. I never know when the rage will hit. And every time I try to stop smoking it comes up big time no matter what else is going on.

I was baptized in a swimming pool in the fall, and changed my name to Ariel Constance, and my connection to God keeps me going. Connie came to the baptism, I know I'm special to her. She has an office in town now, and I'm getting used to it but don't like it nearly as much. I wrote a poem about her old office:

For three and a half years
I've had this place to go dumping all my garbage, leaving refreshed
I call this place my comfort zone
A little red building tucked away in the woods
Looking just like I thought it should
Compact and homey, with curtains in the window
With only outside plumbing

Seeing the smoke from the chimneys, as I drive up
Knowing my angel was there to listen, no matter what I said
Watching all God's beauty about me
All nestled in my comfort zone, sometimes only in my head

Collecting all the garbage to overflowing
Racing to get to my place of safety and security
Seated in our chairs of placement
That I changed a couple of times

We sorted through my garbage
Sometimes with much laughter
Many times a lot of tears
Something I'd not done for many, many years

Those walls never seemed to close in on me
Always there, remaining open, no matter what I said
Allowed to leave behind what I could no longer carry
Knowing it would be there if I needed it in a hurry

The smell of fresh wood burning will always remain with me

Always reminding me of the garbage that was dumped
With no messy piles left behind for anyone to see
Leaving my comfort zone, allowed just to be me

My days going to my comfort zone have come to an end
Although I'll always carry it in my head
I need to tell the walls goodbye
And thanks for letting me in

I need to put the lock in the door
Admitting to myself I cannot go back in time
Saying goodbye to my garbage, leaving it behind
Keeping all the good that's come within the walls of my
comfort zone

My painting is complete
I need to stand back and look
Sign the canvas where the work was done
Leaving my comfort zone complete

When I wrote the poem I thought I was finished with Connie, that I didn't need to see her any more and anyway didn't want to if she was going to be in a different place. That lasted about four days.

I may be finally done with my grandfather. I wrote a eulogy, better late than never as they say, and read it to Connie. It was hard to write but after I wrote it and read it out loud I felt finished with him.

### Eulogy for Bernard Durstan

*Eulogy for Bernard Durstan, a man who left this earth thirty—two years ago. He left behind a little girl so frightened, so alone, with secrets she couldn't share. Her body aching, afraid of the pain of touch, afraid of love (the only kind she knew) yet found herself desperately wanting it.*

*Yes, you told this little girl how special love was between a man and a woman. Yes, you showed this little girl how special love was between a man and a woman. Yes, you told this little girl you sometimes hurt the ones you love. Yes, you told this little girl how you could teach her how to love so any man would appreciate having her. You told this little girl how other women loved being touched by you, and other men.*

*You told this little girl if she didn't love people would be angry with her and she would be sent away. You told this little girl how to tell when people told the truth and you always looked in my eyes and told this little girl how much she liked being loved.*

*This little girl so lonely, so physically mutilated where no one could see, so scarred emotionally, so desperate for touch, so confused, learned all about hate. She wanted to tell you this. She wanted to scream at you, no longer to be silent. She wanted to beat you, hurt your body as you hurt hers. She wanted others to hate you as she did.*

*You left this earth before she could do this. You left a very angry little girl on this earth. Others put you to rest but you remained very much alive in this little girl. She heard you talking to her in that soft seductive voice even when you weren't there. She felt the pain of your touch when she dared let others close out of her need to feel loved. People did become angry with her when she didn't love. She was sent away, not to be loved, many times.*

*Bernard Durstan left this earth a cunning liar and thief. He did not tell this little girl that love is very special without sex, and acceptable. He did not tell this little girl her feelings about his love were TRUE, it was* **wrong!** *He did not tell this little girl she was lovable just as she was. He did not tell this little girl he was taking something very precious from her.*

*He stole this little girl's worthiness. He stole this little girl's choice with whom she would share her body.*

*He stole this little girl's virginity, never telling her how integral it was. This little girl found how important and precious a true love and relationship of giving oneself with great love was robbed from her. She was robbed of having this gift to give.*

*He stole this little girl's trust in people.*

*He stole this little girl's ability to have healthy relationships with anyone especially men.*

*This little girl was enraged feeling raped and he left her to go on alone the best she could, ill equipped.*

*I have found this little girl and have come to her rescue. She is very frightened and hurt and angry but my hand is out to her. She doesn't really want to hurt anyone. She just doesn't want to hurt. I can embrace her, she is very embraceable. We are learning to trust together. We are learning our feelings of right are not always wrong.*

*Notice I saw we as "we" are joining together loving one another.*

*"We" may still hear Bernard Durstan but we don't have to listen. We see him as he was, a liar, thief, and very very sick.*

*We on this day April 10 1989 lay this man to rest. A grandfather in name only. To say may he rest in peace is difficult but we have kept him alive 32 years. It is now time for us to let him go. We offer him up to God setting us free from his wickedness so we can follow the light of Jesus without his burden.*

*May he now rest in peace now that we feel the peace of God's grace. Thank God.*

*Dust to dust, ashes to ashes, blow them away and let my child out to play.*

As I said, I felt done with him. But I don't know if I really am. I don't know what's happening to me in the past few weeks, but something is, and I don't know if it's physical or emotional or both, but it's very scary and I don't know what to do about it. I hurt all over, my face and the muscles in my hands and arms and legs ache and there are sharper small pains throughout my body. I don't know exactly when it started, but it's been getting worse and worse. I had asked Connie if she thought some body work would help me and she said yes, if it's the right person, so I went ahead and made an appointment on impulse with a man who does Shiatzu. I didn't check it out with anyone first and thinking back on it the pain may have started right after that but I'm not really sure, I do know I went into a rage the night after I had the Shiatzu. Anyway,

I finally went to the doctor because I started feeling as if if I closed my eyes I wouldn't wake up, and I almost collapsed in church last week. My body feels as if someone beat me. Dr. Moore did a lot of tests, first he thought it was Lyme disease but it isn't, and said I have polymyalgia and connective tissue disease. He said it's related to rheumatoid arthritis but not the same. He put me on Prednisone a couple of days ago but I don't notice any change yet. The pain is up and down my spine and in the large muscles of my arms and legs. I don't think Connie understands what is going on with me but at least she seems to believe me. I'm so afraid everyone will think I'm crazy, or making it up, just like they did when I was a kid. I'm not making it up.

I feel that my friends at church love and support me, and so does my sister most of the time, and so does Connie. And I know God loves me. But why do I feel like I'm being punished? I feel like I need to be forgiven for my anger, and I need to know what the lesson I'm supposed to learn in this life is. There has to be a reason for this much suffering.

I talked to Connie about all of this, and she thought it would be a good idea to go back to the Shiatzu person since I'd started a process with him even though she wouldn't have recommended that form of body work right away since it often affects people very deeply. So I went back, and the same thing happened as the first time which is that I got very relaxed and felt like a rag doll. I can't explain it, but I went completely limp. Dan said he felt a pulsing lump in my abdomen which he thought was related to liver and spleen, and anger, and when he worked on my back, to the left of my spine, he felt a lump burst, or release. Afterward and still now I feel as if my muscles are sagging, even the muscles in my face hurt after I talk. I feel exhausted after any exertion. I hope the Prednisone works.

I quit my job, felt totally unsupported there. And I stopped taking vitamins, maybe I was taking too many? And I started smoking again. I'll stop when I'm ready. Last week I thought about suicide again, but I always tell myself God will take me when he's ready.

Please God, help me to understand why I'm in such pain. Am I healing all the emotional pain only to have physical pain in its place? I hope not.

# Connie

My dreams continue to lead me—where? The individuation process feels more like a labyrinth sometimes than anything else. Twisting and turning, circling around and around the same issues, leaping forward only to find myself in a blind alley, falling back. Bodily aches and pains when I forcibly halt my tears in session because it's "not convenient" to cry when I have a full day of patients ahead of me. Murderous dreams when I refuse to acknowledge rage because I want to cling to the belief that if I understand, I shouldn't be angry. Wild horse dreams when I repress my sexuality and power. If I ever had any doubts about the reality of the unconscious, they have been completely dispelled. I know I am stumbling my way toward connecting with lost parts of myself, gathering up soul fragments, moving toward wholeness. Often I feel like Demeter, the Mothering One; yet I know that parts of the maiden me, Persephone, are still deep in the underworld. And "she" alternates between acceptance of her captive state, rage at Hades, and longing for reunion.

Three recent dreams are indicative of the themes running through this process:

*I am pregnant, huge with child. I am on a table and give birth to a young child (not an infant), a girl with beautiful brown eyes and brown bangs. Then I am pregnant again, and the mound in my abdomen is higher and more defined in a left-right, low to high fashion. Once again I am on the delivery table, only this time there is an I.V. on the right. Somehow the I.V. tube gets cut; I have a hand in it, and I don't deliver.*

*I am standing in my kitchen—a different one from mine now—more reminiscent of the last house I lived in—and looking out the window. A large turquoise feather with a white center and a black dot within floats down in front of the window. I look up and see what appears to be the tail of a large bird hanging over the edge of the roof. I wonder what the bird is doing there. I go outside with others and see that there is a kind of niche in the wooden-shingled roof and the bird is nestled there. He is very large with a golden-yellow beak, turquoise body, and long, feathery tail. He reminds me of a peacock.*

*A western scene—a house with sliding glass doors right at the foot of a mountain. Children in the house, a sense of wildness and wild animals outside. There are three roads leading up the mountain, one in the middle, one around each side. I see a lioness outside, standing on a hill. Then I see her shadow on the door, and I lock the door because of the children. I am concerned but not very afraid. I know she is waiting for me.*

I've been thinking more and more about learning some form of hands on healing. I've looked into half a dozen different programs that teach body-oriented psychotherapy, but so far nothing seems quite right. So I called Lynn again and set up a session by phone with her in hopes I can get some guidance. Lynn herself is delightful and highly spiritual; I feel such a loving energy emanating from her. She also says a prayer at the beginning and end of sessions. I like that. She said I need to "learn the systems" and then practice. And then the guides began to speak through her:

*Practice, you need to practice. If you lay your hands on the one with the big feet you will find the shifting that takes place will be profound and you will record for yourself what you are capable of doing . What you call your higher self will take you to the place of highest knowledge and there you will be guided. So take in what you must for a short time , you will need to know the systems but then lay them aside and work with the particular bodies that are presented to you, because the people you work with move their energy in a different pattern. You have not yet seen that you are the teacher, you are the mentor. And others will be learned by you but you must first practice with others. Put your hands on the big feet and you will feel the opening that will take place. Take yourself into the company of others that will show you your own body and its patterns so that you may establish how it is that the spirit moves through the body and then your eyes will begin to open and you will see the different patterns and many new learnings will come from this. You are the teacher and you are the mentor. You are on a new realm and there is new excitement about this thing that you learn. Those with the big feet will be blessed by your touch and will know that you have given them a profound encounter. We are knowing your capacity and working with you and excited about your opening, and we are taking you into those who can help you. We are available to you.*

What am I to make of this? As I listened I found myself catching my breath, tears streaming down my cheeks. It made no sense to my rational mind, yet I felt the profound truth of what I heard. Then, later, I thought about my patients and who might have big feet, and in fact I do have a young woman patient who has big feet. But I am a traditional psychotherapist, and I can't just say to this person, let me hold your feet for a few minutes! How do I move from sitting a few feet from my patients and, except for an occasional hug at the end of a session, scarcely touching them, to working with their energy directly, laying hands on their bodies? Is it even possible? It seems like an enormous leap, even if I knew how to work that way. And I don't. I am so moved and inspired by the channeled message; yet I know I have to wait until I have some training to incorporate any of this into my work. How can I be the teacher when I haven't yet been the student?

## Ariel

I've been back to Dan twice for Shiatzu and also Swedish Massage, and the pain in my face has subsided somewhat. I still have no energy, feel like a sack of potatoes a lot of the time. There is a constant feeling of sadness, like a backdrop to everything else, and I wonder if it will always be like this. Dr. Moore has kept me on the Prednisone and I think it's helping a little, but he doesn't seem to know exactly what's wrong either. He wanted to do a lot of blood tests and even a CAT scan, but I can't afford all that and I don't want to owe any more money, especially if it's all in my head. Connie told me about a psychic some people she knows have talked to and trust, and I decided to call her. It kind of blew me away, I feel like I'm still in shock from some of the things I learned and don't know whether to believe it or not but it sure made sense and felt true. This is what Lynn said:

*I see a combination of tentativeness and persistence. You keep chipping away. I see you carving a piece of stone, creating something you see you want. You have staying power. As the figure emerges you keep working on it, you have a dream and keep working on it. You look like you're not quite home with yourself, not completely solid.*

*The feeling I have is that there is a child within you that says to me "she won't look at me and she won't listen." She has a blank look on her face and big eyes. It's like a physical presence here. It feels desperate, and very separated from you, like you're estranged from that child. It's not going to give up, it's going to hang in there. Do you feel something happened to this child that you don't know?*

I told her no, I only know she's been hurt.

*She seems a little locked into her belief system, almost like a recording, like she doesn't recognize changes in you. Now I see her more like four years old, she's clinging to me like a little monkey. What happened to her at four or five?*

I told Lynn I was sexually abused by my grandfather, but I don't know when it started.

*Four is the age that keeps coming. I see adults walking out the door, leaving her, maybe leaving her with someone she doesn't want to be with. She keeps saying "Take me with you, take me with you." She's very frightened. Maybe you were left in a place where you perceived it was going to get worse. The vision is of a little girl clinging to me, and adults are walking out the door, and all she can see are their backs. She's terrified, absolutely terrified. She's in complete turmoil. Did anyone know?*

No, I said, as far as I know. I went to my mother when I was twelve and she didn't believe me.

*You may have gone to her at four, too. There was some physical change at that time. You were penetrated deeper, or torn open, and invaded. There's a small aperture, and all of a sudden it's opened and invaded. You know about it, but all of a sudden you're very aware of it. It's very intrusive, and I see your eyes just get huge. You're shocked, completely shocked.*

I began to feel sick to my stomach.

*She was invaded more severely. It is the truth, it is the truth Ariel. Opening without will, giving in to protect yourself, giving in knowing there was no safety and no protection. Wanting others to see and feeling of loss, knowing there is no power. The intrusion became worse and your eyes became big with sorrow, wanting others to recognize the pain and make the pain go away. Not recognizing at the earliest time the intrusion was dark and later, at a later age, recognizing it as a dark and shameful thing. Feeling as though you were tainted from the inside out, feeling as though you had been violated and your body was made of straw to be burnt or tormented by others. This experience and knowledge became more apparent when you were not yet five. You were hurt, you were hurt.. You protect yourself by relaxing in order to make the pain less intense.*

*You will find you are capable of reclaiming what is yours and belongs to you and the healing will take place from deep within you. The blending of the foul energy will shift away from you. You will walk with greater freedom. There will be forgiveness in you. This will not come for some time but it will be yours and you will pass it like salt scattered in the wind. There is no need for you to be sorry for the ways that you have moved or protected yourself, there is only need now for you to heal yourself and in the process you will find a great forgiveness in you. You must forgive the child within you for her capacity to give in. Gaze into her hollow face and say you have done well, you have protected yourself in the most blessed way. You gave to yourself the capacity to heal even in the moment of greatest pain. You gave to yourself the capacity to open so that you would be less harmed in your flesh and your tissue even when you did not know in your mind what was happening to you. Say this to the child that lives within you and give her no criticism of what she has done. It is the criticism within yourself that causes you the greatest pain and this must be alleviated. Say to the child you are strong in the way that you move your muscles and protect your body. It is wrong what is done but it is wise what you do to defend yourself, and then the child within you will begin to smile, and she will say to you You have heard my voice and you have seen my face, and the critical knowing will separate from you and go to a distant place and there will be peacefulness held within you.*

*If you say these things to yourself often a great abundance will come to you and the forgiveness will be like salt in your hand and you will throw it into the air and the gentle wind will blow it away. You will feel yourself relieved and you will know and claim an aspect of your body that you could not see or claim in a previous time. You will find yourself capable to be blessed and great healing will take place in you. There is no need to speak of these things, there is only the need to listen and say you are forgiven, you have done a good thing and by your beauty you are powerful. I see the goodness that you have brought forth*

*and I know the value that you bring here and these things will heal you
and give you the understanding that you need.*

*Your mother will know that the transformation has taken place
and she will sense within her a turning and the freedom will come from
yet another level. She will know the turning has taken place even though
the words cannot be spoken. She will feel with gratitude the cleansing
that has occurred. You are on the right track with what you do for
yourself and the horror will grow more profound but soon will come a
time, like a great wound it will burst from the inside out and though it
is painful and there is great burning sensation you will free yourself,
your body will be yours again.*

I couldn't stop crying when I heard this. Lynn sent me the
tape and I listened to it three times so I could take it all in. I can't
believe he raped me when I was four. But I know it's true, I KNOW
it. Lynn said she felt that my mother knew but didn't want to
believe what was happening, and she can't tolerate that she didn't
protect me. That's why she can't talk about it, that's why we can't
talk about anything but the weather.

I told her about the pain, that sometimes I can't hold my jaw
closed and sometimes my extremities don't feel like they're mine,
and she said she can't diagnose and wasn't comfortable being specific about physical ailments, but what she kept hearing was Virus, Virus, Virus, and she sensed that there was a virus nestled in a
crucial spot that affects my muscles, a place that's the cornerstone
of sensation about muscle activity. And she said she felt that I had
lost myself, or I'm out of control and that it's also part of the
healing process that I'm in. And then the guides spoke again:

*A sense of regaining control, a sense of loss of control. Not being
able to feel or sense what is happening within your muscular structure
and then having it return to you and regaining it. This is disease but it
is also connected with the healing process you are undergoing in your
psychology. The period around age four is crucial in this because it was
during this period that you lost control and lost sensation, began to*

*separate from your body and it felt as though it was not yours. This is a*
*period of reclaiming. The physical manifestation is to pass you through*
*this realm, and you will pass through it. It is of utmost importance that*
*you care for yourself and take extreme caution to rest large portions of*
*your hours. You must rest and relieve yourself often, flush out your system*
*with great quantities of water. Rest even when you do not feel weary.*
*This is a time of sickness within you and it will be alleviated, but your*
*body must fight it away in its own time and in its own way. You will*
*heal yourself from this particular dilemma. There is a name for what*
*you undergo but the name will be of little consequence.*

What does this mean? Am I dying? Is it possible I will recover
from all this physical and emotional pain? I keep getting this real
strong sense that I don't have much longer here, and I know I
don't want to come back. I don't know if it's just a death wish, or
something else. I feel such a strong, direct, connection with God,
and I want to be with him. I know God's time is different from
time the way I know it, and my feeling that I don't have much
longer here could be fifty years. Lynn said it could also be about a
death of something within myself that I'm perceiving, that union
with God is already happening and doesn't mean I'm going to die
in my physical body soon. I wish I understood all this better.

At the end Lynn asked me if I ever confronted my grandfather,
and when I told her he died years ago she suggested I could communicate with him even though he's passed on. Is that possible?
Holy Shit! She was willing to help me right then but I got really
scared and decided not to. I don't know if I could do that, though
if it would finally rid me of him I think I'd be willing. But I'd need
someone next to me, not just talking to Lynn three thousand miles
away, even though she feels so much closer when we talk. Maybe
Connie would do it.

## Connie

Ariel—whose name change I'm beginning to get used to even though I have mixed feelings about her use of Constance as a middle name—is very depressed again, or rather, still. I listened to the tape of her session with Lynn which, like mine, was extraordinary in terms of offering a broader, more spiritual perspective on what's going on. I have so many questions and doubts about the idea of guides, and channels; it so defies my sense of logic. And yet it feels as though Lynn is aligned with and receptive to information from a higher spiritual reality than most of us can access. Maybe we just don't know how.

For the past month most of the work with Ariel has focused on her relationship to the inner child she abandoned so long ago. It has been deep and painful work for her. What I keep reminding myself is that the process of reconnecting with split-off parts of herself will lead to healing, even when in the short run it increases her pain. It is my experience, and the experience of the women I work with.

Ariel is in almost constant physical distress: pain in her facial muscles, painful twitching of the muscles in her arms and legs, fleeting pains throughout her body, extreme fatigue. Her desire to "die and be with God" comes close to overcoming her desire to remain here and recover if at all possible. I've discussed with Dr. Z., again, the benefits and risks of antidepressant medication, and we both agree that in view of her history of abuse, suicidal ideation, and past allergic reactions to various drugs that medication will be used only as a last resort. The lack of a certain diagnosis and effective treatment and her inability to have more extensive testing because the cost is prohibitive only add to her already depressed state. And once again her living and work situations are deteriorating, this time apparently through no fault of her own.

Three weeks ago I suggested that we do some active imagination with her inner child, and she was fearful but receptive. I've been doing more and more imaginal work, so I was comfortable with the idea and enlisted the help of my three-foot high Raggedy Ann doll, who usually sits quietly in a corner of the couch next to Pierre the Bear. I "became" Ariel's inner child, speaking through Raggedy Ann, and Ariel responded to her as if she were, in fact, the wounded, split-off part of herself she has been so separated from. As with so many people who have been abused, the imaginal realm is quite accessible to Ariel, so she had little difficulty with the IDEA of dialoguing with a doll. She wouldn't look at Raggedy Ann, however, and after a minute or so her eyes glazed over and she went into another spontaneous regression, this time wordless. I talked to her as best I could in the words and tone of voice a young child would use in these circumstances, and at one point asked her if she would hold "me", but she pushed Raggedy Ann away and began sucking her thumb in the corner of the couch, eyes closed and breathing fast. I asked her in my adult voice where she was, but she didn't answer, just gasped for breath. Because I had gone through regressions with her before, I wasn't frightened this time, and after a few minutes with no verbal response from her I said (as inner child) that I would like to talk to her and be close to her when she is ready, and that it's o.k. if she's not ready yet. Ariel's breathing slowly subsided, she slowly returned. and she was very present and oriented when she left. We didn't have a chance to discuss what had happened until the next session, when she told me she had been very angry at every child she saw for the next few days.

"I don't know what to do," she said tearfully. "If I embrace the child I have to embrace her pain. I don't want to do that."

We talked about what that would be like, and her terror of it. She had clearly BECOME the child in the regression; her resistance to integration was strong.

"I caught a glimpse of her. It was horrible. She was absolutely beautiful, but she had hollow eyes. I can't look at her. I just feel overwhelmed by sadness."

"What happened when she was talking to you?" I asked.

"There were no pictures, only feelings. I thought I was going to die, I couldn't catch my breath. It was so bad, overwhelming. So much pain. I had to get my breath or I would die. I remember pushing the doll away. There were no visions, but I felt like I was running. When you said where are you I felt I was hiding under or behind a couch. I could see his feet and his huge boots. He was laughing."

I just listened, feeling rage well up inside me. The man was a beast.

"When I left, and for the next couple of days, my legs felt strange. The pain in my legs was different, and my muscles were weak. My fingers hurt, and I had sharp pains and cramps in my legs but they weren't continuous. I feel like I have to pretend everything's all right, but the sadness is like a deep pit inside me, it doesn't go away."

We talked about her mixed feelings towards her inner child and her inability to talk or listen to her. I asked her if she thought she could write a letter to little Mary Ellen when she went home, and not only was she able to do it, she also wrote a poignant response from the point of view of the child, and an answer to that. She shared the letters with me, weeping.

> Dear Mary Ellen,
>
>     I know you're in a lot of pain, I know all your sadness. It isn't I don't hear you, it's just I don't know how to help you through it. I feel so inadequate and so helpless. I just want to scream at you to stop or to do things so I don't hear you. I'm supposed to be adult, and I don't want Mom's recordings in my head but I try to be tender and become very frightened as I then feel engulfed by your feelings. I feel like I'm missing that middle ground. I'm either childlike or horrid like Mom. If I shut out feelings I can go along and be o.k. But now I'm bouncing all over trying to merge, then trying to shut you out. The physical pain makes me so angry and distracts me from working on us. You've been through enough, I've been through enough and I'm tired of carrying the two of us. You felt the rejection at four, I've

felt it all the rest of the time and even today and it's all your fault. You felt it for four years, I've felt it for 41 years. Where do you get off having everyone feel sorry for that little girl and making me the culprit? The one that's supposed to understand and be grown up. Damn you, I'm just as confused and probably more so than you because I don't remember everything, you do, but I carry it somewhere. I don't have answers and you expect me to. I tell you I want to love you but don't know how and you don't hear me. Cause I'm supposed to know, right? That's why I hate you because you expect me to know things, to know what to do and I don't, not for what you did. Sometimes I just wish you had died at four and we both would be out of our misery.

How can Connie help us? I don't know what to ask her. I no longer know what I need from her to help us. I feel I've asked too much of her already. You're too demanding. If I keep it up she's going to get mad at me, not you, and I'd rather die first. When I no longer have her then who will believe us? She keeps giving me hope and I believe her, then you demand more. I can't keep going, I don't want to have that hope or believe, it seems too endless and it is just more fairy tale stuff. Cinderella was a movie made by people with imagination, not reality, and when you realize it's not going to happen to us and life is just going to continue as it always has you won't want any part of it either. Yes, I've turned cold and hard but life is that way.

I feel like it's all impossible, it's not like I haven't tried. We have too many hurts, rejections, pain, and scars to pick up now and be o.k. I've done the best I can but it's just not good enough. It isn't you, it's me, that's just losing the will to keep trying.

I do love you, but I'm just too tired to take care of you anymore.

Regretfully,
Ariel

*Dear Ariel,*

*Please hold me, please take care of me, please don't shut me out anymore. Please let others hold us, it feels so good and I can sleep. You want to be held too but you keep blaming me. I hate you and you're going to feel my pain. I've stayed hidden long enough. I don't care if I get locked up, I hurt too bad to care anymore. I've waited and waited while you went off on your way shutting me out. You filled your head so you wouldn't know I was there.*

*Connie is trying to help me and you keep taking her away. If we want to live she's my only hope. I beg you to let her help. I don't know so much but you can teach me if you let her help.*

*I don't feel sorry for Mommy, she heard me. I tried to tell her how I hurt after being with Grampa and she knew. I hate her, she wouldn't give me what was mine to have. She turned her back on me, her an adult that was my mother afraid of what other people would say cause she let it happen. She left me at four to do the best I could. I had to give in, I couldn't die and no one would stop him. I had no family, just people that were supposed to be. I wanted to go away but the home never let those kids out. I looked and looked but they were never out. I have to be outside to feel good, to breathe, to smell. I wanted Miss Holbrook or Mr. Stimson to take me home to be my family. They didn't have anyone and neither did I. They liked me but felt sorry for me cause I couldn't tell them what's wrong.*

*When I realized nobody was going to help me, going to a home for mothers wasn't so bad. I saw a movie about them and people loved them and helped them. But Daddy lied to me and he let me get married. He was glad to get rid of me. He hated me. Then you grew up and left me when I would try to talk to you you wouldn't listen but I was driving you crazy. You were killing both of us. I hurt I hurt I hurt and saved you and you were killing us. That's not fair. How can you do that to us?*

*I won't shut up 'till our last breath you have to hear me. People really like us and you're too cold to feel it and believe it.*

*We weren't bad. We weren't. Grampa was bad, he was a devil you knew it when he smiled others knew he was bad but no one would help us. Thought I was bad. I wasn't bad but they wouldn't listen. Don't you stop. Don't you dare or I'll hate you forever. I don't know if our pain will stop but I promise if you listen if you hold me and love me like Connie showe you I promise I will stop crying but I will keep it up 'till you listen to me. I can't breathe anymore, I can't stay like this. I'm getting tired, I want to sleep and I'll never wake up.*

*Don't hate me don't shut me out. Please let me be loved before we leave here and we'll always remember it and God will take care of both of us I promise. He loves me, he's been with me, he keeps telling me not to give up. He knows all about us trust him trust Connie and help us to know love here. Jesus did it you can do it. Please help me. Please.*
*Mary Ellen*


*Dear Mary Ellen,*

*I'm sorry I haven't listened to you or looked at you. I haven't known what to do for you. When I look at you I then feel the pain. I haven't been good to you or taken good care of you and when I tried to help you it hurt so bad and I had to drown you out. I've tried to kill you so many times. Your pain makes me want to throw up. I'm understanding more but too many pieces are missing. I have needed to keep a distance from other people as it brings up your pain of having no one when you needed them. If I hold you it makes me so sad and I can't stop crying.*

*I want to let you up now but I'm finding so much confusion. I know you hate me as I have hated you. I don't hate you anymore but I'm so scared and feel like I don't know how to take care of us. My hands hurt when I write now and that has been my only way of really communicating my feelings. I know I need to use my mouth and scream and yell but it doesn't come. I want to scream for your pain, for my pain, but I'm held back by something, I don't know what.*

*I'm missing a part of me, but is it you I'm missing? How can we merge together, you with your pain and me with my pain of today. Will we be engulfed in pain? Will we be able to find happiness anywhere here on earth?*

*I am angry with Mommy and what she did to you but I'm now to put that aside and forgive her. How can I go back and make everything o.k. and still do as God wishes for us?*

*Mommy didn't mean you would be locked up. You misunderstood her. She said you would be sent away to a children's home and she would be locked up if you said one word. My eyes hurt from crying so much but needing to be quiet so no one will hear.*

*Will Grampa give us any answers or will he also tell us we're lying and exaggerating? I always believed Mommy would come to us someday and hold us and love us and want us. I have now accepted that she won't, can you accept this? If I treat you like our mother did how can I mother you?*

*Will you suffer from culture shock when we merge? I don't know what fear is left. I've married, the children are grown and distant, not sure what direction to go. We've done everything before our time and I feel it's all over. I haven't prospered, no education, what can I offer us? More sadness, more hard times, more lowliness. Tell me if it can be different but use no flowery words or childish imagination fairy tale stuff.*

*I want to love you but don't know how.*

*Ariel*

# CHAPTER VII

## *Help from Heaven*

## Fall 1989

### Ariel

I've thought for a long time that Connie is an angel, my special angel, and now I feel that Lynn is another angel who's come into my life. I know Connie hesitated to tell me about her—she laughed and said giving the name of a psychic to a patient was "unorthodox, to say the least"—but the guides Lynn channels, I KNOW they're angels, so wise and loving and knowing things only real angels could know. I don't think Connie talks about these things with her other patients, and I don't even know if she's ever had a session with Lynn, but as soon as I get the tapes I bring them to her and we listen together. She says what the guides say through Lynn is helping her a lot to understand what's going on with me and how to help me better. We laugh and cry when we listen, and it's like we have a spiritual bond because we both know about these things.

So I called Lynn and set up another appointment for last week and told her that for a long time after our last session I felt a kind of bubble around me, but that lately I've been feeling such despair and frustration I don't even feel close to my Christian friends. I haven't known how to replace the feeling of despair, what to replace it with. I feel like I should get busy, go do something, but I feel so awful in my body I can't do much. And I can't go around crying all the time.

She told me to breathe down into my belly, and when I did that I felt really, really sad. She tried to help me get in touch with anger, but the sadness was easier to feel.

And then all of a sudden the guides started talking:

*We would offer to you at this time that there is a darkness that lives in you and in the space above your head and it is the darkness that is given to you by others. You carry it because in your willful mind you cannot see the possibility of ridding yourself of the darkness that is buried there. We give to you these understandings so that you will see yourself with great clarity and know the power that you carry within you.*

*You have been carried a great distance without supper or water and it is necessary for you to rest yourself and carry yourself to the stream where you may drink and heal yourself. You see yourself as vile and destructive and you do not know the beauty you have carried within you. You have carried a gray and shadowed bag along with you, a sac that is filled with sadness and darkness, and yet deep within this sac there is a luminescent pearly light that shines forth with a powerful essence that is soft and strong. This is your essence of who you are. It is important for you to reach down into the shadowy depths and bring forth what is hidden there and then you will find that the glowing takes place all around you and you see with a different eye. You are in deep need of a ritual cleansing so that you will carry with you only yourself.*

*You ask who we might be. We are the voices of gentle knowing that carry you across the dreary waters which you have swum through and brought yourself to this marshy shore. You do not see that you have brought yourself through shark-infested waters and from a place of great poison and even now you walk through sticky mud to bring yourself to a place of greater light. The journey is not finished, nor is it close to the beginning. You are in the middle of a pathway that will take you to an understanding that cannot come through the mind and could not come from your earliest experience. You bring with you your mother's shadowy misunderstanding and she too holds within herself the feeling that all will be well if she keeps herself silent and speaks not the truth. You must say what is the truth with you and make it known to all around you, for in so doing your understanding will come forth and you will see yourself in yet a different way. Take yourself from the house of sorrow and walk in the light and when you return you will have brightness and a clearer voice and will know what needs to be said. Take close to you the flowers that give you joy and make sure your eye falls upon them often. You must say to someone near to you how deeply you have felt and all that has gone with you and all you have experienced, and in so doing you will take the truth away from you and it will fall away and disappear down the river and to a different place.*

*Your sadness hides the brutal anger that you carry deep within you. The anger festers and grows like a great infection and poisons your blood and takes itself into your heart and then you feel that a demon has poisoned you from within. An infection must bring itself to the surface or be absorbed slowly and the anger within you is so deep and strong it takes itself to the bloodstream and causes a red line of fury that creates poison throughout your system. You are now feeling the sickness of anger not brought to the surface nor released in its proper way. It is important to lance the wound and bring out what is there so you know you are capable of bringing it forth and healing.*

*You will find that your sense of dark foreboding comes from early hours when you could not claim yourself or speak in your rightful voice, when you wished to tell a truth that could not be heard, and your voice fell silent and you could not say it, and you grew in a rageful fear around you and you knew that if you spoke the repercussions would be worse than the experience in its first wave.*

*We are giving you these understandings so that you will know that you have done no wrong. You will see yourself as one who has filled up a glass with dark water and it is necessary to tip it sideways to spill out the water. The clear glass feels its grief and its sorrow and feels the emptiness as the darkness spills from it and then comes the clear light that fills the glass and makes itself sparkle . You in your essence are not dark, but what is spilled upon you is . You carry with you the sadness of others. It is yours in part but belongs to others and the rage within you also must be spilled and taken out. You must think in your mind what you would do with this rage and allow your body to lay dormant as the thoughts pass through your mind. You may bring to your surface the thoughts and images that will give you great release and understanding. If you pound your feet upon the pavement and throw the stone at the wall you will take from you the energy that belongs to others. And then you must light a candle to your fear and all will be well.*

*The angels of mercy and understanding are over your shoulder and know full well what you have encountered. The angels of forgiveness walk in front of you and ask you to step closer to them, not asking you to forgive those who have perpetrated sorrow against you, but to forgive yourself for the vile thoughts that have entered into your head. There is no need for forgiveness to others at this time. They are taken to a place of peacefulness but it is important that you forgive yourself the violence that courses through your veins, the poison you carry within is vile to your body and must be spat forth and make itself to come out, for in so doing it will cleanse your system and you will be healed.*

*There is a voice that lives within you, it is the voice of patience and great understanding . You must say to yourself inside I am an orphaned child and I do not know my true parentage, and in so doing the most profound healing will take place. And the mother and father who have loved you over a long distance of time, they will step forward in spirit and make themselves known. You are wise in your desire to be part of a family and a wider community, for you see the goodness that you are capable of bringing forth in others.*

*You have lived in isolation for a long distance and carried yourself in sorrowful, painful pathways where others could not travel with you for too long a distance. Make yourself enjoyable and connected to those around you and feel yourself part of a whole that is outside of you but encompasses and includes you and in so doing like the woman who walks through the village and knows the names of all the people there, she knows her place and knows she is exalted and knows that if she took herself to the river and flung herself into sorrow and made her head to break open against the rock and her body were to float down a great wailing of sorrow would come from the village, the cry of death would be heard. She knows those who would kneel beside her and grieve over their loss and she would not do this thing but go instead to the river and gather the water in her baskets and take it back to water the plants that she had planted, and though the thought would flicker through her mind she would say and then my body would come around the river and come up in a spot, and the women who had gone there to wash their clothes, and the children who had gone to wash their feet, they would be filled with grief, and the sadness would overtake them and the cry would be a sorrowful sound. And she would say my soul would not go to a place of peaceful resting, for I would live in their cries, and so she says to herself it is a thought that went through my mind, and it must pass over to the land of death. I myself will gather my baskets and gather the water and as I pass back through the village I will see the other villagers, the men and women who would weep at my death, and I will wave my hand to them and over them some of my water, and when my crops have grown I will not remember the sorrowful thought that entered my head. And this woman knows that she is wanted and understood. She tends to what is in her garden, and yet she feels herself to be part of the community. This is what is needed here, a gentleness of community, to provide comfort.*

*In your earliest hours you did not know yourself to be of value and you felt yourself to be the object of others' needs only, and your soul went to live on a distant hill to become like a hermit and to live under the dark rock. Now your soul returns and stands on the hill windblown and in great sorrow and she clutches her cloak about her, standing underneath the cloak and says I cannot find my way back to the village and the woman who is the object, the self that is the object, lives in the village and says I cannot find my true self, I am wishing to take myself to death, and in truth it is the uniting of the self that is banished and sent away and the self that is object, the desire to bring them together and make them as one. That is your purpose now, to bring together the part that was abandoned and left, the part that was sent to the far place to live, to take this part and incorporate it and make it part of the object. And then the two will be one and there will be a great rejoicing within.*

*You will not take yourself to the door of death though the thought enters your head often. But you will take yourself instead to the process of healing and cleansing. We are here beside you and stand in front of you also. We grab hold of the dark knot within your stomach and shake it until the poisonous attachments fly free within your system. And soon will come the hour when fingers of joyous light will reach into you and disintegrate the hard knot and pull it through you and with a great sadness and retching, but it will be pulled from you and your dark hour will be retreated. We are here for you, our little pumpkin seed, and plant you in the earth and watch what comes up from you. You are to us not a thing, an object, but a soul that is filled with light. We hold in our hands the pearl that you are and ask you to find us here where we enclose the gentle light that lives within you. We will stand at the doorway where darkness dwells and kick and scream until the darkness has lifted itself off. We are here for you in the dreariest hour. We are here, we are here, we are here.*

# Connie

## *Treatment Summary, September 1989*

Ariel (formerly Mary Ellen) has been drug-free and sober since beginning treatment with me approximately three years ago. Bulimic symptoms have gradually abated, and she has been in remission for about a year, with a gradual normalization of eating patterns. Normal weight, within a five-pound range, has been maintained during most of that time, and menses are fairly regular. Treatment has included completion of the Evergreen inpatient program as well as hospitalization at Carter House for severe depression approximately one and a half years ago.

Ariel has been employed during most of this time: as an office worker, salesperson, and market researcher. She has been active in AA and had a conversion experience about a year and half ago that resulted in her becoming a born-again Christian. Her active involvement in a church has apparently provided her with a great deal of support and comfort until quite recently, when she has expressed some dissatisfaction with the church and a sense of "Jesus Christ being farther away from me."

Over the course of therapy, with sessions usually two times per week, Ariel has worked through many of the feelings and issues surrounding an apparently extensive (infancy through age 12) incestuous relationship with her grandfather; her sense of abandonment and rejection by her mother; emotional and physical abuse by her father, and many other family of origin issues. She has developed a strong, sustaining relationship with her sister Denise, a sense of identity as a woman, and, although shaky at times, a growing sense of herself as an intelligent and capable person.

Ariel continues to have difficulty with interpersonal relationships and to exhibit many typically borderline traits, i.e., abandonment depression, splitting, rage, and self-destructive thoughts. She experiences chronic suicidal ideation and periodically, before treatment here, has made active suicide attempts. Currently she reports many suicidal thoughts but says she does not intend to act on them. She reports great difficulty at times resisting the impulse to "escape from this life and be with God," and in other ways manifests a schizoid defense pattern.

My treatment with her has included Jungian dream interpretation, trance-induced age regression, and spontaneous regressions during which she has reexperienced the incest trauma. She has also learned to use a journal and has drawn her feelings and memories. A lot of our work has focused on her wounded inner child, a part of her that she associates with shame, pity, and fear.

For the past five to six months Ariel has complained of intermittent muscle pain, particularly in her face and legs; extreme fatigue, extreme sadness, hopelessness, and helplessness, and strong recurring suicidal thoughts. She has consulted several different physicians during this time, and apparently aside from some muscle weakness and flaccidity, tests have been normal. Some relief has been afforded by daily Prednisone, 10 mg. She recently quit her job because she could not sustain her energy level for a full day, and now lives with a family as an au pair. A definitive diagnosis has been impossible to obtain, and her frustration and discomfort have deepened her depression. Her symptoms apparently began around the time she had a Shiatzu session with a male practitioner. After the session she experienced extreme rage, which required several extra sessions with me to work through. Apparently the penetrating nature of the Shiatzu had recreated her incestuous experience, including an overall muscle response of exaggerated relaxation followed by pain.

Ariel, feeling quite "stuck" with her physical symptoms and her depression, had a telephone session with a psychic in California. I listened to the tape of this session, which suggested that as early as four or five years old Ariel had been vaginally penetrated by her grandfather, who was a very large man. Apparently to survive the pain, she learned how to relax her muscles and continued to do this during other incestuous assaults. A suggestion was made that Ariel's current muscular flaccidity and pain were related to those experiences. In another session with the psychic it was suggested that healing will come when the accumulated negative experience is released. All of this fits with my understanding of Ariel's history and the profound psyche-soma connection that exists.

As a result of listening to these tapes and much discussion with Ariel, I have agreed to have a phone session with the psychic and Ariel from my office, in an attempt to help Ariel find some relief from the physical and emotional torment from which she suffers. I am aware that this is a highly unusual, unorthodox approach.

Constance Simpson Myslik, RN, ACSW

With some anxiety but even more excited anticipation, I arranged the session and set it up so Lynn was on my office speakerphone and Ariel and I were sitting nearby. After Lynn asked Ariel and me to breathe deeply, she did what she called a "check-in", tuning in to each of us energetically, and asked each of us what we were experiencing.

"Anxiety comes and goes in waves," Ariel reported. "Otherwise I feel as if I could go to sleep."

"Are you hazy?"

Ariel laughed. "Either that or I want to escape."

"How about you, Connie?"

"I'm feeling pretty grounded. A little lightheaded, but comfortable."

"Are your eyes perceiving in any way other than normal?" Lynn asked.

"Yes," I told her, "but I don't know how to describe it."

"Say thank you, thank you for my eyes, thank you for my hands. Then let your hands go to wherever they want to go. Then let your eyes go kind of half mast and see if any pictures or anything comes about Ariel's body. Any images."

I followed her instructions and somewhere inside my brain

had an image of Ariel all curled up. I told Lynn.

"How old is she?" she asked.

"Partly her own age, and partly much, much smaller." I couldn't believe answers were coming to me like this. From where?

"How does that feel, Ariel?" Lynn asked.

Ariel hesitated. "I'm wanting to hold on to Connie."

"Is that o.k., Connie?" Lynn asked me.

"Yes," I told her. "Part of what I was imagining was that she was curled up and I was cradling her."

Ariel and I moved to the floor, and I cradled her, describing what was happening to Lynn.

"There's a very powerful guide or presence with you, Connie. Can you feel that at all?"

"Yes, I can." I felt the presence of strong energy at my right shoulder. It was almost palpable.

"Is there any sense of what it's asking or guiding you to do?"

"The words that come are—it's almost like I need to gather her up, which I'm kind of doing."

"What's happening with you, Ariel?"

"There's a voice inside me saying Help me, help me."

"What does your guidance tell you to do about that, Connie?"

I felt uncertain, incompetent. "I'm not sure," I told her.

"Say those words to Connie, Ariel: help me, help me, help me."

There was a long silence. I could feel, rather than hear, Ariel pleading with me for help.

"I'm not sure what to do," I said rather helplessly.

"Just be with her," Lynn said. "Imagine she's about four years old and something has happened, and she can't tell you what it is. You both know something has happened."

"I won't let anyone hurt you any more," I said to Ariel.

"What do you want to do with your hands? I keep seeing you holding her head to your chest. Put your hand that's on her shoulder, if you feel like it, down to her solar plexus. Just sit there with it for a minute and see what you feel."

Ariel nodded permission, and I put one hand on her solar plexus. It felt tight, and I told Lynn that.

"What do you feel, Ariel?"

"It feels like there's a knot, but the pain just moved up to my throat."

"Take Connie's hand and put it in the spot where it feels most comfortable, where it touches most the place that needs to be touched."

"There are two places, I can't tell."

"Where are they?"

"The heart and the throat."

"O.K., put Connie's hands there, and Connie, pay attention to what you feel as you touch those places."

I moved my hands to her heart and her throat.

"I'm going to say something that doesn't make sense to me. . . . the heart is open and there's something stuck in the throat." I had no idea where my words were coming from.

"How does that sound, Ariel?" Lynn asked.

"Absolutely."

"As you say it, does it shift or change at all?"

"It becomes more clear," I told her.

"Is there a vision?"

"Something needs to be said."

"Is there something, Ariel?"

"I just hurt so bad in the throat."

"So Connie, is it words or a sound?"

"It might be a sound," I said.

"Say, may I hear the sound?"

"May I hear the sound? . . . there's no sound."

"Just hold your hand at her throat," Lynn instructed, "and ask that it be released. It doesn't matter that she can't say it, just ask that all the energy there be released and move to its rightful place. And pay attention to what you feel, sense, and see as you say those things.

I did as she said.

"It feels like the heart and throat are trying to connect."

"What are you feeling with your hands?"

"It feels like there's some relaxation."

"What are you feeling, Ariel?"

"Like there's a shifting back and forth between my heart and my throat."

"What you can say, Connie, and Ariel, you also, is "May her heart be filled with light, may her throat be filled with light, may the space between the two be filled with light.""

Ariel and I spoke the words together.

Lynn continued, "May the energy that moves within her heal and bless her, may the most holy light live within her body, may she be free of all that is not hers, all that does not serve her. May the residue of others that no longer loves her and serves her be bathed in the light and taken to its rightful place. May the most healing light live in each of her organs. May the most healing light live in each of her passageways. May all that is here that does not serve be gone. May the most healing light live within her. May she be blessed and nurtured and fed. May she have all that she needs. . . . Did anything happen for either one of you as I was saying those things?

"Yes," Ariel answered, "there was a horrible pain in my breast-bone."

"I had the sense of some energy shifting," I said.

"Is there a way to put the speaker closer to you guys? And take some time to rearrange yourselves, it's important to be comfortable."

I moved the speaker, and Ariel and I shifted positions.

"How is the pain in your chest?" she asked Ariel.

"It's gone. Connie moved her hand and it left."

"O.K. Check your hand, Connie. Did you sense the pain when she felt it?"

"Right now I'm looking at my hand and I have a pain in the center of my right palm."

"Can you see it or feel it?"

"Both," I answered, aware that a part of myself was watching and listening to all of this with absolute incredulity.

"I'm going to ask you some questions, give me the first answer that comes to mind. Ariel, you may have an answer too. Take your own hands and put them where the pain was. Connie, is this pain yours?"

"No."

"Does it belong to Ariel?"

"I don't know."

"Did someone give her this pain?"

"Yes."

"What must be done with it now?"

"It has to be thrown away."

"Do you know how to do that?"

"No. I just had an image of throwing a ball."

"Look across the room from you, the opposite of where you're sitting. Half close your eyes, and there may be a funnel or opening of some sort, like a corridor. Do you see it?"

"No."

"Look around the room and see if you see it."

"I want to throw it toward the window." I made a throwing motion toward the window.

"How does your hand feel now?"

"There's a little left at the base of my thumb."

"O.K., let your hands move in whatever way they want to."

"I just brushed it away. Now my hands are all tingly."

"May all that is here that does not heal and bless be gone," Lynn said. "What's happening with you, Ariel?"

"Tears are just flowing out of my eyes and thoughts, no more like understandings. I just keep hearing this little voice that says My heart was broken by Mommy, she wouldn't help me. I have to hide my own bottom."

"Poor little thing," Lynn said compassionately. "Connie, stay with your hands. What do your hands feel like doing?"

"They want to touch her."

"Is that o.k. with you, Ariel?"

"Yes."

"Then, Connie, let your hands go where they want to."

"I have one hand on her abdomen and one hand on her forehead."

"O.K.," Lynn said. "And Ariel, how does that feel to you?"

"My head is full of thoughts coming in. It's the same little voice, saying, I'll let him have it, and then it won't hurt so bad."

"Say it again."

"I'll let him have it, and then," Ariel cried, "then it won't . . . hurt so bad."

"Connie, when she says that, what happens in your hands?"

"Nothing, I just feel very sad."

"What do you feel like saying to her?"

"I'm so sorry, I'm so sorry you had to do that."

"What I want to say to you, Ariel," Lynn said strongly, "is he's not supposed to be doing that, that's not right. . . . how are your hands feeling, Connie?"

"Like I want to do something, like I want to stop it. I feel angry."

"Don't try to stop the anger, let the anger guide you. Look inside her body and use your hands as a scan. Find the place where that energy, his energy, is. Where the residue is of what he put on her. Ask for help. . . . Ariel, stay in your body, don't leave."

I silently asked for help, then spoke.

"My impulse is to put one hand on her abdomen and one hand on her back. It's like . . . it's like . . . it's between the lower part of her back and her abdomen."

"How does that feel to you, Ariel?" Lynn asked.

"I'm just lying her, feeling like, I can't feel from the waist down. My ears are filling up with fluid, like I've been swimming."

"I've got to tell you honestly what's been happening for me now," Lynn said. "I just had a rush of absolute fury and anger. This is a little bit unconventional. I'm going to say the things that are in my mind. You two just be honest with the way you feel. You may feel a variety of things, so just be aware of what any images. Connie, where are your hands?"

"My left hand is on her lower back and my rig... her lower abdomen."

"Great. Ariel, be aware of the space between your legs, like four inches from your vaginal opening."

Lynn began to speak loudly and strongly, and as she did I could feel the anger well up inside of me also.

"I feel so ANGRY," she said. "Leave her alone you filthy son of a bitch! Leave her alone! Can't you see what you've done? This has got to stop! I know what's been happening, and it's got to stop, don't you ever, ever look at her that way again! Don't you ever touch her in that way again! It's finished!. . . . O.k. My whole insides are quivering."

"I feel the same way," I told her.

"How do you feel, Ariel?" Lynn asked.

"I was getting some pain up through my vagina, and I keep hearing her voice saying He won't listen."

"What it feels to me," Lynn spoke, "is like a splitting that happened in you while I was saying that. Like you became a compassionate person who said if this stops I won't have him at all, and don't talk like that, it's a bad way to talk, and there were different parts of you. Does that sound accurate?"

"Yes," Ariel answered.

"How about you, Connie, do you get any confirmation of that?"

"Yes, it feels accurate. And when you said stop it and Ariel said he won't listen I wanted to say I'll kill him if he won't listen."

"Yes, I had the same impulse, and what I saw was a little girl in terror if I said that. Oh, it's getting clearer. The little girl splits off. She hears the mother say "Don't you do it again, I'll kill you," and she becomes responsible for blood and death. And how do you feel when I say that, Ariel?"

"Very sad."

"Yes, and there's a little voice in you, and what does the little voice say?"

"Now there's nobody."

"Yeah, yeah . . . o.k., and what was the decision your body made at that time?"

"I'll do what I have to do, I can take it."

"And Connie., what's happening with your hands?"

"They want to go someplace else but I'm not sure where."

"O.K. Separate them from the body about half an inch and they'll take you where you need to go."

"O.K. I've got my hands on her back, both of them kind of on her spine from the waist up."

"How does that feel to you, Ariel?"

"My whole right side is quivering."

"O.K., I'm going to ask a couple of questions and both of you pay attention to the first answer that comes into your mind. Is something trying to escape?"

"No," Ariel answered.

"Maybe," I said.

"I keep having this feeling that your body made a very, very powerful decision a long time ago and it's a decision that's outside of any kind of consciousness as we think about it. But it doesn't know if it can exist if it gives up this decision. If it changes it's mind, it's not sure that it'll exist. Does that make sense to either one of you?"

"YES," Ariel and I said in chorus. We all laughed. This had to be one of the strangest experiences of my life.

Lynn continued as guide.

"O.k. So Connie, use your hands so the body can feel what it's like to exist beyond this decision. What does it feel like to exist without this decision?"

I hesitated, waited for internal guidance.

"What I want to do is put her arms up and put my hands on her shoulders and chest so that area will expand. I don't know what it means."

"I feel resistance," Ariel said. "I don't know why."

"O.K. Feel your feet, Ariel, point your toes out and then in, stretch them straight out, arch them, move them back. Feel the muscles in your legs as you do that, feel what happens in your bottom and your abdomen. Does anything happen when you do that?"

Ariel followed Lynn's instructions and then spoke.

"They're less tense."

"Roll your feet in and out. Pay attention to what happens in her body, Connie, as she's doing this. Do you feel any shifting? Do you understand what happened, there, Connie?"

"No," I answered truthfully and humbly, amazed at how much Lynn was picking up from three thousand miles away. How could she do that? It was as if she was moving through space and time in a way that upset all my linear notions of what those words meant.

"All of her energy was coming up to letting go, and it's very frightening to let go because her body . . . she made decisions very early in her body that this is what it means to be alive, this is what I have to do to exist, and whatever that involved . . . I have to take on others' energy, things can be done to me and I have to receive whatever's given. And when you start to open it up, it's not just a matter of releasing what's there, it's about releasing a whole concept about the body which then means annihilation."

"Yes, I understand," I said, awed by the depths to which we were going.

"Do you understand, Ariel?"

"Partially," she answered.

"What I felt," Lynn continued, "was that when she got resistant . . . the lower part of her body is a grounding device . . . and all her energy was separating from her legs and coming up into her chest, trying to hold onto something. What we did was take the focus away from where it was happening and to where the energy of the earth will support her and guide her and open up those channels so that she's receiving energy from a different level. So what she experienced was a lessening of anxiety and more of a willingness to let go . . . o.k., Ariel, what are you experiencing now?"

"A lot of thoughts, and a lot of cramping in the middle part of my back. I think it had to do with what you were saying."

"If if feels right to you, Connie, take your hands down to her abdomen, to her pubic bone, and touch the heel of your hand to her pubic bone. Is that o.k. with you, Ariel?"

"Only because it's Connie."

"O.K. So touch her lower back in the same place with the heel of your hand and then work your hands up, like you're kneading something, like snake them up, and go all the way up to her throat, and see how that feels."

I followed instructions. Then Ariel spoke.

"As she was doing it, it felt like part of it was coming and part of it was slipping back."

"Which part is slipping back?"

"The fear of letting go."

"Which part is going out?" Lynn asked.

"The me of today."

"Would it help for me to do it again?" I asked Ariel.

"How does it feel?" Lynn asked me.

"Strange . . . reminds me of being a nurse."

We all laughed.

"What do you experience, Ariel?"

"I don't know . . . I don't know what it is," Ariel said tentatively.

"Stay in your body, Ariel, stay in your body," Lynn directed her. "What are you doing with your hands, Connie?"

"I'm repeating what I did before. I'm sensing there's something in the middle of her back, at the base of the spine . . . something."

"It hurts," Ariel said.

"Put your hands on it. What do your hands want to do?" Lynn asked me.

"Put pressure on it. . . . "

"Say this to yourself and see what happens. "Use my hands, thy will be done.""

I repeated her words silently to myself, waited, and then began to move my hands up Ariel's back near her spine with a fair amount of pressure. I told Lynn what I was doing.

"How does that feel, Ariel?"

"Good."

"Stay in your body, Ariel, say to yourself, 'It's my body.' . . . what's happening?"

"I have one hand on her lower back and one hand on the back of her neck," I said.

"What are you feeling, Ariel?"

"It feels very good, and I keep hearing voices."

"What do they say?"

Ariel began sobbing. "I want to be alive but I don't want my body . . . it doesn't belong to me."

"It does belong to you, and even after all this time you can take it back. It is your body . . . what's happening now?"

I spoke. "I want to tell her to take it back. Take it back, Ariel . . . What can she do to take it back?"

"I don't know," Lynn answered. "The picture I have is of her running . . . I see a man that's very big and scary. He's not only scary, he's nice too."

Ariel sobbed harder. I rocked her back and forth, stroking her hair.

"He possesses something that's hers," Lynn said, "and I see her as a child. It's like Jack and the Beanstalk, and Jack has to run from the giant, steals something from the giant. I see her going into this open space and stealing it and running like crazy. But the thing is that once she touches this object that he guards over, once she touches it she becomes more powerful and bigger and her legs are stronger and she runs faster.

"Like he's guarding the gold?" I asked, seeing the images very clearly.

"Yeah," Lynn said. "Does that story mean anything to you, Ariel?"

"No," she answered, still crying. "But I knew you were talking about my grandfather. He was a big man, like a giant to me."

"Can you see yourself going into a space that he guards and

stealing something back?"

"I have to take myself from him and I don't know how to do it."

"What happens if he catches you taking it?"

"I'm done."

"Well, I don't think you're done, but I don't think the little girl is convinced about that. What's the tool or weapon that you could use to take back what you need to take back?"

Ariel laughed. "I'll take Connie."

"You'll take Connie? O.K."

"Just before you asked that," I broke in, "my image was that this little girl needs someone to go with her. It's not so much a tool as it is someone else, to hold her hand. She needs to chop down the beanstalk or, first get the gold and then chop down the beanstalk. She can do it, but only if someone is by her side."

"Right," Lynn said.

"Someone has to be watching over him to be sure he's asleep while she steals back the gold," I continued

"Does it have to be someone who won't kill him?" Lynn asked.

Ariel answered. "It has to be someone who will make me safe but won't make him die."

"Do you understand that, Connie?"

"Yes. I wouldn't kill him. I would want to but I wouldn't actually kill him."

"What I'm getting," Lynn said, " is that a lot of the terror is that even if somebody does find out she will be responsible for death.

"Yes," I said. "And it ties in with the reality that if her father had found out, he would have killed her grandfather. Is that true Ariel?"

"Yes."

"It's real important to understand that a lot of the decisions made in the body had to do not only with the body's own preservation but the preservation of life beyond that body's life," Lynn emphasized. "So all this splitting takes place, like I'm saving my life by not being in my body, and I'm saving yours by allowing this to happen."

"I feel all that splitting. I don't know which part to hold onto."

"It might help to draw all the different parts and what all those messages are to all those different parts."

"She did that once, a while ago," I told Lynn. "There were a lot of parts, and they didn't come together very well."

"Yeah . . . It's almost like they need a village, so they can be close but not all together at once," Lynn said.

"But I don't want that," Ariel protested. "Then I don't know which one to be."

"Right," Lynn reassured her. "You're not going to be any one of them, you're going to be yourself. They were all decisions that were made after things started to happen to you. There's another Self that lives underneath those . . . you're not any one of those."

"You know that, Ariel, don't you?" I asked. We had discussed this, the gathering up of sub-personalities, none of which was the True Self.

"Yes, but I want to scream, I don't want pieces, I want to be whole!"

"That's right, that's right," Lynn affirmed. "You're in the process of finding how to get to that. Close your eyes, Ariel. Connie hold your hands up to Ariel, like she's a screen, and you're reading the screen with your hands."

I moved away from Ariel a bit and did as Lynn suggested. "O.K."

"Now, Connie, what do you feel in that space around her?"

"Even two feet away, I feel a lot of energy."

"What do you feel, Ariel?"

"My body feels very heavy."

"I'm going to say a couple of words, and just notice if anything happens. O.K. . . . May the space around her body be freed and cleared of all that does not heal and bless her. May the channels be opened, may the doorways and pathways be opened, may all that does not heal and bless be taken to its rightful place. May the presence of the most divine be with her. May the space around her be full of her own essence, may it be hers alone. May she have herself alone. May the most holy light live here, may the most holy light bathe the energies and the forms that are not hers and take them to their rightful place. . . . Stay in your body, Ariel. What do you feel, Connie?"

"Just a tremendous amount of energy. My hands are at least two feet away, and there's a tremendous amount of energy."

"What do you want to do with your hands?"

"I want to put them on either side of her head."

"O.K. Did anything shift or change or move when I said those things?"

"All I feel is a strong energy field."

"Ariel, could you repeat after me?" Lynn asked.

"Yes."

"Say this: May I have myself alone."

"May I have myself alone."

"May I know my most true self."

"May I know my most true self."

"What do you feel?"

"Waves of light going across my eyes."

"She looks very peaceful," I told Lynn.

"It's like angels' wings brushing across my eyes," Ariel said, smiling softly.

"I'll vote for that," Lynn said. "Say thank you."

"They're white!" Ariel exclaimed. "White angels' wings."

We were all silent for a moment.

"I keep feeling that there's a voice or an energy that wants to talk to you, Ariel. Do you feel that at all?"

"Yes. I've been having that feeling and I'm afraid of it."

"O.K. Is it all right for it to talk to you?"

"Yes."

"Put your hand on her, Connie."

"I'm holding her hand," I said, as I took Ariel's hand gently in mine.

"Is she touching you enough, Ariel?"

"Yes," Ariel answered, her voice trembling.

"What does the voice say?"

"It's looking at me. I'm afraid, but I want to hug him at the same time . . . " she sobbed. "It's my grandfather."

"O.k, o.k. . . . can I talk to your grandfather?"

"Oh . . . do it for me," Ariel cried.

"You want me to talk to him?"

"Yes," Ariel said, gripping my hand.

"Grampa Durstan, look at me," Lynn said. "She's trying to become herself, alone. It's time to separate from her, to take all your energy back, everything that was done and said to her, every look and every gesture that is yours, take back and hold it with yourself. And I ask you also to send to her the support and the help she needs to know herself separate from you that she can know love that invigorates her and enlivens her and doesn't take anything from her. She's trying to heal herself, she's trying to heal herself. Take yourself to the pool of forgiveness and drink there."

"I have to know if he loved me or hated me, it's all mixed up," Ariel pleaded.

"What I see is that he loved you and he also, I don't know, it's like he had a cloud in his head and he refused to see that he was hurting you. He refused to acknowledge what your real experience was. . . . Grampa, can you see this now? . . . There's a kind of intermediary who speaks for him and says he sees it small, he sees it in small ways.

*He is coming to retrieve the energy forms he left with the child not knowing the poison that he left there. The doorways are open and he wishes to retrieve the aspects that were tainted and take them back as his own. He is wishing to cleanse himself and given the task to return to the places of poison. You are not the only child poisoned by this man. There were others too who do not speak, who stand in silence . He knew you as an object and yet in great love for you also gave you things of goodness.*

*You knew in an earlier time his love for you and have confused what is love and what is stealing.*

*You do not know the capacity to give love without giving fully of the self in a way that is detrimental and harmful. It is your task now during this period to learn the difference of knowing that the self is greatly loved and there is giving also. It is not selfishness to claim a space for yourself. These things are the tasks that you must learn. You will learn this before your time here is finished but your body is holding many memories that must be freed.*

*To the one who heals* ("This is for you, Connie," Lynn interrupted.") *we would say do not expect that these will come as conscious understandings. That is why you are guided to deal with them as energetic blossomings. The flower does not know it is a flower and still it blooms. The energy that was given there cannot be named because it lay outside experience that could be given dimension in the mind. It must be moved energetically and the girl will feel a different experience. She is wishing to reclaim herself, to know herself in her soul. Her angels are quite present and will give you the guidance that you need. You must give up on her and tell her to go her own way. See her continually and be with her but demand of her that she look within her and find the path she must take. You are the one who will bring forth the presence of the loving spirit but the command must come from within her. She must kick her grandfather in the tail and say to him be gone and you will stand near to her and place a steady hand upon her and she will be guided in her essence and will know herself. He was one who did many things for her and she remained innocent and then her body became his. Do not allow her to give herself to you instead of claiming it for her own. You must stand by her in the sheltered woods as she runs across the open meadow and with her hair flying and fear flailing about within her she takes the invisible thing and claims it as her own. There are many confusions here but the pathway is open and clear. The work is good and we are here for both of you, we are always present.*

There was a long silence, and I reminded myself to breathe. I felt dazed, and Ariel sat with her back against the couch, eyes closed.

"O.K., o.k.," Lynn said finally. "Wow. Where have we been?"

"I think it's time for lunch," I said, suddenly aware of hunger. We all laughed, breaking the spell.

"It seems late," Lynn said. "I have to get oriented here. All right. I'm in California, you guys are in Princeton, New Jersey, it's 1989. I've been many places . . . in a fairy tale, and in Ariel's childhood and . . . many places. Also different time zones . . . Ariel, how are you doing? And Connie?"

"I feel confused but at the same time very directed," Ariel said slowly.

I took a deep breath. "Whew!" I said. "I think I'm fine . . . we've been together two hours . . . I thank you for this."

"You're welcome," Lynn said warmly. "I'm so grateful to be part of this . . . it feels like it's real important for all of us."

We all said our goodbyes and I hung up the phone. Ariel reached out her arms, and I gave her a big hug.

"I'll never be the same," she smiled weakly as she turned to go.

"Nor I," I said, shaking my head to clear it.

# CHAPTER VIII

## *Reclamation*

### Fall 1989

### Ariel

So much has happened the last couple of weeks. When I woke up the morning after the session with Lynn and Connie everything looked different, felt different. For the first time in my life I felt like I was part of the human race. I'm one of them! I kept saying to myself. My ear was still running, but my muscles were cramping much less. I felt different, more hopeful and more powerful. I was awe struck by the process.

When I saw Connie later that week she said I looked very well, and I knew it had to be true, because I felt very well. I kept saying my body is mine, my body is mine. At last. Because I knew something got moved in the session. But I knew it wasn't completely gone, that the tree limb there would wait things out and attack again. What kept coming up when I was with Connie is I needed to scream, but I couldn't in her office and not when alone.

The weird thing is I really felt my grandfather cared for me except when he abused me. But I understand now he defined love for me, and if I give that up I don't know what love is. It's like there's nothing. If I give that up, all my concepts are topsy-turvy. It's real scary, because if I let go I have no anchor. That's not true but it feels like that, like it's a piece that's been such a part of me for so long that I'll fall apart without it. I know I'm not making sense again but I am.

Then for a few days, I was aware of a lot of tension. When I breathed deeply, I felt my lower chakras opening, and it felt as if I was one big hole, like my vagina and anus were open and everyone could see right up to my throat. It was awful and uncomfortable to notice this, it felt unsafe. It was hard to share with Connie, I can't believe the things we can talk about, but I did. I really did make a decision to turn my body over to my grandfather since my mother wouldn't or couldn't help me. Connie and I talked about the session and what my grandfather looked like when he was in the room, and I drew a picture of him. He had sad eyes, no mouth, white hair. I can't believe he was there, but he was. As real as if he'd never died.

I never liked Jack and the Beanstalk, I was always afraid of the giant. My impulse is to take back what was stolen by confrontation rather than sneaking, but sneaking would be safer. I want to say, give me back what's mine, but I'm terrified. If I confront him, even if I get that piece of myself back it seems he'll take it again. Why can't I just say this is my body and confront him and go on? We talked about this, and it feels like they're empty words. The words have been there since he died—it's never made any difference whether he was alive or dead. Maybe if it wasn't him it would be someone else.

Connie asked me what I needed that would give me back my body, and I told her that if I could have had the courage to kill him, that would have done it. At Evergreen others screamed and yelled at him in role play, and I couldn't do it. I guess from the fear of losing something I couldn't live without, it's so sick but true.

For about a week I could feel a buildup of emotion, I was restless and then nauseous and my feet started tingling and I got real lightheaded, dizzy. Then the facial pain returned and my lower legs hurt, my feet cramped, and I thought for sure I'd throw up a couple of times. Not because I wanted to but because I was so nauseous. I didn't know what to do with the way I was feeling, couldn't sleep, kept feeling pressure on my bladder and having to urinate all the time. And then I knew that there was something there, something to do with my grandfather, and I was so scared, and I didn't want to remember anymore. So I had a stern talk with myself and said if you don't let yourself remember you're going to stay sick, you'll keep being haunted by it. And I don't want to be haunted anymore. By the time I went to see Connie I was in some kind of state, couldn't sit still, and after a few minutes I started remembering and then couldn't talk fast enough and then went into another regression. And it was awful what happened, horrible. Somehow a part of me always stands back and watches and remembers even though when I'm there I'm reliving it like a child and it's happening right then with all the pain and all the terror. I was little, probably four, and I was swinging on a swing, and my grandfather came and held me on his lap and was touching me and rubbing me and then I felt something big and hard going inside me, in my vagina, and it didn't go in, it didn't fit, but he kept pushing and pushing it in and in and it felt like I was being ripped open, the pain was excruciating, and I was crying and telling him to stop and he wouldn't, and he held his huge hand over my mouth so I wouldn't make any noise and just kept thrusting it in me until he stopped. It was the most awful pain, I didn't understand why he was hurting me and I threw up in Connie's wastebasket and cried and cried until there were no more tears. How could anyone do that to a child?

And then, the miracle is, I went home and slept fourteen straight hours and woke up feeling much better. My feet were still cramping, my lower left back hurt, and there was still pressure on my bladder, as well as some pain in my face, but none of it bad. I felt drained, but the fear was gone. For some reason I have a very bad rash under both arms, maybe because I was sweating so much. I saw Connie, and I was able to talk about what happened while looking at her. The shame is gone. I feel as though something has happened, a shifting of some sense. Realizing having Christ in my life today is making such a difference in my understanding and outlook of my life past, present and future. Also in talking with Connie realize I did struggle with my grandfather but was against a greater force and had no one to rescue me. I did not just give in as I had imagined but struggled and was able to leave my body so as to survive.

I just want to be me. To do the best I can in giving and receiving love. I want to keep working on this area of therapy, important not to leave it until it is complete. I do have my body back. I have reclaimed it after allowing him to rule it for forty-five years. He still has my voice, he took away my ability to express anger, to yell and scream. I want so many things, I guess to make up for all those years of emptiness, feeling of worthlessness. I feel so full, so directed, so excited but know God will direct me and give me all I need. I have nothing to fear, nothing more horrifying or horrible than what happened to me as a four-year old defenseless, abandoned child. I feel cheated in relationships and life, and great sadness because of this, but I know I chose this, even the abuse, because I needed to learn unconditional love. God loves me even though I suffered and hated, and knowing that helps to take away the hate I have felt toward my grandfather.

I wonder if sex could ever be different for me.

## Connie

The session with Lynn was extraordinary, and extraordinarily help-ful. She feels like a very old friend, a sister, and I'm so thankful she appeared in my life. Not too long after we had our three-way ses-sion Ariel relived the rape at four—something I still have a hard time registering, it seems so inhuman, so incomprehensible to me—and her physical pain lessened somewhat. But then she got pneu-monia—she was smoking like a chimney—and that really set her back. She's going for acupuncture, and I hope it helps, but I'm not sure she's ready to give up cigarettes. She's frustrated with her financial situation as well as her health, including her doctor's diagnosis of fibromyalgia and Sjogren's syndrome. There is little but symptomatic relief offered, and little of that without over medicating.

Despite her physical dis-ease, there is a lot of movement. Ariel's perception of herself in relation to her grandfather has truly shifted, partly in response to the work we did with Lynn and partly as a result of a psychodrama process we did. On impulse, I bought a colorfully illustrated copy of *JACK AND THE BEANSTALK* , took it to the office, and read it to Ariel. She sat by my side on the sofa, and I think she was a little embarrassed and uncomfortable at first but then became quite childlike and absorbed in the story. She told me later that though her mother never read to her occasionally her grandmother did, and she had a remembered sense of wide-eyed wonder as she listened. She had strong associations to the giant and the treasures he had stolen, and talked about her awareness that she had had to stay in a magical world to survive. Then, in adolescence, the childhood magic no longer worked. Alcohol, drugs, and bulimia became her magic; her one healthy escape was music.

I told her that all magic eventually fails: "Sooner or later we all have to confront the giant." We talked about how she might do that, and I suggested, if Dr. Z. was willing, perhaps he could play the role of the giant.

"Oh, no," she said, "No, no, no. He reminds me too much of my grandfather."

"How?"

"Well, he's really tall, and he speaks softly . . . maybe that's why I never want to have anything to do with him. He scares the shit out of me, excuse my language."

I thought of Dr. Z. as a kind and gentle man. No wonder she'd never wanted to call him in my absence! To her, he was a monster, the same as her grandfather. Little did he realize what she had projected onto him.

"All the more reason for him to be the giant," I said, aware as I spoke that he might be a very reluctant giant. I hadn't asked his permission to volunteer him and knew this wasn't what he usually did. However, we had a good relationship, and maybe he'd agree. Ariel and I laughed, imagining him playing the role of giant, then settled down to the serious business of planning the encounter. I knew from the safety of my office we could make light of it, but that Ariel was actually quite frightened. "We could use Raggedy Ann," I suggested, and as we talked it became clear that there was tremendous potential for healing in acting this out. We set it up for the next session if Dr. Z. would agree to participate. As Ariel left, I could see the fear beginning to build, and I reassured her that I would stay with her during the entire process.

Dr. Z., when he heard the plan, was willing to be the giant. I coached him, and at the appointed hour he burst into the room where Ariel, Raggedy Ann, and I were waiting.

"Give me that child," he demanded of Ariel, sounding reasonably ferocious.

Ariel, frozen with terror, clutched Raggedy Ann to her chest.

"Give her to me!" Dr. Z. repeated, stepping closer to Ariel.

Ariel held out the doll without a word. Dr. Z. grabbed Raggedy Ann, turned on his heel, and left. Only a moment had passed, but it felt like hours.

"I don't know if I can do it," she said, beginning to weep. "I'm so scared."

"I'll stay right with you," I reassured her. "Take a couple of deep breaths, and let's go. You've been waiting all your life to do this."

Ariel walked shakily out the door, with me right behind her, and down the hall to Dr. Z.'s office. She gripped my hand tightly for a minute, as if for strength, and then opened the door and walked toward his desk, where he was sitting with Raggedy Ann on his lap.

"Give her back to me", she said unconvincingly.

"No," he answered. "She's mine."

"I want her," Ariel said, a little louder.

"No," Dr. Z. replied stonily.

I could feel Ariel's anger and power mounting.

"You pitiful old man!" she said strongly. "You give her back to me, she's mine and I need her!"

"No, I have no intention of giving her back," he insisted. "I want her."

"I DEMAND that you give her to me!" Ariel shouted. "Just because you have her doesn't mean she belongs to you. You give her to me right now!"

She took a step toward Dr. Z., and he handed Raggedy Ann to her. She held the doll close, shaking visibly, and stepped back.

"I HATE YOU!" Ariel shouted, beginning to sob uncontrollably. "SHE'S MINE, MINE, MINE!" She stood there, crying and shaking, until she could speak again. Dr. Z. just sat quietly, impassively.

"You can't hurt me any more," she said finally, firmly. "I'm free of you, WE'RE free of you. You don't have any power over me any more, not over me or this child you hurt so bad. You're just a pitiful old man, and you can't hurt us ever again."

With that she turned around and walked out of the room. Symbolically, it was done.

And me, what parts of myself am I in the process of reclaiming? It seems that what got stolen, or abandoned, was some part of my feminine nature, the part that reminded my father of my mother. I remember his words so well after we went to live with him:

"Cut your hair, you're starting to look like your mother", "Don't talk like that, you sound like your mother," "Behave yourself, you're acting like your mother, and if you don't straighten up you'll grow up to be like her. She's a witch, a whore, is that what you want to be?" I was already terrified of him, and now added to that was terror of being like my mother. Was she really a bad person? I didn't believe it, fought him tooth and nail. But then, the second time she came to see us, something shifted, and I started to believe all the horrible things he said about her even though they contradicted my memory of her.

It was winter, it must have been right after Christmas. I had only seen her once since the summer, when she came to the school playground and later to the house we'd moved to with our father and soon-to-be stepmother. She was beautiful, the way I remembered her, and I ran to her joyfully. She smelled the same, a soft fragrance, and I remember her pretty blouse. I had missed her so much. But when she came to the house later to see my brother, who was home with the chicken pox, she and my father fought, and he threw her off the patio, ripping her blouse. I was devastated, frightened beyond words. I remember watching from a doorway.

And then the Christmas visit, a couple of months later. I was in my classroom, sixth grade, and the principal called me out to the hallway. He said my mother was waiting outside, but my father had given strict instructions that my sister and I were to walk right past her, directly to the schoolbus. He took me by the arm and led me down the hall and out the door. My mother was standing to the left of the cement steps with a huge box filled with brightly wrapped Christmas presents. She looked awful. Her usually beautiful auburn hair was straggly, her face was pale and thin, her clothes were disheveled. She didn't look like my mother, it couldn't be my mother, she had turned into a hag. I walked past her, got on the bus, and cried hysterically all the way home and for hours afterward. That was the beginning of becoming the good girl my father wanted me to be.

I've had a couple of dreams lately that seem directly related to recovering the parts of myself that I lost:

*I'm in a bus filled with people, sitting at the front right. A man is driving, and there is an unknown woman behind him, across the aisle from me. The man is middle aged, rough, and somewhat disheveled in appearance. He sits with his back to the side window of the bus and talks to people as he drives. We are on a highway and the road curves to the right high above water. The driver is not paying attention and the bus goes off to the left and then we are over the water. It is dark, but I know we will hit the water and try to think of what to do. We splash into the water and begin sinking quickly. I break the window in front of me and swim out. Then I am in the water, swimming. I know there are others swimming around but can see nothing. I call out and the woman next to me answers. I ask her name and she tells me. I forget and ask again, and again she tells me. We swim toward shore and once again I forget her name and have to ask. It is very important that I remember her name. Then we are on land, walking outside houses trying to find one where we can go in. A dog barks from one and I'm frightened, so we walk by. Finally we are inside a house. There is a family there, and children, and it is very light.*

*I walk into a nightclub in an elegant, sexy, slinky red dress. There is a dance floor ahead of me. There are many people in the nightclub, and I know there is a man in the nightclub who will get me—kill me?—if I dance. He has a gun. I awaken, terrified.*

*I am walking down a country lane—a dirt road. There are fields on both sides, and there are horses in the fields. Suddenly I realize there are no fences, and the horses are wild, and they are loose. I stop on the road, afraid. I turn back.*

# Winter 1990

## Ariel

Well here it is a New Year and I'm still alive and sober and sick and sick of being sick. I feel like I did when I was a kid and no-one believed me, how much I hurt, because they couldn't see anything on the outside. I feel like I'm on a treadmill that's getting nowhere, and being ill I feel so disconnected and just want to get to the end, to wherever I'm going so I can finally feel that love at the end. I just don't understand what's going on with me. I feel isolated even when I go to meetings, not even my sponsor understands. I know Connie is trying to but she doesn't really understand this physical stuff. Sometimes I feel like this therapy doesn't get me anywhere but then other times a lot happens, I never know. There are days when I'm real hopeful, when I feel a little better but it doesn't last because I feel so exhausted and in pain so much of the time it's real hard to keep the faith. And then I feel worse, guilty because feel I'm wallowing in self pity and that never got anyone anywhere. I'm dreaming a lot and we spend more time on the dreams, that's interesting and sometimes teaches a lot, sometimes makes me cry. Here's a weird dream:

*I have an appointment to see Connie. I'm afraid I'll be late. At 4 a.m. I'm walking the streets of Princeton or my sister's town. I go to an office and my sister is working there. She asks me what I'm doing there and I tell her I have an appointment with Connie. She says it's only 4:30. I say I know, I'm afraid I'll go to sleep and not wake up and I'll miss my appointment. Then I'm in Connie's office and I have to see her. I'm talking to her and I'm hurting in my vulva. I go to the bathroom to find out what's hurting. I rub it and the skin opens up. I pull out an old, broken, corroded knife. I say oh my god where did this come from? I knew it had been there a long time. I'm horrified. Denise and Connie appear. I'm shaking and show it to them. Connie says profoundly, it's been there a long, long time. She takes the knife and shows it to Dr. Z. Then I'm in Connie's office, Denise is gone. Connie comes in, concerned. She says stand up and let me look, and tells me to turn around and she touches the lower right side of my back. It hurts! I say don't touch it again! She asks how long it's been swollen, and I say I didn't know it was. She says it's been there a long time and you're full of infection and it's going to take time to come out.*

I've always been afraid of knives. They're sharp and deadly weapons and Dad always said they were more dangerous than guns. I did cut myself accidentally yesterday when I was slicing a carrot, that's what I get for trying to eat healthy. I know the knife in the dream had something to do with my grandfather.

I called Lynn Breedlove again in California thinking maybe she could find something out about all the pain I'm having and also Connie said if Lynn was willing we could set up another session with the three of us. It's already been five months since the last one. She fit me in a few days later, and she said it's like I'm hibernating, kind of like it's winter for me, which means there will be a spring also. The guides said I would feel better about myself if I give some time to others in service, but also to take care of myself. Then they said:

*You are learning the art of living and this will be a time of renewal and coming forth in you. The springtime will bring great flowering within your soul and within your spirit and you will feel the jubilation of newfound and newborn life. You are in need of touch in a powerful and healing way and this will bring to you the understanding and the patience that you need. We are with you at this time; we are an aspect of the holy spirit that is not easily recalled or recorded. We are the communicating aspects between what is most divine and most holy and what is most human and most separate from what is remembering its holiness. You are in a place now of falling away from your power of knowing and you have lost the ability to feel that all is well and all is good. You will experience from time to time a wind that blows across your soul, a chill wind that goes to the bone and makes you sorry that you have been born and come to this place but always you will find the doorways to close out the wind and you will stand warmed by the hearth knowing that the wind is nearby. You will feel the warm glow and the connection with others. You are in the process of healing and this is not easily or quickly done. It is not the time now for you to take on any projects other than for you to do what is important to you, a small piece at a time. Walk slowly and rest like the tree or the bulb that rests quietly in the winter. This is an evolution that wishes to come forth.*

*You do not know the goodness and the gladness that we celebrate for the distance that you have come and the power that you have to brought to others in the silence of their misery and grief. You do not see that the channels that your direction takes and the power that you bring forth, but we are offering you the understanding that by your capacity to heal yourself hundreds more across the plains who are injured and denied, who are lonely and severed off from their holiness, these awaken within themselves and feel a hopefulness that they cannot claim and they say I give homage to and thankfulness to a woman that I do not know who has climbed out of the abyss with her fingers bloody and shamefulness within her pocket. She has climbed out and brought herself to the edge of the cliff. There she sits, perched, uncertain of her worthiness, feeling the cold wind of sorrow as it blows up from the dark depths into her face. But if she can climb up and feel the soft wind of gentle human support then I too may know that this is possible. I give thanks to her feet, for all I can see is the bottom of her feet as she ascends to the top. She will be my model and my worthy mentor though she rests in silence and does not know the gift she brings to me.*

*This has happened at a level of understanding that is not possible to bring into human consciousness fully but we would say to you it is as though there is a channel of understanding through which your story is told and it reverberates across the earth and others who are weary raise their heads and have hopefulness when they see the distance you have come. Suffice it to say that the angels who watch over those who are hurt hold up your picture and your story and others are guided by this also.*

*Understand that it is of great value. It is what heals the many, the understanding that one is healed.*

When I heard those words I felt so hopeful, like some good is going to come out of all of this, and then after a day or so I don't believe it any more, it sounds pie in the sky, airy fairy, and I wonder why I called Lynn. The words are so beautiful, like hearing someone read the bible, but it's hard to hold onto as real for me.

I told Lynn that Connie doesn't feel comfortable doing body or energy work alone but would do it with her, and she laughed and said the guides were clapping their hands and saying "Oh Yes"! She said she thought it would be helpful and we're going to set up a session sometime in the next few weeks.

# Connie

Yesterday I had my third session with Stephen, a healer in his fourth year at the Barbara Brennan School of healing. He's channeling energy to the different energy centers (chakras) of my body, and specifically working to release energy from what he called a "black hole" just above my second chakra, which is in my lower abdomen. If all this seems weird, it does to me too! But, as Lynn predicted, things are moving.

I bought Barbara Brennan's book, *HANDS OF LIGHT*, just before Christmas at a conference on the interface between psychology and spirituality and read it over vacation. I got through the first fifteen pages and wept, knowing it is what I've been waiting for, searching for. It's about spiritual healing, addresses issues related to mind, body, emotions, and spirit, and teaches knowledge and techniques to work directly with the human energy field. I told Stephen I cried when I read it and he said it's because I recognize it as the key to my soul's deepest longing. It may be true.

I've started seeing Stephen so I can experience healing to see how it's done, and also to facilitate my own process, accelerate the pace of the work I'm doing with Jane. The way it works is we talk for a little while, and then I lie, fully clothed, on a massage table. He stands at my feet and holds them and I immediately feel a charge of energy running up my legs and into my body. There's also a lot of heat emanating from his hands, and they seem to get even hotter as he does the healing. He puts his hands in different places, working his way up the body, energizing the chakras and, he says, helping to balance my energy and dissolve energetic blocks that are in my body. The first and third sessions were soothing, but in the second one he made several small slashes, like steam vents in the black hole of accumulated (negative?) energy. What I felt was his left hand on my lower abdomen and minimal pressure from one or two finger tips while he breathed through his nose. Then, he explained later, he sent rose light into those areas to fill in. Sound crazy? All I know is I developed a two-inch wide band of pain like a menstrual cramp above my pubic bone which lasted off and on all week, and nausea that lasted off and on for three days. As I was leaving his office I started shaking, and by the time I got to my car I had chills, my teeth were chattering, and I felt quite disoriented. In retrospect I shouldn't have driven home, I should have stayed there and told him what I was experiencing. I couldn't get warm driving home even though the heat was blasting full force. I wasn't upset; part of me was standing back watching, and thinking, isn't this fascinating? That night I had a dream:

*I'm in a roller coaster, going downhill. David is on my lap; he's one and a half or two years old. He falls forward, and though he doesn't fall out of the roller coaster, he is wounded. I look at his head and see three small holes, perfectly round, on top of his head. They look dark inside, but there is blood around the edge of each. Then I'm walking somewhere with my husband, and there is a young dog off to the right, in a wire pen. He is there because he's wounded. He is really David transformed into a dog—but he wants to be out of the pen. Somehow he breaks free and runs toward us.*

When I went back for the next appointment and told Stephen what had happened he seemed concerned and upset and couldn't understand why I drove home feeling the way I did, didn't call him and let him know, and why I came back! He said he had done too much, gone too fast—"you fooled me"—and would work much more slowly from now on. He hadn't expected that kind of reaction. Neither had I!

The band of pain across my lower abdomen returned while he was doing the chelation (running energy) yesterday, but it wasn't nearly as bad. He said what's going on in the area of my second chakra is related to early issues of trust and betrayal, that the black hole developed around the age of two and was complete around ten years later. He knew that I had learned very early to be a good, responsible caretaker (I should bring pictures of me as a little girl,

I'm always holding a doll or an animal)—and he told me th
piece of mySelf missing. After all this work! He could sense ...
alternate throughout life between being like my mother and my
father. My life task is to find mySelf, and equilibrium. All this
makes sense. I know I'm very defended regarding the repressed
emotions from my early childhood, and want to get to them as
quickly as I can tolerate.

I'm going to attend a four-day workshop in April to check out
the school. If I still feel that this is what I've been searching for, I'll
apply and hope I'm accepted for September. I'm *VERY* excited about
the possibility. The classes are held four days six times a year, with
a lot of homework including practice healings in between. I'll be
finished with my second year at Wainwright House this summer,
so the timing is good. Could I do it? A lot of time, a lot of energy,
a lot of money would have to be invested. How would it affect my
practice and my relationship with my husband? Would he be supportive? A lot of unknowns . . .

In the meantime, the work with Stephen is very stimulating
to my dream life; the night after each session I've awakened with
powerful dreams and a lot of emotion:

*I'm in a house. There's a kind of valley in front of it, and another
house across the valley, and a pond or small lake in between. There are
children in the other house, including mine. I go for a walk, and when
I approach the first house I see the water in the pond rising, water
pouring down the hill into it. I see it, but it is as if my eyes are half
closed. I don't see it as dangerous. I'm uneasy about it, but only after I'm
in the house for a while do I look again, and I panic because I suddenly
know the children are trapped on an island now and there's no way
they can escape. I'm terrified, I run to the edge of the water. Then David
(my younger son) appears. He is grown, strong. He's carrying Suzie (my
daughter) in his arms—she is unconscious and pregnant. He has
struggled to rescue her. I'm frantic, can't believe I didn't recognize the
danger.*

*I'm in a room upstairs, looking over the top of a Dutch door with others. The top part of the Dutch door isn't really a door—it's flimsy, paper, and only covers part of the opening. The latch is broken. In front of me is a wide stairway going down and curving to the right. There are wild animals in this museum-like building. A pride of lions ascends the stairs towards us—a large male on the right, facing me, a female beside him, others behind. I think I should close the door, but it's inadequate. Someone suggests we just watch them.*

*I'm in an L-shaped room lined with very deep lockers. There is an enemy army outside, and I am hiding here with several children, including David, who are playing at one end. They are laughing and running around noisily. I hear the army approaching and tell the children they must get in the lockers and hide; they must be absolutely quiet so we won't be discovered. They don't take me seriously and I am afraid. With great difficulty I get them into the lockers, but I'm not at all sure they will stay quiet. I'm very anxious about this.*

# CHAPTER IX

## *Expulsion*

### Spring 1990

### Ariel

Still physically sick and struggling to make ends meet but at times feel hopeful, then sink back into why not just go home. I keep trying to do whatever I need to do to get better and in some areas I am, in others I can't seem to. Each time I try to stop smoking whether it's a patch, hypnosis, therapy, whatever I lose it, get enraged, overeat, and finally give in and smoke again and then hate myself. Connie doesn't push me, says it's a lot to give up the smoking when I've already given up all the other things that soothed me or helped me escape when life got tough, but I really want to stop. I cough a lot and people are turned off by the smell on my clothes and my skin. It's a disgusting habit. And even though I'm not bingeing anymore, or hardly ever, every once in a while Connie asks me what I'm eating, and when I talk about it I see it's not real healthy food a lot of the time. My excuse is I can't afford healthy food, but I know it's more than that, it's part laziness and part I don't think about it much, just eat what I feel like. At Evergreen I had a food plan but I can't seem to stay on one. Or don't want to, it never seems important enough. Anyway, I eat a lot of white bread and spaghetti, hoagies, things like that and hardly ever vegetables or salad or fruit. Connie reminds me that after all the years

of abuse my body might welcome especially healthy foods, but so
far I'm not doing it.

We had another session with Lynn a few weeks ago to help
with what Connie called the physical residue from the sexual abuse.
One of the first things she said was that Connie seemed bigger and
stronger, that her hands were huge and filled with light. She said
they were like Mickey Mouse hands, and that they were separated
from her body, kind of floating nearby. I couldn't see it even though
I looked hard. And she saw me in a tunnel, like I was a cat crouched
down, waiting to come out. She said a prayer—

> *May all that happens here be good for each of us as individuals, for
> all of us as a team, and for the greater good. All the energies that don't
> heal and bless, may they be nurtured and fed and taken to their rightful
> place, and the energies that will love us and help us be here present with
> us.*

Oh," she said, "there's another presence with you, there's a
feeling of wings flapping rapidly. Who are you?"

> *I am the spirit of therapy. I have many faces, the demon and the
> dark forces and the face of light. I am none of these things but I show
> my face in different forms and in this way I move along the process so
> that the healing takes place. I am here in this hour to guide and to offer
> my assistance. I am not the one who will do the work but rather I am
> like the keeper of the gate who stands and watches to make sure that all
> goes in its proper order. I am the sentinel and the guardian of time.*

Connie asked, "Is this being always present during therapy, or
is it connected to one of us?"

> *I am from as you would call it a tribe of people. I am not really a
> people form but I am of the essence of those who are concerned. I am
> from a pool of logical interpretation of experience and phenomena that
> cannot be explained. I have come to make sure that what cannot be*

*spoken of is framed in a way that is understood. I am the one who translates what cannot be spoken in words into a phrase or movement or understanding so the recipient can be healed in the process. I am with you at all times when you are in the condition of being therapist and present myself here. I know this one well, I have worked with her before. I am one who interprets her energies and gives to you the feedback or the knowledge that you need so that you may follow down the pathway with her to the place where she is crippled and broken and give her a hand of compassion to lift her up so that she might find her way again. I am with you in other situations also. I am not completely like others from my group but I am able to watch interpretations and keep the balance intact. I am the one who jolts you into understanding. When you do not know how you got to a certain place it is because I have kicked hard and shoved you into truly experiencing what is in the other's mind.*

"Does that make sense to you?" Lynn asked.

"Yes," Connie answered.

"Well, he seems ready," Lynn said. "Do either of you feel a presence?"

"It's hard to know, I'm not sure what a presence feels like," Connie said, laughing. "Actually I do feel something in this room, I don't know how to describe it."

"I feel butterflies," I said.

"It's sort of funny, he's wearing gray. He's kind of somber, but he seems flexible, like he could change color. I guess the circumstances are somber."

"May I ask you a question?" Connie asked. "Why would my hands seem separate from my body?"

"Oh, because . . . " Lynn started. "There's another voice now . . . "

*Because you are not yet fully in association with the power that you hold there, you are not yet fully aware of your ability to transform only through the touch. You are greatly identified with your ability to trans-*

*form through logical understandings. That is why this one, Ariel, comes to you, to teach you that the transformation can take place sometimes only through touch. It cannot always be put through the processes of the mind and the voice. When there is logical understanding and it is brought to consciousness there is one kind of healing. There is another kind of healing that happens in a pre-conscious or not yet arrived at logical consciousness, in the cells. This kind of healing we are guiding you toward and your friend Ariel is much in need of this so that the poison within her will be dissipated and taken down the river. She is wishing to free herself of the darkness. Lay your hand upon her lower belly and there you will find the seeds of darkness as they were planted into her. She carries the darkness of others that she cannot name in her mind and it poisons her voice and her thoughts and gives her a dreariness and a sorrow. Lay your hand upon her, the one left on the front of her and the right on her sacrum. And then you will feel the seeds that are planted there, the dark and slimy seeds of others that are not her own. She is wishing to translate this into an energetic form that will pass through her cells and away from her. It is the touch that will remind her of her blessedness and her love for you that will transform her.*

I lay on my back on the couch, and Connie put one hand on my abdomen and the other on my lower back and explained where we were to Lynn.

"Both of you tune in, breathe deeply," Lynn instructed. "Connie, spread your fingers wide, and then put them together, and pay attention to what you feel. Don't try to feel anything, just pay attention, and be aware of the contents of her body underneath your hands."

"The only thing I'm aware of other than her back being very hard and the breathing motion in her abdomen is . . . it's almost like there's a pulsating, and it's not just a pulse, it's a pulsating."

Lynn laughed. "There are all these guides around you clapping and jumping, saying yaah! O.K. . . . . what are you experiencing, Ariel?"

"I'm feeling very uncomfortable breathing with my stomach. I always get this picture of a helium balloon when I breathe this way."

"Are you uncomfortable because it doesn't look right, or you need to hold yourself together, or what?"

"Hold myself together."

"What would happen if you let yourself balloon out?"

"I used to be afraid of it bursting, but now I wish it would."

"O.K., " Lynn laughed. "What are you feeling right now, Connie?"

"I have the sensation of something very solid between my hands other than the body."

"O.K. . . . I want you to talk to the thing that's solid other than her body. I want you to ask it, are you there?"

"Are you there? . . . It got bigger."

"I feel pregnant," I told her.

"Ariel, now you ask the same question: are you there."

"Are you there? . . . I don't feel the ball anymore."

"It feels like it got smaller when she asked that question," Connie said.

"O.K., so when she asked it it got smaller, and when you asked it got bigger. What does that say to you?"

"I don't know," Connie said. "When I put my attention on it, it gets bigger and harder."

"How does that relate to what it's like being a therapist for Ariel?"

"I don't know what you mean . . . you mean it's amplified?"

"Yeah, and when she focuses on something inside her, it gets more elusive and farther away."

"Hmmmmmm."

"Have you found that to be true?"

"Sometimes. Often when that happens it turns around . . . "

"All of a sudden it seemed a metaphor for what's happening. O.K., so what's happening now underneath your hands?

"Something's moving . . . changing shape."

"When you focus on it, Ariel, does it feel like something you want to be there, something that was given to you? What's it's nature?"

"I don't want it to be there," I told her.

"Does it have a consciousness of its own?"

"Yes. Sometimes it recedes . . . it's almost like a tree limb, reaching up my back. Now I'm feeling very very angry. I just want rid of what's not mine, so I can do what God wants me to do and be myself."

"O.K. . . . . may I give you a suggestion?"

"Yes."

"I suggest that you ask God for help and if this thing is not yours that it be gone from you."

I did what she said, and I heard Release your Anger. I told Lynn.

"So are you saying that in some way it does belong to you?"

"I don't know."

Connie spoke. "My hands feel tingly and there's more warmth, and the thing inside feels like it has a lot of energy."

"Has it shifted?"

"There's a lot of motion, almost continual motion . . . I had an image before of a snake, writhing . . . "

"I saw penis," Lynn said.

"They're pretty close," Connie said. We all laughed.

"O.K.," Lynn said. "Ariel, I'm going to ask you to do something, and if you don't feel like it say so, it's o.k. I want you to imagine that your whole vaginal opening had been packed with cotton, like after you'd had a baby, and I want you to slightly spread your legs and make a motion like you're pulling it out of your body and away from your body. You may feel silly as you do it. And Connie, I want you to imagine that you're mentally helping it to be pulled out. If it's too intrusive or too uncomfortable for either of you I don't want you to do it."

I lay there and tried to do as she suggested, but it was really hard. I felt like I was doing something disgusting.

"This is hard," I told Lynn. "I want to do it but it's hard."

"What I see is that it opens that lower chakra," Lynn said. "What's happening with you, Connie?"

"I'm mentally helping . . . I'm imagining black cotton, it's saturated . . . "

"If you can put your hand under her tailbone and make a motion as if you're helping it leave, showing it a passageway out . . . "

"What I'm seeing . . . it's like a block, and then water behind the block."

"I have a horrible something in my chest now," I said.

"I'm putting my hand right below her breastbone, my left hand."

"What happens when she touches you there, Ariel?"

"I'm just aware of a pulsing in my throat . . . "

Connie said, "I'm putting my right hand on her throat, it feels like there's a lot of anxiety there."

"Does it have a shape or a form?" Lynn asked.

"Something green, I don't know what it is."

"Is there anything you want to say, Ariel?"

"I just want this to leave me."

"What I heard," Lynn said, is 'You're killing me'."

I told her, "That comes before I asked God to take it away. I never say it."

"O.K., what's happening in your abdomen, Ariel? Check it out, see if that other thing that was there is still there.

I told her I felt more open down below.

"O.K. Focus on your throat. Just pretend it's a thing, and ask, "Are you the thing that was in my abdomen?"

I said, "There's more pulsing."

"I started feeling a fluttering feeling in my chest," Connie said.

"This keeps going through my mind," Lynn said. "My feeling is that there is something that's taken hold, and when you get too close to it and it's going to be forced out of her abdomen it moves up into her throat. It's kind of a tricky fellow and doesn't like to moved around. "

"It makes sense to me," Connie said.

Connie kept feeling something in her chest, and Lynn helped her shake it off after they figured out it didn't belong to her. What a trip!

"I want to congratulate you for being so perceptive about what's going on in your body, Connie," Lynn said. "That's what keeps you healthy. Has it gone from you?"

"Mostly," Connie told her. "I feel a heaviness in my stomach . . . maybe it's unrelated."

"It's imperative that you not disregard what's happening in your body, because once you start doing this kind of energetic work you can get yourself in a lot of trouble. It may be looking for an escape hatch, or it's looking for a place to lodge itself."

"Hmmm," Connie said. "So where does energy go if it's not good for it to be here, where can we send it to rest?"

"I encourage you not to use your mind to think of where to send it, but ask for the greater will to take care of it, that it go to its rightful place. 'Cause I don't have the slightest idea where that is."

"Well, I sure don't," Connie said.

"So I encourage you to pray, and ask for help. . . . now tell me how you're feeling."

"Good. I think it's gone."

"Say thank you. . . . Ariel, what's happening to you?"

"I just keep repeating in my head, I'm not going to let you kill me. I had a vision of my grandfather or my dad, maybe both. I wanted to say you take it back."

"I see you laying it down and saying I don't care who this belongs to, just come and get it."

"Kind of like the wrong piece of luggage you got from Newark Airport," Connie said.

I said, "Whatever it is, it's gray, and dark, almost like a tree limb. It seems as if it will never go away. I just get so pissed off."

"I imagine it sort of going crosswise, across her abdomen, and

and then it moves, and when it moves it turns around and goes up. A strange image. But I could see this gray, oblong thing," Connie said.

"What I think I may be seeing is the source of this form," Lynn said. "and what you two are seeing is the energetic manifestation that it's now taking. The intrusion was a penis. What's happening with you Connie, you seem like you're almost in the room with me?"

"I'm, I . . . when you were talking I had an image of what's needed in order to get rid of this, and it's almost as if Ariel has to create herself as intact. It's as if this thing penetrated so early that intactness was never sensed.

"Right, right. It's like when two trees grow together and . . . "

"And the one never knows if it's the one or the other," Connie finished for her.

"Yeah, right," Lynn said. "You have all this stuff in you Ariel, it's kind of like your own self is completely embedded with other, so it's real hard to tell the difference. I keep seeing ritual cleansing being real important."

"I keep getting a strong sense that some act is required to expel this, something that would result in expulsion and the body sort of closing itself so the penetration wouldn't happen again."

"Yes, that's why the ritual with the cotton seemed important."

"How are you feeling right now, Ariel?"

"Very angry and sad."

"You look very sad," Connie said.

I told them, "I'm so frustrated because what happened happened at such an early age and I can't really remember it, and I'm willing to do anything but I don't know what to do. And I don't want it to take years."

Lynn talked to the thing for a while, asked it to break itself up and take itself away from me, and she asked my grandfather and my father to come forward and take back the part that was theirs.

"I would like the forces that can heal this child and bless her to come forward and help her feel her wholeness, so that she has a sense of her own integrity, a sense of her own wholeness. Will you stand near her and guide her so that she doesn't collapse?" she asked.

When she was talking I saw Jesus in a white gown, and children running around, and I knew I was one of them, and the thing was gone. Connie said she had a sense of three men retreating, sort of backing up going someplace, with their hands up. I told her I wanted to say it was gone, but I had a feeling it had receded but wasn't gone. And she said she didn't think it was gone either, but it was less solid. And she encouraged Connie and me to create some physical rituals to encourage the thing to leave.

And then our time was up, and I knew there was more to do but neither Connie nor I were sure of what. I felt it was incomplete but it got something going. I went home and took a nap and when I woke up I felt very sleepy, like I was in a cloud. The lump in my throat was pulsating, feeling like it was pressing on my windpipe, and I couldn't breathe right. I felt angry but my heart kept racing on and off so I thought it was anxiety. My mind was racing. I wanted to go have ice cream, not wanting to just stuff the feelings but work through them thought better of it but angry I couldn't do what I wanted to do. If I couldn't do that then I wanted to eat but knew I'd binge. Just like the feelings feeling like they would take over I knew my eating would run away from me. I was crying, laughing at the same time. Felt out out of control. But I didn't want to stop it. I cried, I wanted to allow someone to hold me even if something inside didn't want to be touched. I want to be able to be as others able to feel touch and love like others without fear, without suspicion. I kept thinking about what I did in Connie's office, why so much guilt and shame? Why was it so difficult it was only symbolic didn't understand the feelings with the action. Then that night I had a dream:

*I was looking for my cat and couldn't find him. All of a sudden I was in Connie's office. I was a little girl and she was talking to me. I was on the floor playing with a white fancy cape swirling it and hum-*

ming. I was breathing funny because I had something in my throat that made it hard to swallow and breathe. I was like in a trance, a world of my own, and Connie just kept talking to me and I pretended I couldn't hear her. Then she said something funny and I tried real hard not to smile but couldn't hold it in so leaned over and put my head down towards her so she couldn't see the smile. She started laughing and reached over to touch me and touched me in a wrong spot around the the breast area. I became furious and hit at her body with my open hands. She just laughed and kept touching me all over my body laughing at me because I was angry and I kept hitting on her. I woke up feeling like I was still asleep and had been through a war.

## Connie

My practice continues to thrive, and though it is very hard work, I also feel extremely privileged to be trusted by the (mostly) women who come to me. I'm also more and more aware of how long it really takes to recover from early wounding. New people often hope or expect that they can do the work of therapy and be "fine" in six months or less, which in my experience doesn't happen with eating disordered patients. At this point I feel that about two years minimum for the first phase of recovery is required, probably much longer for those with severe early trauma or for whom the eating disorder has become a major source of identity.

My own analysis, Jungian supervision, the depth psychology program I've been in, and now working with a healer keep me in constant process myself, and there are times when I feel I could devote full time just to those things. But of course I can't and I don't, I just fit everything in somewhere. Anger with my father, which gets mixed up with anger at my husband, seems to be coming up a lot, and it makes me very uncomfortable but I know I need to deal with it. Dreams continue to lead the way, symbolically expressing attitudes, dilemmas, emotions that are often just out of reach consciously. I'm amazed at some of them, puzzled by some, amused by some, discomfited by a few. Working with the dreams always creates movement in my psyche. Here are some recent ones:

*I'm in a room with another, unknown woman. There's a high table there, and in an adjoining room a woman is giving birth. The other woman and I are washing and dressing the babies, and my job is to dress them and put them on a large bed with a high headboard. I put one, then another, on the bed. Soon there are nine babies on the bed. Some can turn over; some can crawl. They are moving around, and I am concerned about containing them on the bed. One of them looks through an opening in the headboard at a row of stuffed animals and points to a stuffed tiger. She says "Tiger" and I am amazed that she can speak. I give her the stuffed tiger.*

*I'm in a basement, with a baby in my arms. I'm cooking something on the stove. The right front burner overheats and melts down into the stove, and the stove catches fire. It is an electrical fire. I run up the stairs outside and see a huge oil truck close to the house, delivering oil. I tell them to get away quickly or there will be an explosion.*

*I'm in a house with a young child, one or two years old. There's a fire in the fireplace. I see black on one side of the white plaster chimney and it feels hot. Then I look around and see smoke and a few flames near the ceiling and realize the house is on fire. I hold on to the child and run out, taking my purse. I realize my dog, Yukon, is already outside.*

The last session with Ariel and Lynn really stirred the waters for Ariel. Lots of shame and anger to work through. She finally remembered that fellatio had indeed been part of her relationship with her grandfather, and the horror and disgust that that knowledge brought up in her was dramatic. We talked about it at length, and she expressed a great need and desire to do some kind of ritual to cleanse herself of those memories and energies. The Jack and the Beanstalk psychodrama was extremely empowering for her, and she wanted something similar. It was hard to think of what ritual would be effective, but I finally suggested that she bring in a hot dog and symbolically eat it and then refuse to eat it, spit it out. I also suggested that she write something that she could say as she performed the ritual.

"Oh my God!" she exclaimed. "It's perfect, but I don't know if I can do it!"

When Ariel came to the next session she was resolute about wanting to cleanse herself "once and for all." We spent the entire time talking about the ritual, alternating between absolute seriousness and hilarity as we discussed whether one particular brand of hot dog would be better than another, whether it should be cooked or uncooked, and whether mustard or catsup would enhance the experience.

"Maybe it should be a turkey dog," she laughed.

Oh the things I was never taught in graduate school!

The appointed hour arrived, and Ariel walked into my office with not one, but two, hot dogs and her typed declaration of freedom. She looked nervous and shaky, but said she was ready.

"I need a cigarette so bad," she told me, sitting on the edge of a chair.

I brought my plastic-lined wastebasket over and set it on the floor beside her.

"If you need to use this, it's fine," I said, hoping she wouldn't. Watching people vomit made me want to throw up myself.

"O.K.," she said, taking a deep breath. "I'm ready."

Ariel pulled a slimy pinkish hot dog out of the baggie by her side and clutched it in her left hand; in her right hand she held a quivering sheet of paper. She took another deep breath, cleared her throat, and began to read:

This hot dog represents all negative penises that have been forced upon me. Also all of the male negativity I have been forced to take in. Upon eating this hot dog I demand that all negative maleness leave me and go to your places of rest. I thank you for staying with me until I have come to know myself. That time has come. You no longer serve a purpose for me. I no longer need your energies to survive. I have come to know myself as a strong woman, intelligent, with much goodness. Having the Lord as my savior and friend to guide me. I am willing to accept my negative side, my anger, anxiety, impulsiveness. Our energies keep getting entangled and enmeshed, which feels like a battle to me, not being able to sort out mine from yours. Having been sent to Connie to help sort and find me, to guide me as a human example in putting the pieces together to fill in what was not learned as a child, a bond has been made between us of trust, respect, and her good will for me with a promise of continuing to be here for me as long as is needed.

Ariel paused and looked at me, as if to gather strength. I simply nodded yes, it's o.k., go on.

Grampa Durstan, I ask that your energies leave me now. Take them, they no longer serve any purpose in my life today. Take the shame, the guilt, the painful memories, they are yours. Any residue in my body left behind, let it be for the good of all. I forgive you, as I believe you did not know all the harm you were causing me. I do not understand all of your reasons but no longer have a need to know. It is time we go our separate ways.

Dad, I ask that your negative energies be released from within my body. I forgive you for not being able to emotionally bond with me. I feel sadness for what you saw when you laid eyes on me and for what I represented to you. I hold your goodness and strengths in my memory. Take your energies back from me and take them with you to where they need to go for all good.

Jake Mansfield, retrieve your negative energies from within my body. I believe I represented a possession that you wanted to hurt. Let your energy be released from me and go for the good of all.

Ceasar, I ask all your negative energies be released from within my body. I pray for good emotional and physical health for you. I forgive you for your harshness and inability to love, honor and cherish. I thank you for staying with me so long. I will remember lessons learned from you. The value of a dollar, strength to continue even under most trying times. I will remember the gentle side that would show itself on occasion that you were unable to share even with me, your wife. The unspeakable feminine side of you. I pray you will face that side of you someday and come to cherish it as a wonderful side of you.

To any and all negative energies within me that do not belong within me: I eat this negative, forced, penis today for the last time. After eating of it, I will purge myself of it and with it all negative energies which it represents. Any and all residue left will be left for the good of all concerned. I accept that.

Be with me God. Thank you for your goodness.

Ariel held the hot dog up to her mouth and took a big bite, then chewed as if to swallow. But she began to gag, and leaned over the basket to spit it out. She shook her head from side to side, shivering, and then took another bite, aggressively, held it in her mouth for a moment, and spit that, too, into the basket. The remainder of the hot dog she broke it into pieces, flinging them into the basket angrily.

"Never again!" she said. Her face glistened with sweat.

"Well done," I told her. She had never felt she had the right or the capacity to refuse before. From now on, she would.

# CHAPTER X
## *Healing Dreams*

### Fall 1990

#### Ariel

*I'm in a house like the house I lived in when my kids were little. There are all these kids, and my sister is there. I'm pregnant! I'm amazed. My son and daughter, six and eight years old, are there and a girl nine or ten. I'm taking care of these kids. The mother of the nine or ten year old wants her to spend the night. I say I'm pregnant, just can't do it. I say I don't mind taking care of them but they can't stay here. Denise says it'll be o.k., I'll help you. We go out to get the mail and walking down the sidewalk comes Connie. She stops by the mailbox and says I just came by to bring you a gift and say hello. I'm amazed she's there. I ask her in, and she insists I open the gift. It's shaped like a tiebacks but I don't expect shoes. I open it up and there are foam-pillowy-cushiony insoles for shoes. They're cream colored. I'm very disappointed but say Oh, how nice.*

I had this dream a few weeks ago and in talking with Connie realized that house was one I felt I belonged in. We lived there for more than four years. I felt the girl was the child part of me, and to stay the night meant I would be constantly responsible, like she was my own. I couldn't be pregnant and care for her at the same time. Connie said often pregnancy dreams indicate a part of the self is about to be born, to come to life, and we wondered what part that is. It's like I can't be dragged down by worrying about that needy child and at the same time allow my full grownup self to develop. So I'm not done with her yet. Every time I think I'm ready to quit therapy, or that I've done enough work on something or someone like my inner child it comes around again. Connie says what she calls individuation is like a spiral, and we circle around the same issues in different ways at different times. Sure seems that way. That nine or ten year old causes problems, takes over. I don't want this sobbing little kid on my hands, she sabotages my recovery. The insoles seem to be a gift to cushion my walk, and even though in the dream it wasn't what I wanted or expected, in some ways it's what Connie does. I have to walk the walk, but having her as my therapist makes it a little easier. She said maybe also my unconscious was playing with the word, that maybe I'm becoming ensouled. I looked it up in the dictionary and it means to endow or imbue with soul. Maybe she's helping me walk with soul?

I stopped smoking again and it only takes a few days before I'm furious at God, at society, at myself and thinking about suicide. No money to pay bills, just one monkey wrench after another in my life. And I start feeling alone and hopeless. Sooner or later I smoke again, this last time after eleven days. I wish I could just sign myself in somewhere for twenty-eight days but can't afford it and can't seem to get through the withdrawal by myself. I may have to stay a smoker.

I called Lynn again and talked with her last week and told her that all the tests from the specialist came back negative. I don't want to continue spending all my time and money having tests done that show nothing that can be treated. My blood chemistries are very abnormal, and I'm frustrated. I was thinking it's a process, that I'm in the last stages of my life and need to take care of those things that need to be taken care of. I don't think I'm going to die today or tomorrow, but I'm going to die, and I don't want other people to think I've committed suicide. Lynn said she can't and won't do diagnosis, but I asked her to look into what's going on with me physically.

"The first thing I see," she said, "is a dark ball in your abdomen. It looks like it's turning. Just turning, like it's going to move in some direction. As it turns it triggers other things in your body, makes you feel sick and weary. Your life force is very depleted right now, very flat. Like something isn't functioning except on a thin, thin level. It's as though one part of your body is shutting down completely and yet it kicks in sometimes and starts working again. It's like you're having some problems with your alternator. It kind of putts along on the side of the road and then kicks in and goes on for a while. I see you at a stopping point, everything in your path is catching up to you so you can move on. It looks like everything else, school and the other things you're doing, is going on. Your psyche is waiting for something to happen. Something in your body that's related to your blood looks like it's almost completely shut down. I have a feeling it's one of your organs, like one of your acupuncture meridians is blocked and the organ associated with that meridian is shut down. It's very important for you to get lots of sleep. When the other pieces are together you'll take the next step. There are parts of you that are healed and parts that are at the end of the caravan. Have you seen an acupuncturist?"

"No, I've thought about it."

"One of the nice things about Chinese medicine is that all the pieces are seen."

"I wouldn't know who to go to. I'm so thirsty! I have diarrhea, and I just keep drinking water. My protein is way down, and my white blood count also, and my immune system is depressed, and there are other things about my blood they don't understand."

"In a way your past is catching up to you, the effects of the eating disorder," Lynn said. "I don't see death for you, but what I do see is a great period of resting and a period of reevaluating. Your future has become completely altered as you have dealt with your past. You can't see the future because the choices are so different than you believed they would be. I see the road turning, it takes a sharp turn and you can't see what's beyond that. Your whole world is shifting, all that you have been is dying off. You have to bury it."

"I do see different truths than I used to," I told her.

"I see you in quicksand, and with all the work you've done there's now a platform under your feet. The platform begins to rise and lifts you out of the quicksand and then you step onto solid ground. A whole new self is about to be reborn, and of course it could mean a physical death . . . "

I said, "I've been grieving leaving here . . . a sadness that's almost a good sadness. And I feel that if I'm meant to be here, o.k., God, I'll be here. There are a lot of things about life I can appreciate now that I couldn't before."

We talked about maybe visiting my mother and father with Denise, and then the guides spoke. I love listening to them, they sound like angels to me.

*This is the time to lay all your burdens down before you and realize you cannot take another step forward until you have totally freed yourself of all encumbrances. Concern yourself only with your well being. Rest yourself often and in this way you will see yourself with greater clarity. You will walk a path of sorrow for a short distance and then you will find that you are in a brilliant field with many colors and the joy you feel will be of great healing to you. Be in the company only of those who care for you and support you and do not give in to the push of others to do that which does not heal and bless you. Speak your truth to others and claim yourself to be the orphan that you are. Forgive your father and your mother but do not walk near them if it does not please you. Give them only the understandings that you have and stand quietly beside the aspect of yourself that is hurt. Say to your brothers and sisters stand near this child for a moment and see the great shame that she experienced and the sorrow that she felt and you would know then that I could not abandon her or take her to a place she did not wish to go. They will then over time see you with a greater clarity and understanding than they have in the past.*

*Your sister is a friend to you . Say to her in a strong voice "Stand away from me when I am in the process of healing. Consider me to be like a child who has grown to adulthood and must bear her children. You would not stand as my midwife and say do it in this manner or do it in that manner but you would stand beside me and know that all is well. And the naturalness of the process would teach me in a way that is most profound." In this way she will understand you. Say to her "Do not ask me to do a thing I cannot do. It is the child within me that has suffered and I cannot abandon her. You would ask me to leave my child and visit a mother who did not gaze at me and doesn't see me with clarity. I could not leave this child for a moment, for in the abandonment of her the healing would go backwards and a great wrongdoing would take place. Go to her our mother and give to her compassion and kindness if that is what you wish. Speak my sister of your lowliness and leave my name from the table. You cannot claim for me that I am either sick or well, but say that I am in the process of bringing forth a new essence of myself, and it is this which shall be my greatest salvation. I am mother to myself now and I will find a father also that lives within me. I walk now fully as an orphan and those who have known me as members of my family can walk beside me as friends and call my name and know that all is well within me. When I have claimed myself to be an orphan my greatest healing comes to pass. And I am healed.*

*You will gaze at the stars with a different eye, our little one. You will see the sun and feel its brilliance in a different way. You will gaze at the colors around you and see their beauty. Your body undergoes a memory of near-annihilation and it will take itself down a plunging pathway until it strikes the bottom and then you will be renewed and fulfilled. It is not a light request that you would go to a teacher who would give you the understandings of the workings of your body. There are things that you eat that are not healthy for you and things that you discard that would give you the renewal that you need. It is necessary for you to breathe deeply into yourself each hour of the day so that you bring in the wholeness of life. You must consider that you are one who is taken to the door of death and brought back many times.*

*You have a mother in spirit and a father, too. They know your name and stroke your hair and rock you. These are the ones that will give you what you crave. We are here with you our little child and know the goodness in you and the strength that has not yet told itself to those around you. Call yourself an orphan and call out to the spirit realm: "Be my mother and father and watch over me." And in so doing the healing lights will come forward to you and all will be well. You will not go to the gateway of death in the physical sense but you will walk to the doorway where you see yourself in a new light. You wear many robes of different colors in different realms and different times. Do not complain to those around you of what goes on with you but say simply I am lonely, there is sadness deep within me. I do not know the path I am to take, but I see the goodness in the earth and this memory I will take with me when I go to my grave. Do not look to your physical family, but look to the stars, and the moon, and the trees. Look to the trees that are bare. You tell yourself I have died and there is no life within me but deep within the juices run though more slowly and in the springtime new life is born.*

*Your grandfather walks a darkened path and by your truthfulness you have freed him into a better understanding. Fling to him the stones of sorrow you have carried, and report to your father all the times that you were wounded and say to him this is the manner in which it happened and this is what was done. And your father will weep with sorrow and bury his head in his hands but he will understand the great wrong that was done to you. When he encounters his father on the other side he will shake him and say "Look at the thing you have done, look at the thing you have done." Your grandfather will come to your doorway with your father in command and take back the stones of darkness he has given you. Speak the truth to your father so that when he passes the threshold he takes the fullest message of your pain. It is not finished when the door of death encircles one but the beginning of a new agenda. Your father waits for the truth.*

*We go from this vessel but walk with you still on the other side of your sleep. We treasure you, our little friend. Take yourself into the company of the healer who sees your body as a whole and does not poke at you or fragment you but sees the beauty of the distance you have come. You are one who grows herself out of a toxic wasteland and now comes*

*the hour when you take your tiny seeds and plant them in fertile ground.*
*Walk gently, we stand nearby you.*

They are so wise and loving and accepting, not like so many humans, especially my family except for Denise. When I listen to them I feel like there is still hope for me. I wonder who my father and mother are in spirit? There's so much that comes through Lynn I don't understand, but the part about being an orphan makes sense because then I won't always want and expect my family to be different, they can be whatever way they are and I can get my needs met elsewhere. I wish my spirit parents would show up in some way so I could know they're really near me. I wonder what they look like. Do they have names? Were they my parents in another life, or did they adopt me? None of this makes sense, yet it all does.

I told Lynn about the course Connie's taking and wondered if she could be my healer. Connie said she doesn't know enough yet to do that, but she knows someone close to here I might see. She promised me that as soon as she feels competent enough she will do hands-on healing with me. I really have a strong feeling I need something like that, because there aren't a lot of doctors that see the whole picture. I wish I could believe the part about not really dying.

# Spring 1991

## Connie

Well, I've begun the Barbara Brennan course, and if I love it in June as much as I do now, I'll definitely continue for three more years. In some strange way it feels like what I've been moving toward all my life and also like something I've done before. There's a strong intellectual component, a great deal of reading and written homework, and plenty of opportunity both at school and between classes to practice healing skills. We're learning how to open up our high sense perception, and how to modulate our own energy fields. I'm meditating almost every morning now and keeping my journal much more faithfully.

When we do practice healings on one another a number of people go into deep process while on the table being "healees". I just get the same intense band of pain in the area of my second chakra that I've had during healings with Stephen. But so far I haven't cried during a healing. None of the "rigids" have—those of us (according to Core Energetics classification) who have a lot invested in an outer appearance of competence and calm, and excellent boundaries. We are all recognizable by our perfectly matched clothing, well-coiffed hair (carefully parted), and incessant smiles. We learned how to be "good" at an early age, can be counted on to get things done, and under pressure withdraw emotionally. We feel a lot but have difficulty expressing those feelings. We are very rational, and we like to be right. Yuck.

Meanwhile, I'm following and working closely with my dreams in analysis, and very aware of how energy work activates the dream process. I'm curious about what happens neurophysiologically. How are pathways opened and stimulated by healings? What is happening on the cellular level? Several interesting dreams in the past couple of months, all after chelations either in school or with Stephen:

*I'm in a primitive place with earthen floors and thick walls, no ceilings. I'm in a large, open room with no other people around. Off to the right and in front there is an opening in the wall, door shaped, and as I walk nearby I see a pride of lions in the room. They are standing and lying about. One sees me and begins to approach. It is a large, rangy male lion. I begin to move quickly away, to my left, and he chases me. I run, and he runs after me. I run faster, across a large open space, hoping to reach a door on the other side before he catches me. I run through the door, lock and bolt it, and am safe. A little while later David and some friends knock on the door, and I open it and let them in.*

*There are two fireplaces, and a fire in each. The one on the left begins to burn out of control, and flames leap up on the outside, on the right side of the wall. I repeatedly fill two containers with water—one plastic like the one we use for juice, the other like a hiking thermos— and pour water on the fire to extinguish the flames. But it is totally ineffective, and I panic. I run to find my husband, and yell to him to call the fire department. He just looks at me indifferently, as if there is no cause for alarm.*

*I have been somewhere with my friend Mary, in her car. I get out of the car and begin walking away, across an open area like a parking lot. When I am twenty or thirty feet away, I remember I have left my purse in her car, and I call out to her to tell her. She gets out of the car and throws the purse towards me, but wide to the right, a careless toss. It has been thrown into a canyon, and I look over the edge to see a long ladder leading to the bottom, where my purse is way over to the right. I see grass, and trees, and a house on the left. I hear a dog barking fiercely. It's about a hundred feet down, and I'm terrified. I say to Mary, "you threw it there, you get it." She laughs and says "no", as if it is obvious that I must retrieve it. Then she sits and watches. Another friend, Inez, sits to her right; they chat casually, oblivious to my terror. I descend the ladder, almost paralyzed by fear. I retrieve my purse and climb back up. Tears run down my face; I am hysterical. When I get to the top I am enraged to see Mary just sitting there, watching. I hit her and tear at her face; I want to destroy her. A part of me knows I am being totally irrational; it's not really her fault. I stop, and wake up.*

*I am pregnant, heavy with child. My belly is large, but when I put my hand on either side of it , it feels light, almost disconnected. I am in the doctor's office, and for a minute I'm fearful that the baby has died, but the doctor feels my abdomen and listens for the heartbeat and reassures me that everything is all right and it is almost time. I remind him that it has been twenty-three years since I've delivered a baby and he laughs and says this should be easier than twenty-three years ago. I am excited about having a baby and my fear of the delivery subsides. I think it is a boy.*

*I am somewhere with my husband. There is a carcass of a dog nearby. The flesh is decaying, and there's a large open, rotten area. He puts his hand on the putrid flesh. I am horrified. He acts as if it's a perfectly normal thing to do.*

*I am in a house with my children. They are sleeping in their rooms. I go in Billy's room and see the water has risen past the window. It is flooding. I look in Suzie's room and here, also, the water has flooded and is above the window. I remember it has rained a lot. I look in David's room and the water is below the window. This doesn't make sense to me, but I wake them all up. We must hurry to get out of the house and to safety.*

Fires, flooding, pregnancy, dead rotting dogs! Just in case I had the illusion that I was learning about the healing work just as a way to help my patients by becoming a "better" therapist, I've been thoroughly reawakened to the depth of my own need for healing, body and soul. Sometimes I wonder what it is that pulls me so strongly toward continuing my own healing process. It would be so much easier to coast for a while; this metamorphosis I'm going through disrupts the status quo in every area of my life. But

the impetus to continue toward individuation, to move tov
the light, is irresistible. Where is it leading?

In many ways this past year has to rank as one of the most
difficult and at the same time most extraordinarily transformative
years of my life. Yes, I know , the path of individuation requires
chaos and confusion and pain, at least for a while. But it's been
much harder than I could have guessed, and the pain and upheaval continue. It's time for ANGER, that most difficult of emotions for me to express. Always diluted by UNDERSTANDING!

Richard Bachrach, our psychodynamics instructor, says the
task of being human is to tune the soul to the frequency required
for it to do what it's going to do anyway. I like that. We only need
two tools to return home: faith and free will. According to this
perspective, we choose to be here, to be in duality, to learn our
own lessons, and to bring light into the void. It's possible to create
a bridge between psychodynamic and healing work because there
is a strong connection between psychodynamics and spiritual reality. The more I learn about the energy work, the more convinced I
am that early trauma is impressed on the bones, muscles, and cells
of the body. Even when there is no conscious memory of the trauma,
as with Ariel and other women in my practice who've been abused.

So what is the highest spiritual perspective from which to view
early wounding? If we can see that our wounds are related to our
reason for incarnating, that as we heal we open up the possibility
of connecting with our life task, we can see whatever trauma happened to us as offering potential for healing. We no longer identify
our Self with the wound. As Richard said, "the wound is the road
map back home."

I think one of the reasons this program appeals to me so much
is because there is nothing in it that I'm aware of that's inconsistent with what I already know. Although it seems to me there is a
certain amount of dogmatism that's crept into Jungian analytical
training, when I read Jung himself there is no contradiction. I'm
not sure my analyst agrees with me, but it's because she's been
trained in an orthodox manner. Jane is, I think, doubtful about

the wisdom of path I'm choosing. She has been a steady, grounded presence, a Wise Woman for me for almost five years now and has helped me so much to understand and integrate my own shadow. And yet it often feels as if there's something else I need in addition to analysis. She was visibly disturbed by the last dream I shared with her, which I know has to do with the split that still exists inside me:

*I am in a building with others, taking care of a dog and a young horse. I cannot care for both, so I tend to the dog. Then I go into another room and see the foal, dead, lying in a pool of water. I am very sad.*

I want to be able to relate to, integrate, both dog and horse energy, not have to choose between one and the other.

## Ariel

A couple of weeks ago I decided to have more tests done because I knew something was terribly wrong and getting worse even though I'm seeing Connie and also now have seen Stephen, a healer she recommended. I even started going to a chiropractor. But the tests, a G.I. Series and a bunch of others came back only Sjogrens, not much else they can diagnose. Now I'm taking sulfa for my bladder infection, and Elavil at night so I can get a little sleep, but it feels like my body is getting eaten up from inside. My bones feel hot, like I'm burning up, and my skin is hot to the touch even though I have no fever. It's like there's fire coming out my mouth, and I'm thirsty and drinking all the time. What is going on?

I went to see Stephen last week, and as I lay on the table first on my back and then on my stomach, I could feel a lot happening in my body at first, lots of movement energetically. Kind of a tingling, swirling inside. Electricity moving through me. I lay very still even though I was a little scared with my eyes closed, and then I went away, like I was asleep but I knew I wasn't really. I saw Christ on the cross and he said "it's o.k. I'll take away the pain." Then I saw a lamb, and a voice said "you are the lamb." Then I saw pictures, my family and me, but Dad wasn't there. I heard "he's traveling." I felt as if I was out of my body, and Stephen said later I was. I couldn't feel my body at all except at the very beginning.

It seemed like a long time that he was working on me, starting at my feet and placing his hands in different places all the way up my body. His breathing was odd, like he was working hard. He left me on the table for a while, I don't know how long, after he was finished, and when I sat up I had a headache and I was really confused.

"I'm not surprised you feel the way you do," he said. "The guides operated on your heart chakra, and I took a lot of black gunk from your spine also. You're probably going to feel strange for a few days."

"When you had your hands on my heart I saw my grandmother standing nearby smiling," I told him.

Stephen nodded like he knew this already.

"And I kept hearing a bell ringing!" I said. "What was that?"

"I don't want to try and explain too much right now," he said. "Sometimes people perceive things symbolically and sometimes literally. Let's just say you entered another realm for a while." He smiled reassuringly. "I will talk to Connie about it."

I wondered if I should tell him about the Dragon Lady. Most people would think I was crazy, but if Connie trusted him, maybe I could.

"I don't feel her now, but for a couple of weeks I've felt like there was something inside gripping me in my spine all the way up to my head, and I kept seeing images of a dragon lady . . . I know it sounds stupid .."

"Not at all," Stephen said.

"Well, I was really scared. I kept hearing "it's all over, you can't do it. Fun while it lasted ha ha ha you can only get a glimpse but it's not for you. God doesn't hear you help him out go ahead help him out take an overdose it's o.k. Better yet get in your car drive away cut your jugular vein it will be over quick."

Stephen just stood there looking kindly at me and nodding as if he understood.

"I prayed to God to give me strength to get up to get the pills or drive the car but it didn't come and I fell asleep."

What I didn't tell him is I kept feeling Connie's going to push you away, she's tired of your neediness, you're too draining. I felt like fire, hatred dripping from my mouth and eyes, one minute knowing I'm good, love the new me, and the next feeling such need to be somewhere safe, somewhere so the dragon lady wouldn't destroy me or the ones I love.

"I felt like I would do anything to get rid of the dragon lady, I couldn't be whole with her part of me. Did you get her out of my spine? I don't feel the gripping now."

" I think so," Stephen said.

He asked me to call him in a few days or sooner if I needed to, but I didn't yet. My bones don't hurt as much since I saw him, and I haven't seen the dragon lady again. Only the headache and confusion for a few days, but that's gone now too.

I had such a weird dream the night after I saw Stephen.

*I was in the present just as I am and sick. I was crying and running from place to place and person to person crying I hurt so bad, I feel so bad someone has to help me. No one could help me. I laid down on the ground and cried myself to sleep in a dream I heard a voice say calmly it's o.k. I was not calm. Then the voice said a time bomb is being set. I became panicky, a time bomb, oh God I'm scared. The voice kept saying it's o.k. but I was so scared I woke myself up and actually did wake real scared. I awoke thinking I don't understand a time bomb, how can that be o.k.? I fell right back to sleep. In my dream I was still laying on the ground crying and the voice said A time clock is being reset in your body. And repeated it again and again calmly. Then I awoke feeling confused but calmer I wasn't going to fall apart or blow up.*

# Fall 1991

## Connie

I've started my second year at the Barbara Brennan School and also begun working with a new healer. The time at school is intense, inspiring, sometimes anxiety-provoking, and altogether wonderful, even though by the last day I am usually in tears all day long. The amount of grief that is coming to the surface to be healed is almost overwhelming

My work with patients, even though I'm not doing hands-on healing with any of them yet, is changing because of my new awareness of energy fields, and soon I will offer healings to those who are receptive. That thought in itself causes a knot in my solar plexus (third chakra), as I not only feel a lack of confidence in the new skills I'm learning, I don't know how to make the shift from the way I work to incorporating hands-on healing. Will my patients freak out and leave? I will have to be very discriminating about who I talk to about spiritual healing, as mainstream psychotherapy doesn't yet include an understanding of chakras, auric fields, and spiritual guidance. So I will take tiny steps towards integrating healing into my work—which is already healing but rarely called by that true name—and trust that if I am on the right path, the universe will let me know.

Then there's Ariel. She is asking me to do healings, and so far I have refused, not trusting that I know enough. She doesn't know I've seen Stephen myself; I'm careful to keep my personal process out of the therapy room as much as possible. But she does know I'm learning how to work with the human energy field, and because we have a trusting relationship, seems to think I would be an even better healer for her than those who are more experienced. In terms of the connection we have, and my understanding of her, that could be true. She has been sick for so long—and now she's bleeding rectally and having bouts of severe diarrhea—that she's willing and eager to try anything that might be helpful. The Sjogren's seems to be advancing quickly and affecting more and more of her systems. I'm in the process of finding a supervisor just for the healing work, and as soon as I do I'll discuss with her the possibility of doing chelations with Ariel. Maybe by then I'll be ready.

After my first session with Thomas, my new healer:

*I'm in a large dormitory-type building. There are several buildings like it along a river. They are all connected; there are children in this building. I learn that this river may flood and am very concerned about the children. I must get them to higher ground. I tell them to take the mattresses off the beds, which are neatly made with stuffed animals on them. Each child can use one as a flotation device. We all go toward the right, down a long flight of stairs and up another flight, to higher ground. We are on a porch, supposedly safe. But the river is flooding and a wall of water comes towards us. It is up to my chest. I help the children, but see that David, who is in his playpen, is covered with water. I dive frantically under water to rescue him. I try to swim towards him under water but the water is pushing against me. I wake up, panicked.*

*Then, in another dream, there is a river again, broad, deep, swiftly moving. A group of people, including my husband, is planning to run the river in a rubber raft. I am trying to decide whether to go or not. I know there is white water ahead, and a waterfall. I think I can get off before the waterfall, but I'm not sure. I'm riding in the raft; then I'm in a store, buying special shoes with flat bottoms.*

When I was lying on the table during my second session with Thomas, he channeled a guide who I've sometimes seen on my mindscreen when I meditate. Occasionally I feel her behind me, her arms overlaying mine, as I do healings. I envision her as tall, with blonde hair coiled in a braid on her head and a garland of flowers, like a crown. She wears a long gauzy blue dress and is very beautiful.

"Is there anything you want to say or ask of your mother?" Thomas asked me gently as I lay on the table. "Your guide is right here, and she could serve as intermediary."

I lay there, eyes closed, aware that while Thomas was working on me energetically I had gone into a very regressed place and was still there. We had talked about my mother before he began the healing, and now I felt as if a young part of me was crying inside, sobbing her heart out while I was outwardly composed. But Thomas had seen the few tears that slid silently down my cheeks and into my ears. I was filled with longing for the mother I'd lost at age ten, and terrified of that longing. I'd kept it at bay for so many years, and my adult self wanted to keep it that way. I didn't want Thomas or anyone else to know this vulnerable, heartbroken child inside. I hesitated, and then could only say two things. They came out in a quavering, small child's voice.

"Why did she let me go?"

Thomas was quiet for a moment, and I knew he was waiting for the answer.

"Because she was too weary to go on," he said.

"Does she know I always loved her?" I asked, still in that frail small voice.

"Most certainly," my angel spoke through Thomas.

I sighed deeply, and the tears flowed. I felt my mother in the room, "knew" with certainty that she had been present with me since her death, something I'd not allowed myself to hope for. I sensed that, finally, the abandoned child inside was truly healing.

I realize as I think about how far I have come in my own healing that I am not done yet, that I will always have issues to address. I remind myself that perfection is not the goal, wholeness is. But I am still perfectionistic, trying to please my internalized father—for whom I was never good enough—and vying for "best Mom in the world." It was so obvious on Thanksgiving. Never mind that I'm working full time; I rose at six to cook all morning until time for church, bought the "best" turkey the day before and made an elaborate stuffing, set the table in a fashion fit for royalty.

I wanted my kids and their significant others to notice to what great efforts I'd gone, so I would receive their rave reviews, and felt guilty that I'd only baked the apple pies rather than apple, pumpkin, and mince. Store-bought pies! How could I! My image of self importance tells me I have to do it all, and perfectly, and that extends to being the perfect therapist and the perfect spiritual student. My wise self says give it up, but I, like most people, cling to old ways well beyond coming to consciousness that they are obsolete.

My affirmation for the week is: I am o.k. just as I am. I do not need to be perfect or always have others approve of me to know that I am o.k. I am o.k., a beloved child of God, perfect in my imperfection.

# CHAPTER XI

## *Choices*

### Winter 1991

#### Ariel

Am I dying, physically dying, or not? I've been asking myself this question over and over and sometimes I'm sure I am and I'm glad, and other times it scares the shit out of me, not the idea of dying but the process. And then I have a few days when I feel o.k., less pain and feeling more normal and I get hopeful, and then that scares me. What if I survive this but nothing else gets better and I have to live the rest of my life poor and can't get a decent job? And even if I did then whammy what if I get sick again?

Lynn Breedlove isn't doing any psychic readings for a while, and I asked Connie if there was anyone else because I felt this strong need to find my parents in the spirit world. She said one of her classmates at school talks to someone named Debra Taylor, so I called her and guess what? Now I know who my parents are! Debby connects with my very own personal guides and they talk through her to me. Is that possible? And then she says what she's feeling also and puts the whole thing on tape and sends it to me.

"Who are my guides," I asked her. I hoped they were beautiful.

"Soho and Leana," she channeled.

"Soho? Soho and Leana? What funny names!," I said, half wondering if she made them up.

"I'm especially wondering about the intestinal bleeding I've been having," I said, "and also about work, and finances." Might as well find out as much as I could about everything, I figured.

*It seems as though the bleeding will subside in due time. You may need some help, possibly an operation. We see you progressing gradually with this, with no dramatic move in any particular direction, and over a period of time there will be gradual deterioration. We see you being able to acclimate yourself to each shift in energy without a great deal of difficulty, and becoming less mobile and more centered in spirit. We see you gathering around you a few key individuals who can help you listen to spirit more easily. Any acceleration in any direction that goes beyond what your inner pace is will be disturbing to your physical presence. Try to remain centered and focused, deliberate in your actions.*

*In terms of your financial situation, we see gradually individuals coming to your aid, willing to assist, and we see you seeking public assistance. Know that you may have to go through a bit of an ordeal, as there is some insensitivity around you.*

"I think it's important that you talk to your doctor now," Debby added. "What I'm picking up is extreme fatigue."

"You're right," I told her. "I can't work more than two or three hours without absolute exhaustion, and when I'm bleeding rectally or the pain is real bad I can't work at all. What about the healer, his name is Stephen," I asked.

*"The healing work is good,"* they said. *"And it is also important for you to practice short, controlled breaths to energize yourself. It is not always possible for you to receive what others do from breath."*

I know the smoking is getting in the way and I hate it but still can't stop.

"I made a tape for my father to listen to in the hospital before he died, but the nurses wouldn't let him hear it as far as I know." I wanted to change the subject. "What happened when he died?"

*He heard it and received the thought once he had passed through the veil. We see him knowing and understanding what you had to say. He had regrets over never helping you. We see him blocking the awareness over many years through feelings of shame and anger. He was abused in his own way, and he feared his father even through his older years. We see extreme bitterness in him over this and an unwillingness to release a stream of sorrow. It has gushed from him as he has passed over. He knows your heart and sees you for who you truly are at this time.*

Debby said, "This is Debby. I have the sense of him reaching back and trying to contact you. When he was alive he tried to give an image of indifference or arrogance and I feel him regretting that. There's a tremendous feeling of remorse. I feel him around you, almost like he's another guide, like he's waiting for you. I've never seen it like this. It's like he's not going on to something else until he helps you."

I cried so hard I could hardly ask any more questions, and then finally I asked the one I was most scared of.

"Is it time for me to pass over?"

I could feel Debby hesitating. "Time is different in the realm where the guides are, but I'll ask."

*"There could be a sudden drop or collapse in your systems within the next couple of years after a slow decline."*

Oh great, I thought, two more years of this shit!

"I have a sense," Debby said, "that something wonderful might happen, that around the time you're hovering between this life and the other side you might have a strong sense of both worlds being one and might have a rich spiritual experience."

I didn't understand that at all.

"What about Connie," I asked. " I get the feeling that she doesn't believe or doesn't want to believe I'm dying."

*We see that she is very loving and caring and that she sees you as a teacher just as she is teacher to you. She is learning to watch, to totally pay attention, to never feel that any moment is irrelevant. Every moment, every breath that is taken, every second, every exchange is precious. Also, you may wish to remind her that death is only a change of form and a transformation, and we see each of you teaching each other about this transformation. We see her teaching you about how you can receive more and you teaching her how she can allow, how she can let it be, how she can take it into her belief system that it is possible to choose to do this and not have it be something that is horrible or traumatic. There is great drama attached to dying. It can be healing and strengthening. We see you both altering your perceptions continually and not allowing yourself to be fixed in any one aspect of the process, so that the process of transition is a smoother one, more naturally achieved. We see you explaining this is just something you need to do, and we see it accelerating some as you intensify the fear. So attempt to draw her in to help you relax into the process. And to let it be as slow or as fast as you wish. The slower it is the more you will be able to acclimate to the changes in energy and it will be less painful, less of a wrenching experience.*

"Wow," Debby said. "This is a learning for me, to hear this. I thought it would be easier for it to go quickly! I think what they're saying is that an integration of deterioration would make it easier."

I laughed, the way I do when something hits me really hard. It is all so strange.

*"You need quiet and restful companionship,"* Soho and Leana said. *"It is important to let people help you, that is part of your learning now."*

I had an appointment with Connie a couple of days later and told her what Debby and the guides had said.

"I hope hearing about dying won't create that reality for you," she said in a concerned voice.

"That's not what happened," I told her. "I've believed for the last year or two that I'm dying. Hearing that will make it easier to die."

But I'm still scared. Really scared. I've resigned my job and have information about temporary and permanent disability. At times I feel childlike and frightened, at times centered and accepting. I'm going to sign bankruptcy papers next week, and that makes me feel like I'm worth nothing. I haven't really done much in this life and it's hard to believe there isn't some other purpose here, but if there is I don't know it yet, and it doesn't look like I have a lot of time to figure it out.

## Connie

I'm aware of deep fatigue; often when I meditate I fall asleep. I'm trying to do too much, and it feels exhausting physically, mentally and emotionally. Too much time, energy, money is required to keep up. My process, my metamorphosis, seems to be unfolding at an accelerated pace, with little time to integrate the changes. Do I really have healing hands? Is this program right for me? It 's so difficult to honor the work I'm already doing, my Jungian experience and training, and still find time not just for school but for taking care of myself. I'm sleeping fitfully, barely have time to exercise, shower, and fire up the wood stove before seeing my first patient. Some days, when I'm pressed for time, I do a walking meditation, (at least I don't fall asleep!) and whether I'm walking or sitting in my chair, more and more I have a sense of expanded perception and guides nearby. I write questions in my journal, meditate, and then spontaneously write answers that come from somewhere other than my conscious thought process. In archaic language! I can put myself in an altered state of consciousness and sometimes see people's auric fields, sense what is going on in their bodies, hear words of guidance.

Meditation alters my state of being in such a positive way, and because I'm doing some practice healings with willing family and friends, I'm meditating not only in the morning, but also before each healing. So many of the energy-awareness techniques are becoming natural and effortless; two years ago I never would have guessed that I could feel my chakras spinning, that I could vibrate my own energy field at the level I choose, that I could channel energy through my body and my hands. It's all quite amazing..

And then there's the arduous, heart-rending, and yet fulfilling day to day work with my eating disordered patients, some of whom I've seen through major transformations over the past few years, some of whom leave once they have symptomatic relief, some of whom have such entrenched defenses that progress through talk therapy is painstakingly slow. More and more I'm encouraging my patients to have regular body work in conjunction with therapy; if the massage therapist is good, it really helps the process. And of course, for some, inpatient treatment is necessary.

It's always gratifying to work with people long enough to see them make significant movement towards wholeness, to integrate the various aspects of themselves and move toward self-actualization. The women I work with are by definition split-off, disocciated, with the symptom speaking for them. There's never been a place that's been safe enough for long enough for them to reconnect with the pain, the fear, the anger, the grief that they hold in their bodies, and to release it. The body remembers, and the body speaks when there are no words.

Ariel is the most extreme example of this in my practice, although there are many others who have severe symptoms. I keep asking myself, is all her pain and suffering the physical residue of her abuse coming to the surface to be healed, or is she truly dying? Recently she's had bouts of extreme bloating of her abdomen, which puzzles and disturbs her physician. I talked with him the other day, and he seems to think there is malabsorption of fluid from her intestines due to the Sjogren's; he ordered a cat scan, and it was normal. Ariel is quite concerned that she will not be able to make it to my office much longer and asked if that would be the end of our sessions. I reassured her that I would make house calls if she becomes bedridden. She stopped smoking again, is wearing a nicotine patch and says she's thinking about cigarettes but not craving them. She's also getting food stamps now and is going through the long, slow, laborious process of applying for permanent disability. She looks terrible most of the time—haggard and almost crumpled up—and has begun walking with a cane. One of her legs hardly functions, and she's afraid of losing her balance and falling. Her joint pain is sometimes severe—elbows, knees, etc.,—and though medication helps, with her history it's important for her not to get too dependent on drugs. When her belly swells up there is so much pressure on her diaphragm it interferes with her breathing. Sitting is very uncomfortable, and she's aware of a lot of confusion,

as when she was ill as a child. I must confess I don't unders..
what's going on, and I'm glad she has support at her church and
AA. When there are inconclusive tests, she gets angry and ashamed
and feels that she is causing her symptoms. Is she? On some deep
level she wants to die and doesn't want to take responsibility for
suicide, so perhaps this is her way of choosing death. And if that's
the case, what's my role? I vacillate between wanting her to get
well, to choose life, and accepting that she has the right to choose
death, even this kind of death. It's a difficult challenge for me, to
just be present with loving acceptance, to let go of wanting it to be
any way other than the way it is.

I am coming to understand that at the deepest level we are co-
creators of our lives, and that it is imperative that we be willing to
take responsibility for every aspect of our existence as fully as we
possibly can. "At some level" we have chosen, and continue to
choose, every minute. We may, from the soul perspective, even
choose our parents and the circumstances of our lives specifically
to give us the opportunity to learn the lessons that will enable us
to move closer to the light. But we forget this when we are born,
and it takes most of us an awfully long time to remember why we
came, both in terms of the lessons we have chosen and the gifts
we've brought to give to the earth. All of us have lessons, all are in
need of healing, and all of us have gifts to give. The rub is that we
also have free will, and because we're born into the duality that
defines the earth plane, we don't always choose wisely. And when
we don't, well, the lesson will present itself again! It's like being in
school—if we don't learn what we are taught in first grade, we
make it to second but sooner or later have to learn what we missed
in first. We are in fear so much of the time, forgetting our source!
We have so little faith! But earth is a tough assignment—no wonder so many people are adept at staying out of their bodies.

# Spring 1992

## Ariel

Feel like I'm expanding my understanding of boundaries and old issues with my new realities of myself. My friends seemingly aren't able to deal with my physical deterioration, stay in contact but from a distance and I find old tapes coming up, you're no good, they don't really like you, you're too needy. Then my new tapes come in, you're worthy, God loves you, yes you're ill but you don't exaggerate to convince others. My friends love me and find my illness difficult to handle. In my efforts to confirm my new tape I run to Connie, my stability. I call to hear she's there, she's available, she loves me no matter what. When she doesn't return my calls right away or seems distant my old tapes taunt me but then Soho and Leana reassure me. Soho my director says she will not enable your behavior, you must get beyond continually need-ing her reassurance. Leana my nurturer says she loves you and knows you can be stable without constant contact. Leana holds me and cradles me. Soho told me that with what is going on in Connie's life and her knowing what's going on with you she needs some distance in order to be strong for you. I feel guilty receiving so much from her and giving so little back, and I offered to help her move but she won't let me. Says she needs to keep boundaries intact. Then I get enraged, and want to say fuck it all. But it doesn't last like it used to.

Sometimes I feel like I am between two worlds not by disasso-ciating because I'm aware of my connection and grounding here but I also feel so close to God . I keep getting directed to nature, animals, and birds when I feel down. Spring is so beautiful here, especially May, when everything comes alive and smells so good. A bird flew right in front of my living room window and just flut-tered there yesterday as I was crying and lonely. I saw it and said thank you God for sending me a sign of things to come. The bird flew into the tree I thought oh Ariel you are crazy. With that the bird flew right back and again fluttered in front of that window. I might be crazy to some but I knew God was sending me a sign.

Three weeks ago I bled rectally again after doing too much. My back hurt, I was exhausted, my abdomen was swollen up like a basketball, and I had sharp pains in my mid to low back. And then all of a sudden, blood all over the place. I didn't go to the emergency room because they don't understand this, but I did call my doctor after it stopped. No one knows what's going on.

Meanwhile I have an appointment with the Division of Disability Determinations, actually two appointments one with a medical doctor and one with a psychiatrist, to see if I can get permanent disability. What they put you through to prove you need help shouldn't happen to an animal. It's degrading and depressing.

The best thing that happened was that after my stomach had swelled up again a few days ago Stephen came to Connie's office and they did a healing on me together, they worked on me for two hours and I woke up the next day and my stomach was down to almost normal! I can have the waistband at my waist without hurting, and even though I feel very tired, I feel more peaceful. The only bad part was I had a terrible nightmare that night and woke up knowing something else awful happened in my childhood but don't know what it was. Talked to Connie and felt reassured but searching for clues. Why can't I remember the house I lived in, even when I look at pictures of the house I don't know what the inside was like, not even the furniture or kitchen appliances. Why can't I remember the interior of my own house? I wish I could remember things from my past more naturally. Only through dreams and much therapy. Pisses me off I want to remember me and my childhood like others do, even if it's bad at least I would feel like a person not someone that is here but ghostly. I guess that's what someone with amnesia feels, no past and don't know the future.

Yesterday, two days after the healing, I awoke feeling really good. I had my usual aches and pains but more energized. My mind said yes and my body responded. That's different. I took a ten minute walk in the woods, and called Mom and told her I'm going to visit if I can get cheap tickets. I even went grocery shopping and did some errands, and then I was real tired, I think I overdid. But my stomach is down, what a miracle. Where did it go? What was it? I haven't had any diarrhea or anything. It's o.k. I'm willing to let it go.

I feel I need to make each day count for me. Want to do some things I've never done but have wanted to all my life. I wonder if I will have the time and the energy.

## Connie

I went to New York and had a two-hour astrological update with Linda Martin, who did a natal chart for me a couple of years ag. She said that after I left the last time she was very concerned that I was swallowing my life force, and the "grow or die" messages were so strong in my chart that if I "stuffed it" much longer I would have been in for serious trouble. She sees me entering a whole new phase of life, as having leaped into the abyss and survived. She knew that in the past two years I had made a terrifying descent to the darkest depths of Hades and had come back more alive than I've ever been.

"There's an exultant quality, and a knowing that you can be more vulnerable all the time. You realize you can fly, like a fledgling. By next year I expect you to be attitudinally about as different as could be from the person you were when I last saw you."

"If this transformation continues at the same rate, I won't be surprised at all," I told her. "But it sure isn't easy."

I know that the thing I most need to focus on over the summer is going inward, finding my center and holding it. It means being alone in a new way, trusting that I will be cared for. I need to meditate and pray daily, listen and learn from those who are ahead of me in terms of their own healing, and care for my body to the best of my ability. I'm ready to do healings with any of my patients who are receptive to energy work, and yet I still lack confidence. In classes I'm doing well, passing all the written and skills tests, and some of the healings I've done on classmates have been profound experiences in terms of the guidance I've received and also the physical and emotional healing that has occurred. But to claim my new capacities in my professional life? I'm still afraid.

I called Debra Taylor, whose occasional guidance I have come to look forward to.

"What can I trust in terms of information I receive when I'm doing healings?"

*Your own mind is deterring you from trust. The information is trustworthy. Before you begin, say to yourself in no way will any misperception, doubt, or any distortions of mind interfere with my higher sense perceptions at this time. And so with such a pure intention and with the knowledge that spirit desires for clarity to be your greatest ally, you will know that spirit does not wish for things to be dim, dismal, or doubtful. It would be impossible for you to see from your side why this is so but just know that if you set these intentions clearly and you choose to believe in what you are receiving then trust will no longer be a problem.*

*We see that sometimes you believe that when there is a small bit of the information that has not come through strongly or clearly enough that perhaps you are not tuned in quite properly that day. This is indeed where doubt and uncertainty will cloud your perceptions. So step back from what you receive and look at it as broadly and as impersonally as possible. In terms of improving your reception, you can also sing, we feel that singing will raise your vibrations to a higher frequency and you will feel the clarity more strongly if you are vibrating at a higher rate. Let pleasant sounds come from your mouth, from your heart, find a pleasant, simple melody to repeat again and again and let the sounds radiate. Let your mind, heart, and feelings guide you.*

"Thank you, thank you," I told Debby gratefully. "And I just remembered something from my last Barbara Brennan class. I was lying on the table receiving a practice healing from one of my classmates and suddenly heard a carillon of bells playing exquisite music. Usually a wonderful harpist plays during healings, so I was really surprised by the bells. When I sat up after the healing I asked my healer about it, and she hadn't heard any bells. I asked others in the room, but no one else had heard it either! It was absolutely beautiful, and I don't know where it came from. Can you ask my guides?"

Debby repeated my question for the guides.

*There are bell tones around all human beings at all times, and you were able to pick up on this very strongly and clearly due to a desire to*

*receive and to hear. It was nothing that was extremely out of the ordi-
nary in terms of the subtler levels. There are many clear, high sounds in
the universe that are helping to reorient or shift energies around the
earth. They are purposefully playing consistently, repetitively in subtle
ways, subliminal in your terminology. The origin of the influence is
sound that is set in motion partially by angelics and partially by desire
of divine mind to move energy. So you were feeling and hearing sounds
that have been here for perhaps a century attempting to move negativity.*

"How wonderful! O.K., something else I don't understand.
When I'm doing healings, and sometimes just sitting face to face
with patients, my eyes fill with tears, and my vision changes. I'm
looking through that veil of tears, and I see auras, and sometimes
people's faces appear older or younger than they really are. It's
happened a few times now, and if the person is sitting there looking at me I feel embarrassed with tears running down my face.
Why the tears?"

*It is assistance that is coming to you. Your mind and your vision is
being opened to a different, multidimensional perceptual state. Recognize that as you allow it to happen the tears will be perceived as tears of
empathy. In truth they are tears of mechanical change, tears of in-
creased tolerance for energy vibration. Your tear ducts have expanded
and contracted to allow such vision to come to you. It is being offered to
you by your own highest presence as an opportunity for receiving additional information. See it almost like being able to peek into the past,
future, or present, almost like being given a dossier on an individual.
You are given all their background, their insights, their many aspects,
and it's actually being refined and exposed to you in light of the present
situation. What you are receiving always pertains to the present situation; it is never random. So as you play with it, as you work with it, as
you honor it and let it speak to you, you will learn when to speak to
someone about what is going on and when not to speak to someone. You
will understand that it is an expansion of your perception, and it is
being offered to you as an assistance from above. Go with it and do not*

*be concerned about losing your mind. This is a major concern, al-*
*though you have not verbalized it, a fear that if you lose your cognitive*
*presence you will miss what is being said or lose a hold on being a*
*healer in the situation.*

I had not been consciously aware of my strong need to hold on
to my cognitive capacities and how that might actually interfere
with my high sense perception, but as they spoke I felt an AHA! I
need to let go more of mental control.

I feel so humble in the face of the energies I am connecting
with, and at the same time there is so much that feels wonderfully
familiar. It reminds me of when I was a little girl and my father
took us to the Christian Science church he belonged to, maybe for
the first time, and I listened joyfully to the sermon and bible readings and hymns. I remember my distinct thought was "oh, someone else knows this too!" I must have been five or six years old, and
it was as if I already knew everything they were saying, and there
had never been anyone to talk to about it. I sense that I have been
a monk, a nun, a healer in past lives.

I don't remember ever going to church with my father after
that except the day he married my stepmother, and that was in an
Episcopal church. I don't even remember that very well. We were
certainly not brought up as practicing Christian Scientists, and
with his smoking and drinking and hatred and bitterness, it's hard
to believe he had faith in that or any other religion. He didn't
seem to mind that my stepmother had us baptized and confirmed
as Episcopalians; he just never participated in any way. Never even
talked about it. But then, there was a no-talk rule in our house
about a lot of things. Certainly we weren't allowed to talk about
our mother. We had to pretend our stepmother was our mother,
even at school, and we just went along with it. It was as if my
childhood, from birth to ten, had never happened! Somewhere in
my psyche I encapsulated my memories of my mother; I think it's
what enabled me to survive living with my father. But in the first
few months after we went to live with him I tried to hold on to

her, wanted to believe she'd come back for us, and when he refused to allow any contact at all I stopped eating, was well on my way to becoming anorexic at ten. I'd always been skinny anyway, and I've been told everyone was very worried about me. My sister Pat would go into the kitchen and say "Connie won't eat that," whatever it was. I persisted in my hunger strike until my father began forcing me to eat, standing behind me while I sat at the table pushing my food around the plate, slowly taking off his belt, watching the clock, counting down fifteen minutes to clean my plate or else. With a huge knot in my stomach, terrified he would hit me, I began to eat. After a while I lost all sense of when I was hungry and when I was full; all I knew was that whatever was put on my plate, I had to eat it or else. I understand now that my appestat began to malfunction, and though I was always so physically active that I didn't get fat, by the time I was adolescent I was eating mindlessly, with no regard to hunger. And then, as I became aware of my body and the cultural imperative to be thin, I began dieting off and on; that lasted many years. I gained a lot of weight with my pregnancies, and after I stopped nursing took amphetamines to lose the weight. They worked, but made me nervous and irritable. When I couldn't stand the sleeplessness and racing heart any longer I'd stop and immediately regain the weight. Few people would have called me fat, but I always felt like a blimp, and I struggled constantly to get down to what I thought was "normal"—meaning, of course, perfect. Bingeing, dieting, a period of "normalcy", and then the whole struggle would begin again. When I look back on those years, I realize my obsession with food and weight dominated my life. I don't think anyone around me knew that, not even my husband, but in the last few years I've discussed it with my children, and they remember the Ayds—little square chewable taffies—that I ate before meals to reduce my appetite. My kids loved them; when I wasn't around they'd search the kitchen cabinets, find the Ayds, and eat them like candy! They say they remember me as very patient, but I remember being strung out a lot of the time, and I wonder sometimes what effect that had on them. It is still hard for me to forgive my father for forcing me to eat. On the other hand, I would not have the visceral understanding I do of eating disordered women had my life been different.

And then there was the iodine. I used to chew my fingernails down to the quick, and my father's answer to that was to paint my fingers with iodine, which tasted dreadful. I wasn't allowed to wash it off, and if I cried when he slapped me he'd cup his hands and say sarcastically "cry me a cupful of tears." I learned early not to cry.

He was such a perfectionist. I remember being beaten when I was ten because he ran his gloved finger over the top of the china closet and there was dust on it. Of course I swore I'd dusted it (I hadn't), which infuriated him even more. I wonder sometimes how many generations of dysfunction led to his cruelty. I know now that he was terrified of life, but as a child all I knew was my own terror of him.

Recently, when I was with my new healer and a lot of anger toward my father came up, he put some pillows on the floor and gave me a tennis racket so I could beat the pillows. In my imagination the tennis racquet turned into an ax. I cut off my father's limbs one at a time, then his penis, then gouged out his eyes and smashed his body to a pulp. I had never done anything like that before, and it released tears to exhaustion afterward. But I didn't feel guilty, not for two days, and then I was even able to let that go. All my life I've had compassion for him, but the rage was there too, and almost impossible for me to bring to consciousness. When I "identified with the aggressor" I did it quite thoroughly; the anger disappeared! At least from consciousness. After I'd expressed it so violently with Thomas, a more genuine forgiveness emerged.

I've been thinking of switching from Jane to a male analyst to complete the work around my issues with my father. The man I'm thinking of going to is excellent and also somewhat scary to me; he reminds me somewhat of my father, which is a good reason to go to him. I get to have a father transference. Oh, joy! Seriously, I've taken a couple of courses with him and read his books, and I think

it's time. I think I've gone as far as I can go with Jane. So I asked
the guides about him—Abraham is his name:

*It is good for you to listen to your heart, for your growth now defi-
nitely circles around your father's influence. We feel that you will free
yourself through your relationship with Abraham. He's very intuitive,
and he is able to distance himself and yet remain very present. We see
him being able to sustain a feeling of strength while you work through
deep feelings of anger and hatred around experience with your father.
We feel that you will come out the other side very transformed and
renewed and very grateful to Abraham for his constancy. You will be at
times very disconcerted with his way but he will hold true to himself and
not adjust for you , so that you will experience yourself most fully.*

"He feels like a rock to me," Debby said. "I anticipate that it
will be very intense. He's not afraid to cut into something, and he
won't be raw if you're bleeding . . . you're going to have a powerful
experience with this man."

A powerful experience. That could mean any one of a number
of things. I feel some anxiety about making a change; it would be
much easier to stay with Jane. But if I'm ever to heal my father
wound, why not now? And who better than Abraham? I just hope
I don't fall in love with him; I don't want to deal with that kind of
transference. One of my friends laughed when I told her I was
going to work with him. "Remember," she said, "fools rush in
where angels fear to tread." Am I being wise or foolish?

"Could I have some general guidance for the next few months?"
I asked my guides. I'd learned that this was a good final question
to ask in a session.

*Feel that your being is reaching up to your own mind for guidance,
in order to be able to receive more, to open your receptacle for love. That
is a major focus, a major metaphor for you at this time, and as you
begin to notice changes in yourself, remembering this metaphor will
help you to stay in balance. When you feel an aching, a starvation, it is*

*not necessarily that you need to have that ache filled, it could possibly be that there is an opening to receive more taking place, and it will help you n the future. Stay with it and know that you are being directly guided from within and above. Your heart is the ruling factor here. Even though you are processing mentally, your heart is the one that is leading you, and this is where the inner wisdom springs forth like a fountain. Remember that you are loved, blessed, and supported constantly; you are never without loving, blessing, and support from your own spiritual nature.*

# Summer 1992

## Ariel

Even though I'm sick and in pain and exhausted all the time, unable to walk more than fifty feet even with my cane, a lot has happened. I believe I'm being guided so I can make a decision if I should want to go on or not, I'm at a crossroads and neither decision is wrong. I feel sure I had a past life experience as a spirit that was supposed to unconditionally love and protect God's son. I became so angry with God that he allowed his only son to be crucified that I abandoned him in his time of greatest need. It has been necessary for me to experience this in human form in order to know of God's goodness and his love. I have continued to be angry with God and felt abandoned, but now God is comforting me and I'm very aware of his presence. But the evidence of human persecution sometimes still overwhelms me. Less than it ever used to, but I still feel it and get angry.

I want to make a difference here to better earth but I know it's not what God is asking of me. I really want to make a difference so my family will be proud. To show them I did it in spite of them. That's not the right reason I know deep inside. I don't feel comfortable here on earth because it's not my home, it's never felt like my home. Home is with God. My body hurts, my body is tired and weary, as good as I now take care of it it doesn't seem to be enough. It's worn out. The love I long for can only come through God and I can't seem to find it here on earth. But I can now love even though I feel bad, I can now love even if there are judgments and hate around me. It's been a difficult lesson to learn. It's difficult to detach from those I love and love me like Connie (earth mother), Stephen, my dog Shakespeare, my children. But I can be near them from afar, I've learned that. And now I wonder if any of what I just wrote makes any sense, probably not to most.

In my heart I want to go home but I feel there's a piece I'm missing. Should I struggle to get that piece or let go and go home? Have I accomplished God's mission? That's the piece I'm missing. I need to know.

Connie finally said she was ready to do a healing, which I've been waiting for for so long. And now she's using one session a week out of our two to do a chelation and work on my chakras and my auric field. She asked me to pay attention to my sensations, any images, and feelings that came up while she was channeling the energy into my body, so as I lay there the first time with my eyes closed I paid close attention and wrote it all down as soon as I got home and my head got clear.

She started by holding my feet, and as they were being held I began to feel lite, as though I was floating, except for my right leg. My right leg felt like a very heavy weight, a blob. I kept thinking "My left leg is grounded but why is my right leg so heavy? It feels dead." When my right leg only was being held I could feel activity, energy moving from my leg to my back. I felt pain moving but it didn't feel intolerable. Suddenly I felt a bubble move into my lower back, left side. It was painful but felt peculiar. I thought "This bubble is going to burst and the pain will stop." Where the bubble was in my back felt like that was the focal point of my intestinal problems. I'm not sure if this is when Connie moved her hands to my abdomen. The pain lessened but did not disappear. I heard "hold the pain—embrace it." I felt puzzled, confused. I felt if I hold the pain and love it I must want it, I must be bad. I said this out loud and was given reassurance that I wasn't bad, I could let go of it and concentrate on what was going on at the moment. With her hands on my abdomen I could feel a rocking motion, almost volcanic and kneading. My abdomen felt thick, dense. I tried to envision what I was feeling, but all I could see was darkness. Then I felt the rocking motion again, and I could feel tension releasing in my body. When her hands were on my upper body I envisioned a man's head with long white curly hair and a beard. His hair seemed to be flowing or moving in the wind. He was smiling at me like a proud father. I felt a deep sadness and wanted to be touched by him. I told him I was not afraid. I knew I meant I was not afraid of what I needed to go through to my final transformation. I kept trying to get closer to this man to recognize him. I kept hearing the name Thor but that made no sense to me. I was brought back to the room by being told to breathe. When Connie's hands were on my throat, I kept thinking how can I do anything, my body feels so broken. How can I do God's will if I can't get around? I hear loud and clear "you will be given speech". This touched my funny bone since I've been communicating with the congressman and talking to everyone about the disability but feel like I'm babbling most of the time. As this was going through my head I had the sense that that statement didn't mean voice but that I was being given the gift of speech that will be heard for the good of all. I could see white—white before my eyes. Then her hands were on the middle of my chest and I heard "you have a good heart". I remember thinking well I guess I'm not going to die from a heart attack. I was also aware of discomfort in my lower back. I had a strong sense that the statement I had a good heart had nothing to do with my physical status. When I felt hands on my shoulders I felt tension released, warm and comfortable, thinking "this feels good." Then her hands were on the sides of my head, and there was an immediate prayer in my head. I can't remember it all. "May Jesus Christ's presence be with you. May Jesus remain in your heart". I remember thinking Thank you thank you. Then the white cleared from my eyes, and I was back on the table, talking with Connie.

I know I can't get my hopes up that the energy work will make me well. Connie says she doesn't know what to expect, that she will ask for guidance and keep herself as clear as possible so that whatever healing energies are needed will come through her. I don't want to get my hopes up but want to trust as much as possible.

The night after the healing I had a dream:

*I was walking down the street carrying a little girl. I was walking with three people, one tall man and a little midget. I told them I couldn't keep carrying this little girl but I loved her so much what was I going to do. I couldn't trust just anybody with her. The tall man (he reminded me of my minister Ken) kept encouraging me . The midget was trying to find a solution so I wouldn't have to keep carrying her. He knew what I said was the truth, I was too exhausted. The third person I don't remember except a sense of support and strength. I thought the little girl was my granddaughter but then I realized the little girl I was carrying was all crippled up and was not able to walk on her own. I think that little girl was my inner child, the wounded one. The tall man kept telling me I needed to trust. I knew I couldn't keep going on but how could I leave her. We went to this nice looking van. Inside was all carpeted. The tall man and midget were seated. There was a padded lined seat with a seat belt. The man said put her here and we'll take her on an adventure so wonderful that she will always remember. I don't remember putting her down but I ran out of the van and down the street crying and exhausted. I stopped on the corner. People came up to me saying look! you can't trust them pointing in the direction I came from. I turned and saw the van moving and turning a corner. I woke up feeling I have to trust, I have to give in but puzzled by the dream.*

# CHAPTER XII

## *Seeds of Regeneration*

### Fall 1992

### Connie

An exquisite fall. Cool, fresh breezes lifting and tossing brilliant red, yellow, gold leaves from maples, dogwoods, poplars, oaks. It's quite invigorating after the long, hot summer, and as always for me, autumn brings a sense of new beginnings. I will probably always think in terms of academic years.

I've begun offering healings to patients who are receptive, and it's much easier than I anticipated to move from dialogue to having people on the table and working directly with their energy fields. I'm acutely aware of how touching, even without running energy, intensifies the transference; issues of trust, longing, fear, memories of abuse if there was any, are easily triggered. What I'm also noticing is that very often people have what I call "post-healing dreams" that incorporate symbols of energy movement , elements of the transference, and cellular memories that are being released. I'm taking careful notes about what happens during each healing and any dreams that follow, with the idea that this might make a very interesting topic for my Senior Thesis and may also be the bridge for me between Jungian psychotherapy and the healing work. I've asked my patients to keep track of these dreams and their experience of the healings, and I'm finding that very often a post-healing dream will lead directly into the next healing, giving a strong indication of what's happening on the deepest levels and what's needed next.

Most of the chelations I've done so far have been with Ariel, who has been eager for a long time to have me do hands-on work with her. We've had to spend a fair amount of time exploring her expectations and fantasies about this—I think she has been hoping for a miracle, and that I cannot promise. What I'm noticing when I measure her chakras with the pendulum is that there is definitely a pattern of holding in her throat chakra that's consistent from week to week, while other readings fluctuate. She responds very well to chelations, meaning that there is often an energetic and emotional release as well as psychological movement. Before I begin, I ask for guidance, and sometimes I "hear" what is needed (it's my own voice, but it seems to come from elsewhere); more often, I have a sense of knowing which increases as I'm doing the chelation, probably because I reach higher levels of vibration as I go along.

Last week as I was balancing and clearing Ariel's energy field she told me her right leg was getting colder and colder, and my hands felt like ice to her. My hands felt extremely warm to me, as did her skin. I could not see or sense what was going on energetically, but by the time I had completed the healing her right hip, leg, and arm had been completely anesthetized. For three days afterward she had almost no pain. I was not deliberately anesthetizing her; I know the "guides" were working through me to give her relief. If I can be a clear channel, with the clear intention that what happens be for the highest good, healing energy will flow through me, healing where healing is needed. Sometimes what then happens is under my control; for example, if I am repairing a chakra or restructuring one of the levels of the auric field. Other times seemingly miraculous things happen that go beyond my conscious knowledge or intention.

When Ariel came back several days later she was greatly energized and reported a dream in which she was told her throat chakra was opened, and she saw clear white streams of energy shooting out of her head and her feet. When I measured her throat chakra with the pendulum, it was indeed wide open.

One of the hardest things for me specifically with Ariel is that I still feel she has one foot in the door of life and one in the door of death. Until she decides to commit herself to life, I don't think the healing work, even if it brings about temporary change, is going to make a lasting difference. Changes in her energy field as a result of healings will only hold to the extent that she is ready to be healed. So the whole question of "what is healing"? comes up again and again for me. This is one of the greatest challenges to my belief system and my capacity to trust that healing on the spiritual level doesn't necessarily involve holding on to physical health or even the physical form. It is not for me to choose whether Ariel or any-one else lives or dies, or to judge her choice. So then, I ask myself, if she'd rather die, why bother sewing up the tears in the seventh level of her auric field, or restructuring a chakra, or any of the other technical things I can do that MIGHT result in physical heal-ing? I go back and forth about all of this, and ultimately I accept that if she is desirous of healing and I lay my hands on her with compassion and as a clear channel, healing will take place. It might not fit my pictures of what healing is "supposed" to be, but on a level that may go far beyond my limited human understanding, healing will take place. In healing as in dreams, there is always an element of mystery, something happening in the spiritual realms beyond my limited human understanding. If I think I am in con-trol, I am in illusion. What I do know on a very deep level is that Ariel came into my life as much to teach me as I came into hers to be her therapist/healer.

There are other new beginnings this fall. I am living a solitary life for the first time in many years, and though I am lonely, and sometimes fearful, I also feel a deeper, more authentic sense of Self. I finally made the switch from Jane to Abraham, which was diffi-cult, as Jane knows me and has accompanied me as wise woman through a long period of major change and growth. I miss her, the understanding and camaraderie that developed over the past several years. However, being in therapy is a requirement for the entire four years of the Barbara Brennan program, no matter how much inner work we've done before, so this is an opportunity to complete (ha, another illusion) work on my "father stuff".

I was aware during the first two sessions with Abraham that I was somewhat reserved, much less revealing than I had become accustomed to being with Jane. I was not consciously afraid, nor did I feel particularly needy. But the dreams which followed were indicative of the deep process which was beginning:

*I have an office next to Abraham's and an appointment with him at twelve o'clock. I go to do something, to help someone, and forget my appointment. When I come back to my office I walk past Abraham's and when I see him sitting in the chair I realize I've forgotten my appointment. It is ten minutes to twelve. Then I'm sitting in Abraham's office. I'm holding a teddy bear, very worn. The seams are open at the arms and some of the stuffing is showing.*

*There's an elevator with a frayed cord. I try to retie it and realize it is totally worn, falling apart, and the elevator is unsafe. I must walk many flights to get to where I'm going. Then I'm skiing with children. The mountain is steep, the snow is worn away and there are many boulders. Then there's another analyst, a male, talking about fly fishing. I tell him my son Billy likes to fly fish and would enjoy talking with him. Tina, a friend of mine, is there, laughing.*

What a mixture of images! I did have two favorite stuffed animals as a child, a teddy bear and a squirrel named Nutsy, both of which disappeared when I went to live with my father. I've never, to my remembrance, dreamed of my teddy bear before! Billy probably represents my serious, conservative side—but fly fishing is to me a graceful, fluid, highly skilled art form strongly associated with wilderness and freedom. Tina is my Dionysian friend: lusty, impulsive, and seductive. She has been in my dreams before, a shadow part of me I keep hidden most of the time. Frayed elevator cords, bouldered mountain slopes—looks like a lot of elements are already present in the analytical space with Abraham!

As if this new therapeutic relationship weren't enough to deal with, I've started my junior year in the Barbara Brennan program and during the first class session went into deep process during one of the exchange healings. I was being the "healee" while my partner was practicing repairing and restructuring chakras. Ann saw a dark energetic plug in one of the vortices of my second chakra and told Barbara, who suggested she remove it. As I lay on the table, eyes closed, I was quite relaxed and peaceful, in allowing mode. All of a sudden I felt extremely nauseated, and the feeling built until I opened my eyes and told Ann I was going to have to run to the ladies' room. Ann called one of the teachers over, and when she looked at what was going on with me energetically she said the screen had blown off my third chakra (solar plexus area). She replaced the screen and held it there, which reduced the nausea, but resulted in chest pain. By this time my teeth were chattering and my entire body was shaking uncontrollably. I wasn't afraid, just wondering what was going on, and tracking what was happening energetically. When the two of them worked on my heart chakra, the energy moved up to my throat, and at that point I began crying. I had no idea why; there were no memories or images, but I was overcome with racking sobs that lasted for a long time. Ann just stayed by my side, one hand on my third chakra and one on my fourth (heart) until there were no more tears. Finally I had an image: I was eight or nine years old, and home alone. My mother couldn't be with me, and it wasn't safe anywhere else. Not in school, not outside. I was hiding, afraid and lonely, somehow knowing there was an impending separation from my mother.

I remember that time, at least parts of it, but it's always been hard for me to connect with it emotionally. My older sister and I went to court to testify numerous times—I remember putting my hand on the bible and swearing to tell "the truth, the whole truth, and nothing but the truth". Ultimately we were asked to choose who we wanted to live with. Of course I chose my mother, but it didn't make any difference. I remember playing hooky for days and days, walking to the bus stop with my siblings, climbing up a hickory tree and throwing hickory nuts at the bus as it drove off. Then I'd go back to the house and read my sister's books. Finally the school nurse came and dragged me kicking and screaming to the principal's office, where I made up some lie about why I didn't want to go to school. In truth, I was ashamed of my family, the scandalous divorce proceedings that had made the local headlines, and terrified of what was going to happen next.

Those memories and the strong repressed emotions associated with them had created the energetic block in one of the vortices of my second chakra. When the plug was pulled, energy rushed through that vortex and moved upward through my system, affecting each chakra and my physical state on its way toward release. This is one of the ways old wounds can be healed. For the next couple of days, I had an intermittent headache, dizziness, and an upset stomach, all of which were related to the healing that was going on. The night after Ann worked on me, I had the following dream, which to me indicated that the energetic plug that had been removed was related to very early experience as well as to what I had remembered consciously, and that there was new energy flowing through me to parts that had been deprived of it for a long time.

*I'm in a room with two babies, infants. They're in separate beds, bassinets. I'm not sure if they're mine, but they're my responsibility. They're malnourished and something's wrong with them. Also, the room is disheveled and dirty; the babies are unkempt. There's a dirty pacifier in one of the bassinets—I am upset and repulsed by this. At one point I try to take them to the doctor along a windy, hilly road along a river but there has been a hurricane and enormous trees are across the road, so I have to turn back. Then I am in the room with them again and they are very still. I pull back the blanket from the one on the left and see an*

*emaciated, blackened arm. The baby is dead. The other one is also. I
don't know what to do. There's a party in the next room and I don't
want to upset everyone. The babies are dead for two days; then I see the
one on the right moving. I pick it up and it's very hungry. I begin to
nurse him; milk gushes out of my breast. When he is full, I put him
down, and he crawls around on the bed. I pick up the other baby and
it, too, is ravenous. I nurse this baby also, and again milk is gushing
out. When he is satisfied, I put him down and cover him. I wake up.*

As difficult as this entire process is, I can feel my energy flowing more freely, my habitual defenses and holding patterns relaxing, my entire being opening more to fully to life. It's not that I
don't suffer anymore; but there is definitely more joy, more alive-
ness. There's a part of me that's less and less attached to the daily
vicissitudes of life, at peace regardless of the circumstances around
me. Not that I don't have fears, and grief, and lowliness, and frustration, it's just that none of those things are who I am anymore. I
love the meditation we learned in school: "I have a body, but I am
not my body. I am the light. The light surrounds me, the light
protects me, the light flows throughout me. I am the light."

# Winter 1992

## Ariel

It's almost another New Year and I'm ready to go home. I feel the love of those around me so strong sometimes and yet I'm so tired and need a different place to live and my bones feel like they're cooking, they're so hot. The disability hasn't come through so Ken my minister has written a letter to the Congressman Bender, and also at church asked parishioners to write to him because he's the last hope. People have been kinder than I thought people could be, and I go out on calls to the sick with Ken and somehow that makes me feel better. I think that's why he takes me with him, not because I really do anything but I feel like I'm being helpful. And we laugh a lot, even though he's a minister he has a sense of humor and I think really likes my joking around especially when he knows I hurt so much. But people must get sick and tired of me. I'm sick and tired of me a lot of the time.

Connie has been doing a lot of energy work and sometimes it really hurts when the energy moves, like yesterday it felt like a hot poker going up my spine when she was working on my hip area. Sometimes areas that have been hurting go numb and stay numb for hours or days, and that feels good, it's like someone gave me a pain killer with none of the bad effects of a drug. And sometimes I feel such sadness I just cry, and if no one is coming right away she lets me stay on the table for a while. Once in a while it's like I go away someplace, and I see beautiful lights and hear voices, and then it's hard to come back. At times I feel Connie is angry with me because I can't make up my mind whether I want to live or die, and I can feel her pulling away and that feels bad. Other times she says things that make me feel she's o.k. with my dying, but it's confusing because I want her to do the healings and yet what if I get better? No job, no money and even if I had those things it might only be a remission and I couldn't go through all this again.

I know people with Sjogren's have remissions but there's no cure. If I can't be healthy why be alive, why not go home?

I had a dream the day after Christmas that was very strange:

*I came down some stairs in a large area, two connected rooms, like a warehouse but homey. I was so happy it was a party and it was for me. Everyone was there, everyone who has helped me and all my friends and family. As I came to the bottom of the stairs my mother was standing there. I said oh Mama isn't this wonderful, everyone is here. Looking at her I saw something was wrong with her left hip. I said Mama what happened to you? She laughingly said I was cuttin' the rug at the powder puff ball. I said you what? and she repeated what she said. We laughed as she moved her hip and it was fractured but she was o.k. I said Mama everyone's here except Amanda. She didn't come. My mother looked sadly at me then my brother Johnny standing behind Mom looked at me with his know-it-all smile and said she'll be tied up for four years. He was looking at me as if to say what's the matter with you, you fool, you should know that.*

*Still overwhelmed with happiness I said I'm going outside for a minute. I went out the back door and there was my Dad. I was amazed at how good he looked but he had no arms. Because I knew he was dead I couldn't figure out why he was there. I said Daddy why are you here? He said "I'm here for you." I thought oh great I want to die but how come you're taking me when I'm having fun. Then I realized he meant that he was available to me. Then I said Daddy how come you don't have any arms? He smiled and walked over to what looked like his work bench but had nothing on it and flopped his shoulder on it saying I don't need them see I can do anything I want without them. I started crying and said Daddy I hurt so bad, so bad, I can't stand it. When can I come home? He said not much longer, hon, after Christmas. And he promised me something, but I don't know what it was. Still crying I thought but it is after Christmas. I looked up yelling at him I don't understand it is after Christmas. But he had disappeared. He was gone. I kept yelling and crying but it is after Christmas. I woke up sobbing trying to figure out what he meant after Christmas when it was after Christmas.*

I talked to Connie about the dream.

"Why didn't he have any arms?" I wondered.

"What do you think of when you remember him with arms?" Connie asked me.

"Hurting, always hurting me," I told her. "He used his hands and arms to hit me."

"Maybe he was showing you that he can't and won't hurt you anymore," she said.

"What about the Christmas part?"

"I'm not sure," she told me. "But if Christmas is a time of joy and giving to you, maybe you're being shown that Christmas is coming to you before you die. It might be gifts and happiness, or more of the light of Christ. I do believe that we leave our bodies sometimes in sleep and are taken to other realms and shown things we wouldn't see or understand in ordinary reality. You seem to have more of those experiences than most of the people I work with, maybe because you've been close to death for so long, maybe because you're more connected to your guides. You seem to have learned early how to leave your body to escape from the abuse."

It's true that talking with my guides through Debby is helping me connect more and more with them, and lots of times I wake up in the morning and I have the feeling I've been traveling with them. It's odd, but it feels so real. Even my sister thinks I'm nuts when I talk like that, so I don't talk about it. Except Connie understands. Maybe she's crazy too but I don't think so.

I saved enough for another session with Debby and asked what do Soho and Leana look like? She said their names a few times to connect with them, and then they spoke through her:

*I am Soho, I am strong and tall. I am a fortress of energy. Imagine me in tall cylindrical fashion. This approximates my energies. I will attempt to help you visualize a tall warrior, a tall gentle warrior. We are your mother and father from the spirit world.*

*I am Leana. I create a sweet, scintillating energy. See me as a sparkling glittering energy coming to refreshen your mind, body, and spirit. You have been traveling with us in spirit for quite some time so I sometimes call your name to help you reconnect with your own identity and physical form .*

"Do you have any memory of traveling with Leana?" Debby asked me.

I laughed and told her yes, in my dreams. Then they said:

We are going to help you to generate higher energy within yourself. Think about your own source and allow it to bubble down into your body. We see that stresses can be partially relieved and your body can be lightened so that you can sense our presence more completely. When the body holds strong tensions it is difficult for the mind to open to receive higher energies of the spiritual nature. Recognize that as you focus on your source and imagine the energies flowing down into your system, it will help you to allow us to raise you to a level whereby you can feel our energies more completely. Another suggestion is to sing a very high tone that allows you to feel that you are vibrating at a faster rate or in a faster resonance.

Concerning your current situation, things have stepped up a bit. Your experience is requiring more of you; your mind is more keen and sharp and alert, and so we see that you are very clearly tuned into what you have to do and have a strong desire for things to settle down and remain settled down. It's almost as if you have been given an opportunity to balance and to stabilize, and now it is time for you to take the renewed energies that you have created and change and shift and apply them to creating other capacities for experience. We see that you are going to need to enlist the assistance of many of those around you over the coming months and you're going to also need to regenerate yourself quite a bit along the way. Give yourself an opportunity to listen to what others have to say to you, those who are in the body around you, and see that they will have many valid suggestions for you.

"I feel your minister and his wife around you as loving presences," Debby said. "And I also feel the disability will come through soon."

I want to believe that but it hasn't happened yet.

"I also sense something improving , like a light, clear feeling in your heart or lungs."

That sounded good.

"I think Connie is angry with me and this process of dying," I told her.

*She is not angry, she is disappointed that she has not been able to plant the seed of regeneration deeply enough in you that you desire to fully recover. There is an element in her mind that is not totally apparent to her even, that she is very disappointed in your not being able to see that you can find full joy in this experience on earth. In other words, she judges herself.*

"Connie doesn't fully understand why, if you have a chance to get better, you're still invested in going home," Debby said. "And I sense that you fluctuate about this yourself. Connie also pulls back because she's afraid of how she's going to feel when you do go home, but mostly she's upset with herself. It's not that she has a moral judgment of you."

"That's what I feel sometimes," I told her. "I've learned that boundaries are good, but sometimes it feels like hers are really rigid. I get angry and frustrated when I feel her putting up walls. I know it's leftover stuff from my childhood, at least partially, but it feels bad."

*"Your healer does not wish for interdependence. She loves you but*

*believes she needs to keep her professional boundaries to be a good thera-*
*pist.*

Connie has talked about maybe writing a book about psychotherapy and healing and using my story as part of it, and I want
her to, it would make my life worthwhile if what I've suffered
could help other people. But she said she needs to complete the
therapy with me before she writes it, that if she wrote it now it
would affect the therapy and might not be good for me. I wish she
would do it now, what if I die and never get to read it? So of course
I asked the guides about that too, and they even knew about her
writing a book!

*It is no accident that she was led to assist you. There is a purpose for*
*it to be read by another and for it to be presented to others. You have*
*generated creative energy in her. The book will help others and therapy*
*will be affected profoundly and positively.*

So maybe there is a reason for me to be going through what
I'm going through that goes even beyond my learning to love and
forgive myself and others. Maybe I have something to give to the
world after all.

## Connie

I'm afraid. Afraid of being alone, unloved, unsupported. Afraid of being coerced into abandoning myself again, afraid of depending on a man just because I'm afraid to be alone, afraid of being unable to stand up for myself in relationship, afraid of making a mistake. The fear grips me: my solar plexus area is tight, my stomach is upset, I have low back pain that's intensifying every day and that back exercises and a chiropractor haven't helped. I've had some relief from the pain during and immediately after healings, but the fact that it keeps returning means there's something I need to work through and haven't yet.

I asked for guidance about my back, meditated, and then wrote an answer spontaneously. The answer that came through me is that I am trying to defend a deep, young part of myself, that I am tensed up against the fear that I am afraid will rule me. I feel that young part of me to be three or four years old. I need to treat her with the protection, love, and consistency I needed and didn't get when my father was leaving. I've taught so many others to be kind to their inner children; it's time for me to care for mine.

When I am unconscious of my fear, it comes up and overwhelms me through my dreams. Flood dreams, lots of flood dreams.

*I'm in a valley and water is rising. I walk with others up a long path, through fields, over split-rail fences, up a mountain to a refuge in a large log cabin overlooking a valley. I'm not sure if we'll all be welcome. We arrive safely and are warmly welcomed.*

*I'm in a large house, with a man and a woman, maybe others. We go for a walk out the back and into a large grassy meadow towards rocks overlooking the ocean. We are almost there when a huge wave crashes over the rocks, and water rushes towards us. There is a flood; we run back towards the house. Then we are in the house. I look out the back window and the water is up to the windowsill. I look out the front, where the ground is lower, and there is water everywhere, rushing below. I go out on a balcony or porch and the part of the house I'm on separates from the house and begins to wash away. I run down the stairs, through knee-high water, back to the main house. Then I'm in the house. I know my dog and cat have been lost in the flood. I wake up, panicked, heart pounding.*

*I am in a small sailboat with other adults, including my father and two small children. I have been coerced into taking this voyage through stormy seas to get somewhere (unknown). Then we are in a house near the beach, and it is time to return. I look out and see dark sky, mist, and fifteen to twenty foot waves crashing on the beach. I say it is not safe, I don't want to go, and certainly the children shouldn't be taken in the boat. The men mock my caution, say I cannot make this decision because I'm always more fearful than anyone else. We argue; I stand my ground and refuse to go or allow the children to either. The men give in; I take the road instead.*

Why can't I know what is wise, why am I so ambivalent? Why is it that the rest of my life is unfolding so beautifully and I have to struggle so hard with relationship issues? I am so tired of it. On some level I know I recreated a marital relationship that mirrored my relationship with my father to give myself an opportunity to heal the original wound, but when I'm in the middle of the pain and the grief and the fear it's hard to keep that perspective. It's so difficult to deal with my personal issues and my practice at the same time. I can be there for my patients, I can handle the details of life reasonably well, but my body is saying "hey, what about me? I'm holding all the emotions you're not allowing to flow through you and be released." Abraham is a rock, so solid and grounding for me right now, so aware and sensitive to that young, scared, vulnerable part. I don't know what I'd do without him.

The process that is unfolding with Ariel continues to be my greatest professional challenge, although there are many others to whom I feel deeply connected and committed and who have extremely challenging, painful material to work through. I'm still working primarily with eating disordered women, so symptomatology is similar, but each person is unique, each relationship special. The therapeutic relationship holds extraordinary possibilities for deep intimacy, even though it's one-sided in certain ways and excludes sexual union. Jung writes about the conunctio, and I now know what that means from my own experience. On a soul level what is created in the sacred space of therapy goes far deeper than most friendships. I continue to be awed and filled with gratitude that this work, no matter how difficult, is my calling.

On the other hand, I often feel stretched to capacity as a human being, and I can easily understand why there is such a high rate of burnout among therapists. Though one of the wonderful aspects of hands-on healing is that I am actually energized by it; I am channeling energy through me rather than depleting my own energy field as I often seem to do in regular therapy sessions. It can be tiring work, but it's a different kind of fatigue than what I feel when I sit in dialogue all day.

I am so torn between wanting to support Ariel wherever she is, in whatever position she takes about living or dying, and wanting to scream at her "I refuse to accept your dying! I want you alive! I want you to fight for your life! When you die, you die, but I want to work with your life force!" I feel sometimes that she is manipulating me, forcing me to collude with her victim stance, and I hate it. I told her a month or so ago I'm not willing to do any more hands-on healing work with her unless and until she commits to life. But then, of course, I felt really guilty, because I know healing takes place on a level far beyond what I can or should try to control, and who knows what's actually happening when I lay hands on her? So I have continued.

"Ariel," I asked in our last session, "what would make you choose life, really choose life?"

Ariel stared at me intently and then gave me one of her "all right, I'll play your game" smiles.

"Guarantees," she said. "If I knew I'd have a job, and some money, and wouldn't be sick any more, I'd stay."

"That's great," I said, in retrospect with more than a little sarcasm. "Guarantees. Like most people have guarantees."

Ariel's eyes flashed in anger.

"Most people haven't gone through what I have."

"You're right," I said. "Your life has been really hard. There's just no guarantee it's going to get easier . . . so what would make you clearly choose death?"

"If I'm convinced I'm not going to get better."

"What do you think death would be like."

"Peaceful, no more struggle, no pain," she told me, smiling genuinely.

"You know," I mused, "maybe it would be a good idea to list the pros and cons of life and death, so you could decide one way or the other."

Ariel's anger flashed again.

"That's not very funny," she said.

"I'm not trying to be funny," I told her. "It's just really hard to work with you when you keep changing your mind about whether you want to live or die."

"I feel like you're really angry at me," she said, tears filling her eyes.

Suddenly I felt remorseful.

"I'm frustrated," I told her honestly. "From my perspective, the only benefit to dying is that you'll lose your body. The lessons are the same, whether you're here or beyond the veil. We just learn more quickly in the physical body, which is one reason we choose to incarnate. I think you've spent most of your life choosing death instead of life, and now you're on the fence, and I don't want you to die because you can't make up your mind to live. You can choose whatever you want, but I don't want you to die, I want you to live. You matter to me."

Ariel just stared at me, and then she began to cry. I took her hand in mine and held it until she stopped. In my darkest moments I've wanted to say to her get off the damn fence, if you're going to live, choose life, if you really want to die, then for God's sake do it and get it over with. I am ashamed of those thoughts, those feelings, and yet I know I need to acknowledge my own anger and frustration, at least to myself, or it will come out unexpectedly in my work with her. Telling her how I feel, that I really care about her, that her living matters to me, may help her get off the fence, to choose life. But what do I really know about what her soul needs and wants? I need, again, to surrender to not knowing.

There is always a strong element of a mother-daughter relationship in female therapist / female patient therapy, and sometimes I wonder if I'm unconsciously attempting to heal my mother by working with the people I work with. I'm pretty sure, knowing she was depressed for so long, and looking at old photos of her, that she was anorexic for years. Other times I think I'm relating to my patients in the way I wish my mother had been able to relate to me. Maybe I was just born over identified with the mother archetype! I know at the deepest level my work is about helping my patients reconnect with the feminine—the Goddess or Divine Mother. Sometimes the personal mother, always the transpersonal mother. And of course, I am healing myself through this work, of that I am sure.

# CHAPTER XIII

## *Going Home*

## Late Winter 1992

### Ariel

I am happier than I've been in a long time. I'm going home! I know I am, I just know it. It will happen this spring, probably May, and I'm doing everything to get ready. I moved to another house, where I'm renting a room and bath, and it's in the country and owned by people from the church, so I know when I go there will be support around me. I wrote a Living Will, and wrote letters to my daughter and Ceasar and Connie and a few others saying goodbye, so it doesn't matter how much I hurt any more or what happens to my body.

For a few weeks Connie wouldn't do energy work at all, and she finally told me that she was angry with me that I was choosing to die and didn't want me to, and was having to work through a lot of her own feelings about death and what healing means. I kept asking her to though, because there's still a part of me that wants a miracle, and she finally said she would keep on doing healings and surrender to the idea that even if I'm dying the energy work will help me heal spiritually. So she's done a lot of healings lately . Sometimes I have more pain during the chelation, like in my right hip or back and other times parts of my body go numb, and sometimes I go into an altered state and have no idea what's happened

# 254 CONSTANCE SIMPSON MYSLIK


but have trouble coming back to the present and getting off the table. Lots of times I feel better for at least a couple of days, sometimes longer, and then I get scared. What if I got better? She gets a lot of guidance during the healings now, and when I talk to Debby every few weeks I ask my guides about the healings and pass on what they say to Connie.

The last time Debby said it was almost like my body was on fire, like charcoal in my bones, which is what I was feeling. The guides explained what Connie could do and also what happens to the toxins that are released during chelations. I think it helped Connie to listen to the tape. I know she talks to her supervisor about what she's doing with me too. I trust her, if anything am most afraid that what she's doing will make me well. Overall I feel like something's changing but I'm not sure what. Here's what the guides said:

*After chelations the blood carries toxic waste in the same manner as it does when it's doing its normal work. We see that there is an acceleration of toxins and the body does have more work to do as a result of this toxic purification. There is a very strong feeling of movement toward the center. Sometimes it moves toward the center and doesn't quite reach the intestines immediately in your case. The initial processes move at the same time and sometimes at an accelerated rate of speed. However, when it reaches the final stages, the process slows down. Your body has been working this way anyway for quite some time.*

I told them that Connie has a sense that my liver and gall bladder are having difficulty, and they said:

*Your liver has been working very hard for quite some time in order to help you. When it has been difficult for you to allow the body to be nourished we see the liver has had to work extra hard to nourish the body. We also see the liver is held back by old emotional deposits of anger and rage, and so there is some swelling in this area. The gall bladder is impacted by this as well. We see that there is actually more problem in gall bladder than liver at this time. The gall bladder has been stressed and stretched to the limit and sometimes has trouble carrying out its function. Most of the time your gall bladder is in an arrested state and sometimes a spastic state. This accounts for some of the feelings you have in that area.*

*We see that the outer protective layer in your auric field has eroded, and it is important for Connie to see you as needing a protective covering as the first and foremost need spiritually. The outer layer has diminished way before your body has diminished. Working on building up protective energies around you, believe it or not is the first and foremost way to help you through this time. It will also help your body temperature. We see that having a reduced or diminished outer layer spiritually is partially responsible for the increase in consumptive activity in your body. After this layer is strengthened then other areas can be built up in your body.*

*Aside from the liver a priority is the immune system. We see it's not that you need the immune system necessarily to reverse your personal psychological or physiological difficulties now, yet it is needed to help fight off any related or invasive activities and secondary infections that may arise for you. It is enough to deal with what is going on now. These areas are very important because you need to have some nutrition getting to your physical presence and you need to be able to ward off invading influences to the body. This would stabilize your body as long as your body is open to this.*

*We see that there is a great deal of blue-black energy in your auric field and in your physical system. She can work with this, and to work with subtler colors, colors that are not as bright or pungent, colors that are soft and cool, would be very valuable. If she introduces anything that is too pastel, bright, or sunny, either in terms of her mental configurations or in terms of what she is asking from you, it may be too much of a shock to your system. Gradation, starting from where you are and gradually helping you tolerate more light in your energy field is the way we would describe what needs to be done here. There are many ways of looking at this, and some would disagree with us. Anything that can be cool, soft, supportive, and non invasive, and not accelerate your process too rapidly is going to be to your benefit.*

*We see for you to work with your own hands and feet would be excellent at this time. Rub them, sooth them, for these are the areas where you have contact with this earth, and by loving them, honoring them, taking good care of them in all ways you can imagine, it will help ease your progress as well.*

"Thank you," I told Debby. "My father came to me in a dream and he didn't have any arms. He said something about a promise, but I didn't understand."

*Your father wanted **you** to promise to see him being there for you without conditions. His armless state was to show you that he needed nothing, he didn't need to take anything from you, he didn't have anything to hurt you with any longer. He wants you to see him without threats and without fear. He is totally stripped of what he created in terms of negativity for you. Also he wanted you to promise to see that bravery truly lies deep within your spirit and that your mind is no longer one that is putting any fear into this. There is a gradual progression and he sees that happening for you.*

What about Christmas in the dream? I asked.

*There are many views to Christmas, many words that mean celebration of Christ in spirit. Your mind interpreted celebration of Christ as Christmas. In truth your father meant the rising, the birthing of the Christ within you. This all ties in to the theme of the entire dream— releasing of the Christ consciousness or Christ spirit from within yourself can be seen as a mass, can be seen as a celebration. It is all related to the surrender and the letting go.*

When I hear this I wonder am I supposed to surrender to dying or to whatever happens even if it's not going home? I don't understand the difference between surrendering and making a choice and trying to control everything, they're all mixed up inside me. I'm still taking Percoset three times a day and all the other medications including Zanax at night to sleep, sometimes more than one, and I know that bothers Connie because I get foggy and could get addicted but what difference does it make if I'm about to die?

I know Connie cares like no one has ever really cared before, but sometimes I get really pissed about her attitude because even when she says she's trying to support me whatever choice I make I know she thinks I don't have to choose death. We've talked a lot about dying, and what it means to me. She said I can discard my body by leaving the earth plane but that won't necessarily bring my soul closer to the light, that I will simply continue the soul work in some other form. And she says that's a valid choice. But then she said if I were to commit myself to life there could be unlimited possibilities, and I've never done that. And she says it seems like when I feel bad I want to die and then when I feel better I want to live. She says I still want a guarantee that if I commit to life it will be better and easier than it's been and there isn't any guarantee for anyone. So I'm still trying to control the outcome, I'm still bargaining with God based on how I feel day to day, which is different than making a clear choice.

I don't think she believes I'm going to die this spring or wants me to but she'll see. I tell her there are only a few weeks left and she just looks at me, doesn't argue but I can tell she doesn't believe it. I asked her to make house calls and she said no, only if I'm really incapacitated, which I'm not even though I'm walking with a walker now and have to use a wheelchair if I go any distance without a car. I get the feeling sometimes she's pulling back and then I think who needs her? And I want to cancel the next appointment. I wish she could be by my side holding my hand when I go but don't think that will happen.

I feel like my guides are part of me now, Leana and Soho, and more and more when I'm sleeping or sometimes when Connie's doing a healing or I'm lying on my sofa half asleep they come and take me traveling with them. It's almost like I'm practicing, getting ready to go home.

# Spring 1993

## Connie

Ariel's expected appointment with death has come and gone; she'd rented a little cabin for the weekend to die in and awakened the next morning somewhat disappointed and I think a little embarrassed to find herself still quite alive. What an extraordinary challenge it has been for me to come to a place of understanding and accepting that healing is not about whether she lives or dies, recovers physically or not, but is about the continuing evolution of her soul. I've finally surrendered to not knowing, not needing to know, to simply opening myself as a channel to allow the highest good to occur. There is a deep connection between us.

Energetically, I've sewn the torn threads in the seventh level of her auric field, the outer "egg" (which I believe is changing her belief system), repaired and restructured chakras, cleared the emotional layers of the field, done a spine cleaning, and a great deal more. I've tried to pay attention to the guidance I receive from my supervisor, Roseanne, through Debby, and from my own guides before, during, and after sessions, and I feel that my own capacities have expanded tremendously as I've done hands-on healing with her. And others as well. My sense with Ariel is that, despite her protestations and continuing physical deterioration, a shift toward health is occurring. There is both more stability in her energy field and a great deal of old emotional pain that is emerging in and out of sessions. Up until lately she has focused more on her physical pain; now she is connecting more fully with the emotional. She's had chest pain recently, which I urged her to see her medical doctor about, but energetically it's as if there are black spikes around her heart. I will remove them energetically next week. When I think about that I gulp and say to myself "you're going to WHAT?" But I'm more and more confident in the skills I've been so well taught, and as long as I prepare myself by meditating and raising my vibrations to what is needed, and asking for only the highest good, there's a great deal that can happen through me. I know also that because of Ariel's great willingness and because of the severity of her illness, I'm on the cutting edge with her in a way that I might not be with someone healthier. There is not a lot to lose, and a great deal to gain. Sometimes I'm optimistic about her potential for physical healing; other times it seems that even if she were to fully commit to life her body is so damaged it could not be regenerated. When I feel hopeless and angry, I try to avoid getting hooked into either rescuing or punishing her. For the most part she continues to have a very strong positive transference to me, occasionally marked by outbursts of fury when I don't rescue or collude with her.

I've had several guides with me as I learn the healing work; the latest one, according to the guides Debby channels, is Harmony. What a lovely name!

*This guide helps you with your personal spiritual connection. Hueta is still there at times and combines with other energies so is not always easily differentiated. We see that you have become very strong in your ability to connect with your guides, and we see that there is very little that's going to stand in your way in terms of allowing more energies to come through. In terms of recognizing what your connection is with these individuals, the more you are able to feel the connection in yourself, to your clients, the more you are going to be able to feel the presence of the guides. So just keep working with the earth plane, the connection with your clients. Know that everything that comes up, including working with the self, working with your own personal becoming, will facilitate a clearer and more positive opening to your spiritual guardians and opportunities to give more to those who come to you.*

# Ariel

So I didn't die, I guess it wasn't time. I don't know if I'm disappointed or not. I know with all the healing work and people around me now who seem to care it's confusing, almost as if I'm being healed in spite of myself. Not so much my body, but how I think and feel. I stopped the Prednisone, realized I'm up after I take it and down when it wears off, and I'm trying to cut back on the pain medication and Zanax. Then at least if I die I'll die awake instead of in a fucking daze. Excuse my French.

I want to be consistent about wanting to live or die. Am I as sick as I think? Does Dr. Moore think I'm dying or not? Can I live and be well? Can I let go and die? I asked Connie all these questions and she doesn't know the answers either. I asked her to call Dr. Moore and get the straight scoop, and she said I should talk to him directly but finally agreed and he told her that I don't have any immune deficiency, it's really the opposite, auto-immune, which I don't think I ever understood before. And apparently I could go on this way for a long time and not die. And he said with all the damage from my addictions and the bulimia for so long he doesn't know what the prognosis is for real health even if the Sjogren's goes into remission. And he agreed with her that my will to live or not is crucial. So it's all back on my shoulders, and no one really knows anything.

I called Debby and she said she had a sense of things caving in and circulation slowing down or having difficulty getting to major organs. The guides said my body was trying to clear out the effects of medication and stress over a long period of time, and not to be disturbed about the sweating, that it's a natural balancing system. And then they said:

*It's almost as if soul is standing back and waiting for you to decide which way to go, and to be committed to that and to be whole with that. There is of course a natural fear of moving either way, and we see because of this it's been difficult for you to stay consistently with what is happening in your body. As you receive emotional support from those who love you there is a natural healing process that occurs. There are also masses of fear that have collected on the etheric level. Your healer has worked on this already, and it is possible for her to help free you for whatever experience lies ahead by working on this level. You may feel relief as a result of this cleansing process.*

I asked if there were any other specific suggestions for Connie, and they said:

*To work with the lower chakras is very important and to work with aligning the heart with the lower centers. We see there is a great deal of resistance here, and yet to continue to work with this will help build an energy field. Whatever level she feels guided to will be appropriate. This will be very helpful in terms of giving you an opportunity to feel that you are correct wherever you are.*

I told Debby how uncomfortable I feel sometimes talking about my dying with Connie, less so than before but still confused about whether she agrees with me. Maybe it's because I'm inconsistent. But I asked if maybe I should just stop having the energy work, sometimes I think it doesn't make sense and just confuses me more.

*We see you both being blessed by all of the work that you're doing and by experiencing the healing process each of you will open yourselves to greater opportunities for self care and for caring for others. We see that the process that you undertake and experience together will not end here. It will not end in any way. The benefits go on for both of you, so see that whatever you are doing, it is something that you both will carry with you for a long period of time. See that there is a very strong resiliency in each of you to anything that appears to be a blocking of energy. See that even when something appears not to move, the effects of what you are doing continue quite a bit after each session. You are both receiving benefits from what is being done.*

I told Connie that when I die I'll come back as an angel, I'll be one of her guides. We had a good laugh over that.

Last week when she did a healing I had a pain in my chest that kept moving back and forth to my lower back. She had worked on my heart two weeks ago after I went to the doctor because of the pain in my heart and he said there's nothing wrong with my heart. The pain went away after she worked on it but came back last week during the healing. She did most of the energy work on my low back with me lying on my stomach and said it was fifth level surgery, and then had me turn over. She had one hand under my back and one on my heart and then the floodgates opened, I started crying and bawled like a baby for a long time. I heard myself say I just want to be, all my life I've been treading water and I don't want to struggle any more I just want to float, and then I said I surrender, I surrender, it's o.k. to live or die, it's o.k. either way. And then I kept crying, and when I sat up she held me and I put my head on her shoulder and cried some more.

The night after that healing I had the strangest dream:

*Asleep at 12:00 midnight. Began floating, felt so good, was aware that my chest hurt real bad but as I floated I didn't feel it anymore. I kept calling Daddy, Daddy but just kept floating higher and higher with no response. Felt peaceful but aware of being alone and frightened that Dad was not there for me. I said Daddy you told me you would be there for me, where are you? No response. Kept floating higher. I became angry and yelled where are you? Then I was in this room with a lot of people in it some sitting, some lying down, some standing. I didn't recognize anyone. I said Daddy are you here? I looked to my left and a little girl about six or seven was sitting in a child size chair. She was smiling at me. I said angrily, who are you? She said I'm Susan Blake, smiling. I said, well who are you? She said like I should know her, you know Susan Blake from that story. I said oh like I then knew who she was but I didn't know what story she was talking about. There was an older boy standing to the right of her smiling at me. I said to Susan, who's he? She said matter of fact, he's my brother Tim. I asked if they knew where my dad was and told them his name. They looked blankly at me and from behind me I heard a kind voice from behind me say he's over there. I somehow was guided to the far left corner of the room. I saw this man all slumped sitting on the floor with a cap over his face. I said softly Daddy? He hung his head and rolled his shoulders in. I said Daddy? once again. No response. I pulled the hat off his face. It was my Dad and he looked horrible. He looked like a bum and would not look up at me. I said Daddy, it's me, Ariel, you said you would be here for me, what's wrong? No answer. I said Daddy you don't have to be ashamed, I love you. No response. I said Daddy it's o.k. I love you please don't feel ashamed. I started hugging him and kissing him telling him how much I loved him and he did not need to be ashamed. As this was occurring I heard a voice from the one that guided me to Dad say, you will not come to this place, you will go to another place. As all of this was occurring I became aware that I was back in my body and had rolled off my bed and heard a woman say is she gone? and could feel Dr. Moore touching me and had a stethoscope to my neck saying not yet but soon. I felt my tongue all swollen and sticking out of my mouth. I was angry as they were keeping me here and I needed quiet. I left my body once again and was floating higher and higher. Straight ahead I could see this light but it was a long way off and in that light was like a gold dome. I knew that was the place I was going. I became frightened as I was alone. My stomach was queasy as I was floating so fast. I knew I could keep going but opened my eyes just to make sure I was in my bed. Awake, I saw the clock said 2:22. I had to go to the bathroom real bad but I was so dizzy and still floating that I wasn't sure if I could walk to the bathroom but I knew if I went back to sleep I'd wet the bed. I walked to the bathroom. I was so lightheaded and like a drunk but got there and back to bed. I was afraid to go back to sleep, wanted someone to hold my hand while I slept, to feel safe, wanted to call someone but finally went back to sleep.*

Today my abdomen is swollen again, but the chest pain has subsided and the back pain is gone for now. I'm sleeping a lot, very tired after going to New York with a group from church to a play.

They took turns pushing me in my wheelchair, I knew I couldn't walk the ten blocks or so from the bus. Ken said I might be able to get into a Presbyterian Home, he's working on it. One really weird thing that's happened is that all my warts are falling off. Just falling off!

Connie says what's important is to stay with whatever is happening right now, in my body and in my emotions rather than trying to jump ahead to what's going to happen next. She says the only way out of my pain is to release it, it's like the physical pain is really emotional pain that hasn't been released yet. I've blocked it all my life. I am trying to let it go but it's so hard and it feels so overwhelming sometimes.

# Summer 1993

## Connie

I've been feeling very shaky lately, almost like my legs are going to give way unexpectedly. In talking with Abraham I realize that this period of separation from my husband has triggered similar reactions—anxiety, heartache, terror—to what I experienced when I was eight or nine years old and torn between my parents as they fought the last battles of their private and public war with one another. I remember being sick a lot during that time, mostly stomach aches, and lying with a quilted pad under my head on the living room sofa. I would fall asleep eventually and had nightmares of the diamond shapes in the quilting trying to kill each other. I'd awaken drenched with panic. I kept trying to find the right solution, but there wasn't any. Perhaps it was one of the ways I developed my intuitive capacity, an ability to draw on a deeper part of myself that could help me when my mind was frozen for a time and my feelings shattered. There was no right answer, and no one to hold me and tell me everything would be all right. I have that feeling now, that I need someone to hold me and reassure me, but there isn't anyone to do that. Abraham's presence is reassuring, but he's not about to hold me, and I have a feeling that I look so together most of the time that it wouldn't occur to even my closest friends that there's a child inside who needs to be held. Roseanne comes closest to offering that, but she's too far away to physically comfort me.

Ariel has been working through a lot of rage, necessary but not comfortable for either of us, and once again, a few weeks ago, came to a point of such despair that she chose a date to commit suicide, made a plan, and then prayed "God, if you want me here, send me a sign". She must have a direct line, because the next day she received notice that she will receive federal subsidies, enough for her to move to a decent apartment in a nice neighborhood. She moved a couple of weeks ago and can stay two years with a subsidy. Between that and the small alimony she gets, if she's careful she'll be able to manage. So she decided there must be some purpose for her and has contacted an organization that helps people with disabilities to see if she can contribute in some way, and—when she's not raging—seems much more upbeat than she was. All the healing work has brought a great deal of old, very emotional material to the surface, and the remembering and releasing has been exhausting and, in its own way, depleting to her even though in the long run I'm convinced there is healing occurring. It's almost like there's been an explosion and there's debris everywhere that needs to be cleaned up before there can be calm and order again. When she's depressed and in a lot of pain she begins taking the Percoset again, and Zanax, and I can't believe that assists the healing process but seems to be what she needs to do. When she feels really bad she storms and rages at God and me and everyone else around her and can't understand why she doesn't just die.

But today she came in for the first time in over a year without her walker—using only her cane—and said something new: she wants to heal herself so she can be released. She had talked to Debby again (my unwitting co-therapist) when she was desolate and her guides said:

*Spirit is waiting for you to decide what to do. There is no meant to be here. If you choose to go do it with a clear conscience and see it as a choice and not something that is either being decided for you or something to be blamed for.*

*We see there's a great fear that was given you as you were growing up that created shame. We see the shame of feeling wrong about who you are, the shame of feeling wrong about what you think you contributed to what others did to you, the shame of feeling guilty, shame and blame hand in hand in terms of body memories. We see self-reproach, self-degradation, and so the shame is already there. By adding shame to that we mean the feelings of blame and wrongfulness that you would give yourself for contributing to your own passing. This would just heap more layers on when you need to work on what you need to work on on the other side.*

*We see currents and fields of high energy coming around you and we see greater feelings of support coming to you as a result of the chelations. Know that as you break through this period of difficulty surrounding being stuck you will be able to take in the chelations in a different way, feel them more strongly, feel them more purposefully, and feel more relief and substance to yourself as a result of these chelations. This is something that is going to happen over a period of time, not overnight, so prepare yourself for this and be persistent, and we perceive change happening in positive ways in terms of how you experience your own body. We see more receptivity to those that matter to you and less to those that don't and see this as being very positive. So do not be concerned if you feel like being more exclusive regarding those that have not been helpful in the past. You will be drawing individuals to you that seem to understand you and what is going on for you through the healing work.*

I have such a strong sense of the space between and around Ariel and me filled with healing energies, a whole field of healing energies. When I do chelations and am in an altered state, my vision expanded, I see beams of light around the healing table, sometimes several inches wide and several feet long. I sense that my guides and Ariel's are present, and I ask for their help before I begin. I hear words of guidance: which chakra or organ needs work, what colors (vibrational frequencies) to use, etc. For example, today I was guided to use bright green to heal the groin areas and then to do a brain balancing.

When I am done I stand back from the table a little bit and ask if there is any guidance for the person on the table, and very often there is. Usually I pass it on, and almost always it has immediate relevance. Sometimes it's in metaphor, like a dream, and I have only a vague sense of what it means until we talk about it. But I pay close attention to what I hear now, and to the "knowing" that comes to me as I work, because most of the time I'm finding the information I get to be quite accurate and useful. There are still moments and even days of doubt, but I'm more and more trusting.

Ariel has decided to go to a chiropractor and to work with a massage therapist regularly, and I'm very pleased with those decisions, both in terms of the complementarity of their work with mine and in terms of her taking more responsibility for her healing. She's even taking some herbal remedies and nutritional supplements, which I think she's needed for a long time. As she put it to me today, she's taking "kombu up the gazoo"! Her periodic abdominal bloating is sometimes accompanied by pain and followed by small amounts of rectal bleeding, but nothing shows up on x-rays. Her new home should offer her a serenity she's been hard put to find in her recent housing situations. All in all, I find I'm in a much more allowing mode regarding the healing work with her. Her physical body may die, it may not, but I feel pretty sure no matter what happens on the physical level her soul is healing. That's all that really matters.

I talked to Debby myself recently and asked not only about myself, but also Ariel. My guides' response made me quite curious about where Ariel is headed.

*We see Ariel is starting to move into another level of understanding about herself. She is probably going to wonder why things are changing so rapidly. In other words, the way her life will unfold now will not seem to fit her old perceptions of how life has treated her. It's very difficult for her to move away from her concept that life is doing something to her, that life is a large, looming giant that is controlling her. So after a while she is going to see some evidences contrary to her belief system, that grace does happen to individuals who feel that it never happens in their lives. We suggest that you anticipate that this will come up for her, that she's going to feel some confusion about grace, about the grace of life, about spirit's effect on her life. And on everyone's life, and you may want to anticipate how you will help her. Not so much shatter her whole belief system, which would be disarming to her, but to help her find a way to alter it. It's almost as though she's been in a subterranean subterfuge, in a subterranean place of her own making that is beginning to fall apart, and as it does so you have to start pulling away the pieces that are decrepit, that are falling in on her. And yet she still does need this subterranean subterfuge for herself. Contemplate how this applies to her. All of this will help you help her with the apparent difficulties coming up in the not too distant future.*

Uh oh. It sounds as if different problems are going to arise. I wonder what?

I cannot believe that I'm about to begin my Senior Year at the Barbara Brennan School. Along with continuing to learn and practice advanced healing skills, I have a Senior Thesis to write and a major Case Presentation, both of which will require a great deal of extra time, thought, and energy. And then? Perhaps I will finally be able to take some time off to write—maybe a sabbatical. I feel as if I need time to integrate all the learning, all the internal and external changes that have taken place over the past few years. I long for time to rest and reflect, to live and breathe mountain air, to connect deeply to Mother Earth.

# CHAPTER XIV

## *Reunification*

### Winter 1993

### Ariel

So much has happened. For the first time in my life, I want to live.

I kept bleeding, not a lot but enough so I knew something wasn't right. The doctors did tests, more tests, and couldn't find anything so decided it was a hemorrhoid. The easiest diagnosis. I knew it wasn't, the guidance I got was that there was a weakening of the wall of the intestine, it was worn out and giving way. It sounded like I might need surgery, but if I told my doctor angels told me where the bleeding was coming from he'd think I was nuts for sure, so I didn't tell him. But in a dream I heard "they're looking in the wrong place," and I knew. I was afraid I would end up with a colostomy or something, but also afraid I would bleed to death. Then I thought what the hell, I might as well bleed to death as go any other way. Meanwhile Connie was doing lots of energy work, and I was going through rage and tears and getting massages and chiropractic adjustments and everything else I could think of. And knowing I was still pulling in two directions as Connie pointed out, part of me wanting to live and doing all this stuff to get better and the other part wanting to leave yesterday . But not wanting to take responsibility for suicide. And feeling rotten.

I moved into my new apartment, that felt good and was getting settled. A couple of weeks later I was taking care of a friend's cat and lying on the couch watching a video one night when all of a sudden I felt wet down below. I touched my pants and my fingers were bloody. I knew it wasn't my period, that stopped a while ago, it was rectal, and the blood gushed out all over the couch. I got to the bathroom somehow and sat on the toilet and the toilet water turned bright red. By then I was getting real scared. I knew this was no hemorrhoid. I had a cup in the bathroom and put it under me and filled the cup. I don't know whether from fear or loss of blood but I was dizzy and knew if I didn't do something I was probably going to die. This was it, what I'd been hoping and praying for all my life. And then I got real calm and said to myself o.k. you've been waiting for something like this, now's your chance, just lie down and let it happen. And I sat on the floor and knew in that minute I had to decide once and for all if I wanted to live or die. This was it, no more fucking around. Now or never. And suddenly I knew I didn't want to die, I wanted to live, take the risk of choosing life once and for all for as long as I could have life! And even though I knew it might not be the way I wanted it to be, I wanted it. So I crawled to the phone leaving a trail of blood behind me and called the ambulance and they came and got me to the hospital.

The bleeding stopped pretty soon after I got there and the doctor, one I'd never seen before, must have looked at my old records and he treated me like I was a practicing alcoholic with a hemorrhoid wanting a free bed and some pain killers. It was awful, awful, and by the next day I couldn't wait to get out of there. I felt like I did when a kid, no one believing me. In a way I was glad there was blood all over the apartment though, because Connie went to pick up the cat for me and saw it all, said it looked like someone had been murdered in my apartment there was so much blood. She was shocked, but at least she knew the truth.

I left as soon as I could and since then everything is different. I'm still bleeding small amounts every few days and have some back pain and sometimes a headache and joint pains but mostly I feel like there's been some miraculous change in me and the healings are working. I know positive changes in my energy field only last if I'm ready for them, so I guess I'm ready. The next week when Connie did a healing on my intestines, she said she heard that my connection to heaven and earth was complete and strong, my task was complete, and I could go in peace or be reborn. I think I'm being reborn. I had a dream that night:

*I was at home but it was a trailer type home. My sister and mother were there in the kitchen fixing dinner. I had to go see Connie for a session and was running late. Denise couldn't leave yet so I told them I'd walk. I had my cane and started to leave when Mom and Denise tried to stop me because they were afraid I couldn't manage to get that far. I said hey, I can do it she only lives three trailers away. Then I was at Connie's, we were joking and talking like we were friends. She was telling me how good I looked and how good I was doing. She then answered her phone in her kitchen. It was a wall phone. I was teasing her as she was talking. She was laughing but moving away as she was continuing to talk without letting the other person know we were having fun. Then I pinched her on the butt so she would have to acknowledge that I was there. She laughingly said she just pinched me then she turned to me and said why did you do that? She then hung up and said happily they're coming over (her parents) to visit. I was happy because I knew them and wanted to see them too.*

The next week my leg straightened out, and the week after that I put away my cane and started taking fifteen or twenty minute walks. It's like my whole body is physically changing, and the chiropractor couldn't believe it, the bones are moving! I get tired easily, but I stopped taking the Percoset and Zanax once and for all and I hardly hurt. In another session with Connie I was lying on the table with her working on my back and left shoulder and I heard myself say "I don't have the key."

"Ask the guides who has it." Connie said.

I did and they answered "Those watching".

"Guides?" I asked.

"Yes" they answered.

"Who they will give it to?"

"Connie."

I had no idea what we were talking about. Connie and I talked about it and felt it had something to do with my earliest childhood. In the next healing she asked the guides:

"Where is the key?"

"In the drawer, in a small table . . . in the Golden Book," they told her.

"Where?" Connie asked.

"In the house of the mother," they said.

Connie asked how I could get it, and they told her:

"Denise . . . ask Denise to get it. Ariel must not ask the mother."

Connie said she saw a piece of paper, old, in a book. It had writing on it, and she said she felt it had to do with my birth. When she told me, I knew it was my birth certificate. My mother keeps a bible in a bedside table drawer next to her bed, and I think that's the golden book. I know there was something strange about my birth that had to be kept a secret, and it is still a secret. I have a feeling I know what it is, but I'm afraid to say it out loud.

I want to stop smoking, and Connie asked me (I hate to even ask her help with this, I've tried and failed so many times) to write about what smoking means to me. What came was it's a smokescreen, a way to screen out all the bad feelings about my family and to keep myself from going crazy. I still have some fear of what will happen if I stop. I have the sense that for a long time the only way the wounded inner child and I could survive together was to kill the body. But I also know I've wanted to kill off that inner child too because she betrayed me. I might go on antidepressants first as a way to help me give up the smoking. I wouldn't want to depend on them either though.

I talked to Debby last week about everything that's been happening, and also asked if it was a good idea for Connie to do another spine cleaning now because she feels it would be, and this is what they said:

*This is a very good idea. A day or two before it would be helpful for you to have Epson salt baths or compresses on your back, especially the upper and lower back. We see that this will loosen areas where energy will come in and leave. We see that you can also visualize opening at the upper and lower portions of the spine while you are getting the spinal cleansing. We see that she has received guidance on this, and we see that this will help create stabilization in your system in general.*

She did the spine cleaning. It took a long time, she said she worked on all seven levels of energy, and though I had some pain up my back when she did it I felt much better the next day and since.

I asked Soho and Leana what I need to do now to continue healing and as always they knew just what to do. They are so wise and forgiving of my character defects.

*Internally we see a great deal of healing has taken place in terms of membrane. We see that your whole system has gotten the message that your membranes need to be healed. Once the one area in your intestines received the healing then everywhere in your body—all of the membranes and tissues that contain, that have to do with containment, have gotten very busy like little elves. They have been busy repairing many of your structural tissues. We see that there is still fear and pain in you that wants to whittle away at the containers of your system. In a way there's a part of you that is calling out to escape from your body. This is happening on an emotional level and also on a spiritual level. Your need to escape causes your enzyme level to increase rapidly, and there is a tendency for enzymes to deteriorate wherever they find themselves in the body. And so we want you to envision enzymes, research what they look like and what their functions are, and see that once you do this you need to act as if they are troops, as if they are a militia, and you are going to call them to attention, as if they are little soldiers who have for a while been working against you, creating enemy lines, and now they are there for you. You call them to attention to stop chipping away at or destroying the membranes and tissues of your body, especially your stomach area. It is very important that you do this because otherwise chaos will have a tendency to continue to erupt in your body. This is your assignment for your own contribution to your healing process.*

I laughed when I visualized this army of enzymes, but later I talked to them like I was a general and they were going to be courtmartialed if they didn't obey my orders. I hope they listened.

At the end of the session with Debby I felt so hopeful and optimistic. I asked Soho and Leana if there was anything else I should know and they said:

*We see that your own issues around heartbreak are becoming more and more compelling. We want for you to see that you can move through feelings of heartbreak without actually breaking your heart. We see that some feelings of physical pain around experiencing heartbreak can cause you to feel shattered. Know that you have all that you need to put your-self back together, and personal integrity, personal unity, personal re-unification is something that you are well on your way to accomplish-ing. You have felt not only misaligned, misunderstood, and defeated in the past, but you also have felt despair and hopelessness and longings for change. We want for you to see that you are in the midst of pulling yourself out of the worst of all of these feelings, and now you are in the process of reunification. Know that you may always go through periods where you need to put yourself back together. The time bombs that are left may feel emotionally debilitating at times, but we offer you hope around this, because your strength and your having gone all this way in your personal recovery gives you additional strength and additional re-serves from which to draw on. You will find yourself over the next five to six years actually feeling that you don't have major crises as you used to. We offer you this to encourage you reclaiming a place of peace in your life. It's not something you have to wait for spirit to douse you with but is something that will be revealed through your own actions. You will access this within yourself. You will begin to feel more like a team player over time, and actually more spiritually connected as well. Expect to go into some deep valleys at times, and yet when you come out the other side there will be greater feelings of relief and, as we said, reunification than you have ever had in your life.*

Amen.

# Spring 1994

## Connie

Once again the earth is greening itself, reassuring us that even through the darkest, coldest winters there is still life deep beneath the surface of things. Azaleas, magnolias and rhododendron, daffodils and tulips splash their dazzling colors everywhere; flowering apple trees and weeping cherries grace lush verdant lawns. Mockingbirds, towhees, Canadian geese, song sparrows call to one another on soft breezes during the day; at night, the great horned owl behind my home awakens me with his deep, mysterious hoo hoo, hoohooooooo. If the sun shines brightly enough, if the light penetrates deeply enough, for long enough, life returns to the surface and thrives.

And so it is with Ariel. Like a child who has been locked in a dark basement, like Persephone dragged long ago down into the dark underworld by Hades, Ariel is emerging into the light. The world looks quite different than it used to, and she doesn't quite trust that she's free, but with every step she takes the ground underneath her feels more solid. Slowly she is realizing that while she was in the underworld she was abused, identified and merged with the aggressor, and survived. And as she has gathered the broken shards of her soul, she has grown up; she has become woman. All the while she was captive, and subject to Hades, she yearned for the light. She thought the only way to accomplish this was to leave the earth altogether, bypass it as it were, leaving the body that had betrayed her behind, and return to the realm of the Gods. Now she has learned, and will continue to learn, that she can walk the earth in peace and joy, that being human does not necessarily mean a lifelong sentence in the underworld, but can mean being solidly grounded on Mother Earth and simultaneously linked with Heaven . If, as was required by Persephone, reunification with the Mother and reclamation of Persephone requires that a third of her life be spent in the underworld, Ariel has already done that and more. Now it is time for the three parts of the her feminine nature—girl, woman, crone—to become one.

Ariel's healing—physical, emotional, mental, spiritual—has continued at a rapid rate. Good nutrition, massage, chiropractic adjustments, the love of friends, and the healing work have wrought what most people would term a miracle. Her bones and muscles have shifted form, she is almost completely pain-free on the physical level, and not only is she working hard for an agency that helps the homeless, she's planning to return to school in September. We usually meet twice a week, fluidly moving back and forth between "traditional" psychotherapy and hands-on healing. Ariel is gradually cutting down on her cigarette smoking, sometimes substituting clove cigarettes as a way of avoiding nicotine, and she is committed to life and to the evolution of her soul, wherever that might lead her.

And I—I am about to graduate from the Barbara Brennan School and four of the most intense years of my life. Though there are patients who do not even know I've been learning healing techniques, I've integrated the healing work into many of my patients' sessions. Those patients and I have found that hands-on healing has deepened and enhanced both the recovery process and our relationship. It's been an incredible journey.

I have continued to ask for and receive guidance in many forms: in meditation and prayer, journaling, supervision with Roseanne, analysis with Abraham, friends, dreams, synchronicities, high sense perception; and through Debby, my guides Amman, Quaalar, and Adonis, with me from birth; Hueta, Mildred, and Harmony, my healer guides; and Hoonan, an oriental guide who has been with me throughout the writing of this book. As far as I am concerned, they define the word angel.

In a recent session with Debby, I asked how I can open up my high sense perception more, as many of my classmates "see" more than I do, and I am sometimes impatient with my progress:

*One way is to make certain that every day you spend time in quiet, contemplative beingness for at least ten or fifteen minutes a day, preferably at the same time each day. This will help activate on deeper levels your ability to be with spirit. This is very different than working on clients. Being with self in a state of sheer beingness without having to accomplish or think about anything, do anything, just a focus less beingness will help you create a tandem relationship to the spiritual realm. That is implying that you have one foot here in the physical realm and the other in the spiritual realm. Doing it in quiet, by yourself, will encourage you on a deep cellular level to be able to perceive information that's been imprinted on you already. Instead of rushing past the window constantly all day, you're just going to stand and look out the window with nothing to do, nothing to say, nothing to think about. Just stand at the window of your spirit with no agenda. Just say here I am, just observing, just watching. You may have images and thoughts rushing by, perhaps some that linger. Just observe it all. You do not need to record it or do anything with it. We will help to tune you by your just remaining still in this fashion. Doing it every day encourages a commitment to the Self. This is the best way to accelerate your high sense perception. There are many other ways as well.*

*We also see that because you have become more adept at some of the other senses the visual has diminished somewhat. We see that when one spiritual channel is more activated it will have a tendency to mute or diminish the acuity of another perception. As you practice using all your avenues of perception simultaneously this is another route you can use to increase acuity at all perceptual levels. This is a very strong key for you: Use all abilities simultaneously, meaning vision, hearing, feeling, touch. Use all images, all feelings, all sounds simultaneously, and we see that you will be able to create a magnificent synthesis of perceptions that will indeed come together in a holistic fashion to improve the acuity of all the sum of the parts. If you commit yourself to this, over time it will find a level of its own.*

Two nights later I had a vivid dream:

*I'm in a house with family and friends around, maybe a holiday and a party being planned. I'm talking with a man. Then I'm aware that in my head, where my seventh chakra and the sixth, front and back, meet, there is blue light encircling a sphere of white light, and within that circle I see very clear images: a train schedule in Arabic from Cairo, cartoons I saw years ago, other bright, clear images of people, places, and things in rapid succession. I'm very excited, for I know I have finally tapped into visual high sense perception, and all information that exists is available to me. I experiment by asking for a person or an event or a piece of information, and sure enough, it appears on this circular mind screen. I am very happy.*

That dream has stayed with me; even though in waking life nothing like it has occurred yet, I know it is a portend of things to come.

And, though it brings up anxiety, insecurity, and fear of loss in me, I am more and more seriously considering taking time off from my practice—a kind of sabbatical without pay—to live in the Rockies and write. As far as I can see, it's the only way the book I've been contemplating is going to get written. And yet—and yet—could I leave my patients, my friends, my home to do this? I asked my guides, and their response was, as always, loving and insightful:

*We would like to say that it is of very supreme importance that you have time to sort through where you are at this point in your life. You need to feel you are moving from a very genuine space within yourself and not just responding to the needs and requirements of others. And so see that the space to contemplate and to produce creatively is also a place of reformation, reformation and resuscitation, renaissance, rebirth from within yourself. You are entering into a transitional phase whereby through the creative process you will help yourself energize, and come up with modification of ideals and commitments morally and emotionally, mentally, and vocationally. All of this will come through in a composite way, sometimes not as clearly defined as you would like, and yet that's part of the remolding process. You will discover what it is to find this transformationally through your creativity.*

*So see that this is of major importance to you, this time away to contemplate, to become open to the creative centers that will help you to reform and to rebirth yourself as a person committed to ideals and spiritual development. From this you will begin to feel that certain areas are more important to you than others and that this posture may be different than what you have had before. Know that what you are doing when this happens is not only responding to your internal needs, to your personality needs, but you are also stretching and flexing with the energies that are coming through the planet, so you are more clearly aligned with the changes that are taking place beneath you and around you. There are many who are going through this now, and as changes occur planetarily there is a need for reformation on many levels. We see you instrumental in terms of the impact this has on you as well as the impact it has on others that you influence, and who look to you for guidance and support in the future. Know that there is such correctness in what you are doing that nothing can be wrong or become wrongful from any of your actions to have this respite and creative venture.*

# Ariel

If I can stay with not smoking it's the last addiction I have to give up. And in many ways the hardest. Connie and I have spent a lot of time on this, and mapped out a plan to cut back gradually and it's been working pretty well but did buy and smoke some clove cigarettes because I'm gaining weight and can't stand that. But I realize I have a fear of not having enough, and when I crave cigarettes to fill me up and quiet me down I have to do something with my hands. I need to move my hands so sometimes I wring a rag, sometimes I write or do puzzles or cross stitch, sometimes I go out and walk just to get away from temptation. It feels so good to walk again pain free.

I'm finding a lot of anger comes up, like why should I have to give up the one thing that gratifies me? And then of course realize I don't have to, no one is asking me to, if I do it it's only because I want to and know it's best for me. It's my choice. I'm finding also that I feel different when I don't smoke, and part of it is a good feeling but also feel fuzzy headed so getting lots of advice about what to eat and what not to eat, etc. I don't know if I can do it, I can't believe the tobacco companies that say it's not an addiction. What horseshit excuse my French.

Most of the time now I have no pain at all. Not in my bones, not my muscles, not my joints. I stopped coffee and am drinking not even that much tea. Stopped to see Dr. Moore a few days ago just to see the expression on his face and thought he'd faint . "Ariel?" he said, hardly recognizing me. "You look like a different person!" And he called in the nurses and even the secretary and had me turn around and they all oohed and aahed, one saying your leg is straight and another your face looks younger and so forth until I got so embarrassed I had to leave. But so happy and pleased all the changes show!

Connie's still doing lots of healings, one time strengthening the outer layer of my auric field, another time working on my heart chakra and helping me release more of the grief that still feels bottomless, yesterday opening my throat chakra more. A couple of weeks ago she did what she called a Core Star Healing to help me connect to and expand my essence into the far reaches of the universe. What a trip! She says more of the changes in my energy field are holding and I can feel that. Sometimes I just feel rested and relaxed afterward, and then once in a while I go into such an altered state that when she's finished I can hardly get off the table. She needs an extra room where people like me can rest afterward, it's such profound work. I never used to know what that word meant but now I do.

The new thing I'm having to deal with is that Connie told me she might take some time off to write the book she's been talking about and not only that but she'll go out west to do it. I know I'm ready to let go and have others who can help me and support me through whatever else I need, but it's hard to imagine her gone and find there's lots of sadness coming up. I feel it like a knot in my abdomen and Mary my massage therapist said it's old pain and sadness that's getting triggered by the thought of being abandoned. Even though I know it's not really abandonment now. After Mary worked on it it felt a lot better. So I want Connie to write the book, if what I've gone through can help others it makes it all worth something, there's a purpose beyond me.

I think I'm finally o.k. Not that there won't still be pain and suffering, but I'm happy for the first time in my life, and I know I'm finally making a difference for other people as well. I know I am.

# Winter 1995

## Connie

Ariel called me the other day to tell me she had her first session with another healer to help her deal with congestion in her ears and recurrent bouts of tearfulness. I hadn't talked with her in a few weeks, since I saw her in New Jersey. She wanted me to know the healer was understanding and helpful and that she, Ariel, had gotten in touch (again) with a young child part that is still afraid to grow up. After the session she had a dream which she read to me over the phone:

*I'm traveling in my car. I don't know what car. I'm only aware of the interior. It's low to the ground. I'm very comfortable in it. It feels warm. I'm only aware of the color brown, yes, brown leather. I'm traveling down roads that are unfamiliar yet I know where I'm going. There is a very pleasant male friend in the passenger seat. I don't know who he is but I know he's supposed to be there. We are talking about the roads we're taking and just enjoying the scenery. We're relaxed, happy, and just enjoying the ride. I don't know my destination but that doesn't seem to matter. The scenery is very earthy with mountains of stone and brown, lots of brown earth. No houses or people. I want to take a new road that's ahead of me but it's not finished. I say to my friend that road isn't finished yet, oh well, we'll just go the old way, we'll still get there, it's o. k. He said I thought it would be finished by now, I'm really sorry. I knew you wanted to go on that one. I said it's o.k., we'll go our normal way. Look, isn't that new road just beautiful. It's going to be wonderful. The road is on a higher plane than we are. It's on another level. We go on our way and come to another new highway being built. It's just as beautiful and seems to be bridging across the highway I'm on but it's going to the same destination. I say to my friend, look at that highway. I sure wish I could go on that road, it's gorgeous. My friend says I was sure this road would be finished by now. I wanted you to be able to take*

*this one. I say it's o.k., it may be finished the next time we need to take
it. This highway and the way it's being done is wonderful, so beautiful.
I say to my friend, let's go find the man that's building this highway, I
want to meet him. My friend and I get out of the car. Climb up the
earthy mountain to the level of this new road. I see a house shaped like
a lighthouse. I tell my friend, there, there's his house. I'm so excited and
happy to meet this man I've always wanted to know. I go inside the
house. It's larger than it looks from outside with a steep staircase. It's
wood and mahogany, warm and cozy feeling. I climb the stairs, telling
my friend to follow me. I get to the door at the top and knock. I'm so
excited. My friend is behind me and comfortingly says you can't see him,
you're not allowed to see him. I'm not at all disturbed. I turn to leave
and before me are generous shelves of food. Grapes hanging from the
walls inviting you to eat them. Well stocked shelves. I say to my friend,
let's have a little. He feels ashamed, like I'm stealing. I say it's o.k., he's
a generous man and doesn't mind at all. My friend took a yellow apple
and put it in his pocket. I took a bag of candy. It's a bag of candy kisses.
As I leave out the door there are throngs of people outside. I begin throwing and sharing my candy kisses with them. I am so happy and light on
my feet.*

# Summer 1995

## Connie

I've been living in Montana for almost a year now, resting, revitalizing, reflecting, writing. The solitude has given me an opportunity to move to my own rhythms, to find and hold more internal balance between heart and mind, masculine and feminine. It is about integration, about finding my center, about letting go of illusion and claiming the Wise Woman I am becoming—including my limitations, my vulnerabilities, my inescapable human errors.

From my little home on the mountain I watch moose rub antlers on the car only a few feet away from my window, am mesmerized by elk and deer in the meadows along "my" canyon road, listen to coyotes sing to the moon. I've followed cougar tracks through the snow, carry a pepper gun in case of surprising bear on quiet wilderness trails, worn out a pair of hiking boots. The sky is clear blue, the moon and stars bright in this unspoiled part of Mother Earth. I feel close to earth, close to sky; centered, at peace. It is almost time to move back into the quicker streams of life: a practice, a professional identity in this community where I've been just another woman in jeans, or the woman writer who's been living on the mountain. I feel as if I have—finally—gathered the parts of my own soul and know who I am and where I am going; my path is clearly laid out before me. I don't know the exact form it will take, and that doesn't matter. I trust that as long as I seek guidance, I will receive it, that as long as I follow my soul's longing to evolve toward the light, I will be led towards the fulfillment of that longing.

My therapeutic relationship with Ariel tapered off by phone last fall and we had our last session in person in New Jersey during the winter, but she continues to be part of my life, as I am part of hers. With other patients, there was either completion last summer or phone sessions until very recently; with Ariel, because of this book, we have continued to maintain contact long after our formal relationship ended. Her unfolding has continued in ways that few who knew her in the depths of her addictions and despair would have believed possible. She bikes, hikes, has healthy relationships with friends, and works almost full time as a volunteer assisting the homeless. Even her relationship with her daughter Amanda, which seemed hopelessly severed, is healing. Though, like the rest of us, she experiences sadness, anger, and frustration at times, a great deal of the time she is healthy, whole, and happy. A walking miracle.

This summer Ariel acquired a van and set off across the country on a six-week journey with her seven-month old golden retriever, Teddy, to see all the sights she'd never seen. She wanted to visit me, and though I was somewhat hesitant about spending other than professional time with her, as maintaining boundaries with patients has always been high on my list of "musts", I invited her to come to my home to read and respond to this manuscript. She did so, laughing and crying as she relived all that had transpired and made helpful comments as she read. We hiked up a mountain with our dogs, I with my dignified eleven-year old golden retriever Yukon and Ariel with her puppy Teddy, who looks like Yukon's son and was born with cataracts, rendering him partially blind. Yukon introduced Teddy to rushing mountain streams and a clear blue swimmable lake, and Teddy cautiously followed his new mentor's lead. At one point he started to run after Yukon into the forest, and Ariel sprinted—sprinted!—ahead on the trail to catch him. I stopped in my tracks and stood still, watching, remembering, shaking my head in wonder. I never would have believed it if I hadn't been there.